Clinical Applications of Psychophysiology

Clinical Applications of Psychophysiology

DON C. FOWLES
EDITOR

1975
Columbia University Press
NEW YORK AND LONDON

Library of Congress Cataloging in Publication Data
Main entry under title:

Clinical applications of psychophysiology.

  Includes bibliographies and index.
  1. Mental illness—Genetic aspects. 2. Psychology, Physiological. I. Fowles, Don C.,
1939–   [DNLM: 1. Psychophysiology. WL102
C638]
RC469.C56   616.8′9′042   75-15609
ISBN 0-231-03931-X

Contributors

Don C. Fowles is associate professor, Department of Psychology, University of Iowa, and associate editor of *Journal of Biological Psychology.*

Doris A. Chernik is clinical research scientist, Department of Medical Research, Hoffmann-La Roche Inc., Nutley, N.J., and associate, Department of Psychiatry, University of Pennsylvania.

Robert D. Hare is professor, Department of Psychology, University of British Columbia, Canada.

Malcolm H. Lader is a member of the Medical Research Council, U.K. and honorary senior lecturer, Institute of Psychiatry, University of London.

Peter J. Lang is professor, Department of Psychology, University of Wisconsin.

David T. Lykken is professor, Department of Psychiatry and Neurology and Department of Psychology, University of Minnesota.

Joe Mendels is associate professor, Department of Psychiatry, University of Pennsylvania and chief, Depression Research Unit, Philadelphia Veterans Administration Hospital.

Peter H. Venables is professor, Department of Psychology, University of York, England.

Contents

Preface   ix

Introduction
  Don C. Fowles   1

1 The Psychophysiology of Anxious and
   Depressed Patients
   Malcolm Lader   12

2 Psychophysiological Studies of Sleep in
   Depressed Patients: An Overview
   J. Mendels and D. A. Chernik   42

3 Psychophysiological Studies of Psychopathy
   Robert D. Hare   77

4 A Psychophysiological Approach to Research
   in Schizophrenia
   P. H. Venables   106

5 Psychometric Applications of the EEG
   David T. Lykken   139

6 Acquisition of Heart-Rate Control: Method,
   Theory, and Clinical Implications
   Peter J. Lang   167

7 Theoretical Approaches and Methodological
   Problems in Clinical Research
   Don C. Fowles   192

Index   225

Preface

THE FIELD of psychophysiology has been expanding rapidly in the last decade and there has been a concurrent increase in interest in psychophysiology on the part of many professionals and students who would not identify themselves as psychophysiologists. Many of these individuals are interested in applying psychophysiological techniques to problems of their own, while others wish simply to be familiar with a rapidly growing field. In both cases it is difficult to find a source which provides a broad exposure to the use of psychophysiology in a book whose size is suitable for the nonspecialist.

The present volume has chosen to focus on the clinical applications of psychophysiology both because it is the applied area in which there has been the greatest research activity and because the largest audience would find that topic of interest. To that end, the contents were selected with three criteria in mind: (1) that the number of chapters should be kept small so that the size of the book would be in keeping with its intended purpose; (2) that the range of applications would be maximally broad both in the sense of covering a wide range of psychopathology and in the sense of covering many different psychophysiological approaches, and (3) that the authors be selected for their outstanding contributions to clinical research and for their depth of understanding of the field of psychophysiology itself.

The audience for which the book is primarily intended includes psychologists, psychiatrists, and other mental health professionals. Graduate students in these areas should find the book helpful in providing an exposure to an important aspect of both psychophysiology and clinical research, perhaps attracting some of them into the field. It is hoped that the book will not prove too technical for selected advance undergraduates, although it is clear that it would be limited to very specialized courses or seminars. Finally, it is further hoped that the book will be of interest to those concerned with the applications of psychophysiology to areas other than psychopathology on the assumption that there will be a substantial overlap.

I would like to express my appreciation to the many people who helped me to prepare this book, especially to Eileen Wetrich, Christine Hiratzka, and Mary Maxwell, all of whom helped with the various stages in the typing and indexing of the manuscripts. The book was written in connection with a symposium of the same title held in Iowa City, Iowa in November 1972 with the chapters completed during the year following the symposium. The symposium and thus the book were made possible by support from Public Health Service Grant No. 5-T01-MH05062-26 and the Graduate College of the University of Iowa.

Don C. Fowles
June 1975

Introduction

DON C. FOWLES

PSYCHOPHYSIOLOGY as a distinct academic discipline is still in its neonatal stage. The date of conception would be difficult to specify but the gestation period clearly extends back to the early publications of C. W. Darrow, R. C. Davis, and M. A. Wenger in the 1930s and 1940s (Sternbach, 1966). The strong endorsement of the concept of "generalized arousal" and of skin conductance level as an index of arousal in a popular textbook of experimental psychology (Woodworth and Schlosberg, 1954) also nourished the developing fetus. The birth of the field may be dated at approximately 1960 with the formation of the Society for Psychophysiological Research or 1964 with the publication of the journal *Psychophysiology*. A short undergraduate text (Sternbach, 1966) appeared shortly thereafter and 1967 saw the publication of two major handbooks on methodology (Brown, 1967; Venables and Martin, 1967). These handbooks and their early appearance underscored the heavily technological dependence of this field. Recent important developments include the publication of a massive theoretical handbook (Greenfield and Sternbach, 1972) and the establishment in 1973 of *Biological Psychology*, a second journal with a strong emphasis on psychophysiology. In addition, an increasing number of books are appearing which are directly concerned with psychophysiology (e.g., Gullickson, 1973; Prokasy and Raskin, 1973; Thompson and Patterson, 1974a, 1974b; Peeke and Herz, 1973).

During this period of development a substantial portion of psychophysiological research has been concerned with clinical problems, and yet the nature and extent of this clinical research is not widely recognized. Thus it seemed timely to call attention to the "clinical applications of psychophysiology" by bringing together a collection of papers by some of the foremost investigators in this area. It is hoped that this book will serve to expose a wide audience of graduate students and mental health professionals to a sampling of research in this field.

Before describing some of the trends which have already emerged in clinical research, it would be helpful to attempt a clarification of what is meant by the term "psychophysiology." One can start by looking at some examples of psychophysiological research which have appeared in the popular press. These examples will not only illustrate psychophysiological research but will also show how widespread is the impact of this area. One of the best-known of these is research on the physiological aspects of sleep, including the identification of physiological responses associated with dreaming. As a result of physiological recordings, it is now possible to identify several "stages" or types of sleep; to determine the importance of each type by selectively depriving subjects of a particular stage of sleep (such as dream sleep); to monitor changes in a person's sleep over time as a result of psychological stress, medication, or other circumstances which alter sleep; and to investigate developmental changes in sleep from birth onward. Because of widespread concern over insomnia and man's eternal fascination with dreams, articles on sleep appear frequently in popular magazines (*Good Housekeeping,* 1972; *Newsweek,* 1973; *U.S. News & World Report,* 1972; *Vogue,* 1972).

A more recent and even more dramatic topic to hit the popular press is the area known as "biofeedback." Briefly, this involves giving the subject information (feedback) as to how a particular physiological system (e.g., the heart or the brain) is responding, with the expectation that he will be able to acquire control of its responding. Often rewards and/or punishments are delivered as a function of the physiological response. Considerable interest in biofeedback has been aroused because of the possibility that psychosomatic disorders could be treated in this manner. Similarly, psychotherapists have hoped that biofeedback could be used to teach patients to control anxiety. Finally, numerous people have suggested that the brain itself might be controlled in this manner. This has led to controversial attempts to produce conditions described as the "alpha state" or the "theta state." These states are presumed by their more ardent advocates to represent a special and highly desirable state of mental awareness.

A third application of psychophysiology which has come increasingly to the public's attention is that of the assessment of the physiological components of emotions, this time in the form of lie detection. Recent disclosures that job applicants are being screened with lie detectors and asked questions about personal topics such as sexual behavior and drug use have elicited a strong protest (*Harper's Bazaar*, 1972). Similarly, there has been a reaction to the testing of policemen and prospective policemen with lie detectors (*Newsweek*, 1973). Although lie detection per se has been of more interest to the government than to psychophysiologists, the assessment of emotional responses on which lie detection is based is a central concern of psychophysiology.*

With these examples in mind we can now attempt a definition of psychophysiology. The major problem is to differentiate it from the well-established field of physiological psychology. Although both fields are concerned with the interrelationships between physiological variables and those phenomena we normally think of as psychological, the two fields can be distinguished along a number of dimensions (Sternbach, 1966). The first of these and perhaps the most important has to do with the choice of subjects. For the most part psychophysiology has used human subjects, whereas physiological psychology traditionally uses nonhuman subjects. Partly as a function of this choice, the

---

* Readers interested in an excellent discussion of the validity of lie detection tests may wish to consult David Lykken's recent article (*American Psychologist*, 1974, 29:725–739).

variables which are manipulated differ. Physiological psychologists tend to manipulate a physiological variable—e.g., removing or destroying a portion of the brain—and then to see what effect this has on overt behavior. Psychophysiologists tend to reverse this procedure: the independent variable is a psychological or behavioral variable with physiological responses as the dependent measure (Lykken, 1968; Sternbach, 1966; Stern, 1964). Examples of independent variables in psychophysiological research are sleep deprivation, the presentation of stimuli eliciting fear or anger, the comparison of subjects on the basis of psychiatric diagnosis, or the presentation of rewards or punishments contingent upon the subject's physiological responses. Finally, while the physiological psychologist may utilize a number of different recording methods, psychophysiologists almost invariably use a multichanneled recorder known as a polygraph to amplify and record the responses in which they are interested. None of these distinctions are absolute, of course, but collectively they point to clearly discernible differences between these two fields.

From the description just offered one readily sees why psychophysiology has been especially suited for clinical applications: the monitoring of physiological activity in humans opened up numerous avenues to be explored. The strong emphasis on emotional disturbance in psychiatric disorders and the possibility that the physiological component of emotions might be measured with psychophysiological techniques immediately suggests prospective applications in both diagnosis and treatment. Moreover, it became possible to monitor covert bodily processes—such as sleep—which are not inherently emotional. The strongest statement of the potential value of psychophysiological research has been offered by Lader (1971), who argued that accurate measurement is an essential component of scientific method and that psychiatry is almost completely lacking in "valid and reliable estimates of illness" (Lader, 1971, p. 279). By way of comparison, Lader suggests that one would have to imagine "studying anaemia without haemoglobinometers or even fevers without thermometers" (p. 279). Physio-

logical measures of the type described in this book have the potential of providing such estimates of pathology and also offer
the prospect of integrating psychiatry and neurophysiology.

Although psychophysiology has a short history, there are
some modest achievements to date. In supporting his belief that
physiological measures have much to offer psychiatry, Lader
(1971) cites the influence of this type of research on our view of
chronic schizophrenics. Until physiological measures were
taken, the social withdrawal and reduced motor activity of these
patients were taken as an indication of physiological underac-
tivity. Beginning with the early psychophysiological study by
Malmo and his colleagues (Malmo, Shagass, and Smith, 1951),
there has been an accumulation of physiological evidence indicating that these patients are more likely to be overactive
physiologically (Depue and Fowles, 1973; Lader, 1971; Lang
and Buss, 1965; Venables, 1964, 1966). These studies have also
contributed to the delineation of subdivisions within the schizophrenic diagnosis, especially the distinction between paranoid
and nonparanoid schizophrenics.

Another application of psychophysiological techniques
which has had a widespread impact is the assessment of the effects of sleep-inducing drugs on the electroencephalogram
(EEG) during sleep. The effects of hypnotics and of such commonly used drugs as alcohol may be evaluated in terms of
whether they produce a change from normal patterns of physiological activity during sleep (Kales and Berger, 1970; Kales et
al., 1969; Oswald, 1969). Such evaluations are likely to influence the prescription habits of physicians and, consequently,
the type of hypnotic consumed by the public.

An early study by Malmo and Shagass (1949) led to the
hypothesis of "symptom specificity" which has exerted a substantial influence over theories of the etiology of psychosomatic
disorders. In this study physiological responses were recorded
during the presentation of physically painful stimuli to two
groups of psychiatric patients, one group which had previously
reported repeated head and neck pains and the other group
which had a history of cardiovascular symptoms. During the

painful stimulus, each group of patients showed a greater response on measures related to their symptom even though they
were symptom-free at the time of testing, suggesting a disposi-
tion toward excessive responsiveness of a physiological system
directly related to their symptomatology. Thus it has been hypothesized that *in part* the development of a psychosomatic
disorder results from the overactivity of a specific physiological
system. Studies with normal subjects have indeed confirmed
the expectation that individuals differ in the physiological system which responds most strongly during stress, as would be
required if the physiological overreactivity preceded the development of the symptom. Longitudinal studies showing that
these individual differences are predictive of the type of psychosomatic disorder which develops are needed in order to provide direct support for the hypothesis of symptom specificity.
Unfortunately, such studies have not been attempted because of
the excessive cost involved. However, "symptom specificity"
remains as one of the major hypotheses in psychosomatic disorders (Lader, 1970; Sternbach, 1966).

These three applications of psychophysiological techniques
are not exhaustive, but they do illustrate the flavor and the variety of some of the early developments in clinical applications of
psychophysiology. The chapters in this volume were similarly
chosen to reflect a wide range of current clinical research in
psychophysiology—i.e., to encompass a large number of psychiatric populations, to include a number of different psychophysiological techniques, and to bear on a number of important issues. Thus the research in the chapters which follow is
concerned with schizophrenia, depression, psychopathy, anxiety, and psychosomatic disorders. The relative emphasis on different techniques parallels that in the field as a whole: the
major emphasis is on the EEG, electrodermal activity, and heart
rate, with occasional reference to vasomotor activity, the electromyogram, forearm blood flow, two-flash threshold (actually a
perceptual measure but for historical reasons strongly associated with psychophysiology), respiration, and the electro-
oculogram.

In the first paper, Lader reviews the psychophysiology of anxiety and depression. Anxiety neurotics are found to differ from normals on a wide variety of physiological measures in the direction of being more aroused. While that finding will surprise no one, his conclusion that these differences are apparent only when the experiment involves minimal stimulation—i.e., when there is *no* apparent stress—is not so obvious. Patients with phobias are divided into a group with specific phobias, on the one hand, and a group with either social phobias or agoraphobias, on the other hand. These groups differ dramatically in their physiological activity as indicated by electrodermal measures, the specific phobics showing near normal responses while the other phobics are almost as responsive as the anxiety neurotics. Similarly, large differences are found between agitated depressives and retarded depressives, the agitated depressives showing even more electrodermal responsiveness than the anxiety neurotics, contrasted with an almost total absence of electrodermal activity in the retarded depressives. On the basis of these and other results Lader concludes that psychophysiological measures point to the utility of distinguishing between agitated versus retarded depression and to the relative sterility of the endogenous-reactive distinction.

In the next paper, also concerned with depression, Mendels and Chernik examine the nature of the sleep disturbance in depression. Sleep studies have shown that patients' reports of reduced sleep in depression are greatly exaggerated, but that there is an important qualitative difference in their sleep. It is likely that the light, fitful sleep with numerous awakenings characteristic of these patients is responsible for their subjective impression of a greatly reduced quantity of sleep. Earlier reports of a reduction in Stage 4 (or "deep") sleep are confirmed, but carefully controlled longitudinal studies of unmedicated patients indicate higher than normal amounts of REM sleep (i.e., rapid-eye-movement or "dream" sleep). Of considerable importance is the finding of a residual sleep disturbance in several patients even after clinical recovery and discharge from the hospital, suggesting that depression involves a more chronic disturbance than is usually believed. There is also anecdotal evidence in the case of two patients that the sleep disturbance may be exacerbated *prior* to a recurrence of the clinical symptoms. If verified, this evidence would strengthen the hypothesis that biochemical changes are etiologically important, and the ability to predict relapses would make possible attempts at prophylactic intervention.

Hare's paper on psychopathy deals with a psychiatric population which does not report discomfort and which does not seek therapeutic assistance. Whereas most psychiatric groups differ from nonpsychiatric controls in the direction of overarousal, psychopaths appear to differ in the opposite direction. The electrodermal data and a number of behavioral studies are interpreted within the framework of a two-factor learning theory as indicating that psychopaths show poor learning of the conditioned emotional response. That is, they do not learn to respond with fear or anxiety to stimuli previously associated with punishment and, as a result, do not learn the socialized behavior characteristic of people who more readily learn conditioned emotional responses. However, experiments involving cardiovascular measures are not consistent with the other results, raising fundamental questions concerning the choice of physiological measure and the theoretical interpretation of the results with different measures. In addition, perhaps more than any other author, Hare discusses the difficulties of defining both psychiatric and control groups.

In the fourth paper, Venables synthesizes a large body of literature and proposes a major new theory of schizophrenia. The basic hypothesis is that schizophrenics suffer from a disturbance in the functioning of the limbic system and especially of the hippocampus and/or amygdala. This hypothesis is related to evidence from studies of the relationship between pregnancy and birth complications and schizophrenia, clinical reports of psychotic symptoms which are associated with organic brain pathology, and demonstrations of an attentional disturbance in schizophrenia. The clinical reports concerned with organic brain pathology suggest that schizophrenic symptoms are associated with a disturbance in the dominant hemisphere but not the nondominant hemisphere, and Venables presents electrodermal data indicating that laterality differences are indeed found in some schizophrenic patients. A new subdivision of patients within the broad category "schizophrenia" is also suggested on the basis of psychophysiological measures and this subdivision is found not to be related to traditional clinical subdivisions.

The first four papers are largely concerned with the assessment of psychopathology. Although there are suggestions or theories concerning etiology and treatment, these are derived from the attempts to assess psychopathology. In contrast, the next two papers are directly concerned with etiology (Lykken) and with treatment (Lang). Lykken, using normal college students, applies the twin-study methodology, which has had such a strong impact on theories of schizophrenia, to measures of the electrical activity of the brain. A sophisticated computer analysis of samples of the EEG allows him to quantify this measure with almost no loss of information, and a factor analysis shows that a large percentage of this information can be accounted for in terms of six factors. All six of these factors yield estimates of heritability which are extremely high, indicating that inheritance has a strong influence on the EEG and, presumably, those psychological functions revealed by the EEG. Lykken conceptualizes these results in the context of a diathesis-stress model, suggesting that these measures may reflect individual differences (of genetic origin) in psychiatric diathesis. Thus, assuming that the EEG measures something of importance to psychiatric disorders, Lykken's paper is a significant contribution to our understanding of the etiology of a physiological component of those disorders.

As mentioned above, there has been intense interest in the therapeutic applications of biofeedback. Lang points to two potential psychiatric applications: (1) teaching patients with psychosomatic disorders to reduce the overactivity of the disordered system and (2) using biofeedback techniques to directly manipulate the physiological component of anxiety in patients in psychotherapy. In spite of all the publicity in this area, however, we are far from being able to accomplish these goals. We have yet to determine the most effective methods of controlling autonomic responses. To this end, Lang begins with the control of heart rate in normal subjects. He then applies these results to patients with ischemic heart disease because some of the cardiac symptoms in these patients can be affected by changes in heart rate. Although ischemic heart disease is not a psychiatric problem, it is used as a prototype for later applications to technologically more difficult problems such as essential hypertension.

The final paper provides an overview of the research presented in the other six chapters. It calls attention to the view of psychopathology which dominates this research, the theories employed in conceptualizing the results of studies in this area, and the most important methodological issues which arise.

References

Brown, C. C. (ed.). 1967. *Methods in Psychophysiology*. Baltimore: Williams and Wilkins.

Depue, R. A. and D. C. Fowles. 1973. Electrodermal activity as an index of arousal in schizophrenics. *Psychological Bulletin*, 79:233–238.

Greenfield, N. S. and R. A. Sternbach (eds.). 1972. *Handbook of Psychophysiology*. New York: Holt, Rinehart and Winston.

Gullickson, G. R. (ed.). 1973. *The Psychophysiology of Darrow*. New York: Academic Press.

Kales, A. and R. J. Berger. 1970. Psychopathology of sleep. In C. G. Costello (ed.), *Symptoms of Psychopathology: A Handbook*. New York: Wiley.

Kales, A., E. J. Malmstrom, M. B. Scharf, and R. T. Rubin. 1969. Physiological and biochemical changes following use and withdrawal of hypnotics. In A. Kales (ed.), *Sleep: Physiology and Pathology*. Philadelphia: Lippincott.

Lader, M. H. 1970. Psychophysiological and psychosomatic aspects of anxiety. In O. W. Hill (ed.), *Modern Trends in Psychosomatic Medicine*. London: Butterworth.

——. 1971. Physiological measures in psychiatry. *Scientific Basis of Medicine Annual Reviews*, pp. 279–304.

Lang, P. J. and A. H. Buss. 1965. Psychological deficit in schizophrenia. II: Interference and activation. *Journal of Abnormal Psychology*, 70:77–106.

Lykken, D. T. 1968. Neuropsychology and psychophysiology in personality research. In E. F. Borgatta and W. W. Lambert (eds.), *Handbook of Personality Theory and Research*. New York: Rand McNally.

Malmo, R. B. and C. Shagass. 1949. Physiologic study of symptom mechanisms in psychiatric patients under stress. *Psychosomatic Medicine*, 11:25–29.

Malmo, R. B., C. Shagass, and A. A. Smith. 1951. Responsiveness in chronic schizophrenia. *Journal of Personality*, 19:359–373.

Oswald, I. 1969. Sleep and dependence on amphetamine and other drugs. In A. Kales (ed.), *Sleep: Physiology and Pathology*. Philadelphia: Lippincott.

Peeke, H. V. S. and M. J. Herz. 1973. *Habituation*. 2 vols. Vol. I: *Behavioral Studies*. New York: Academic Press.

Prokasy, W. F. and D. C. Raskin (eds.). 1973. *Electrodermal Activity in Psychological Research*. New York: Academic Press.

Stern, J. A. 1964. Toward a definition of psychophysiology. *Psychophysiology*, 1:90–91.

Sternbach, R. A. 1966. *Principles of Psychophysiology*. New York: Academic Press.

Thompson, R. F. and M. M. Patterson. 1974a. *Bioelectric Recording Techniques*. Part B: *Electroencephalography and Human Brain Potentials*. New York: Academic Press.

—— 1974b. *Bioelectric Recording Techniques*. Part C: *Receptor and Effector Processes*. New York: Academic Press.

Venables, P. H. 1964. Input dysfunction in schizophrenia. In B. A. Maher (ed.), *Advances in Experimental Personality Research*, Vol. I. New York: Academic Press.

—— 1966. Psychophysiological aspects of schizophrenia. *British Journal of Medical Psychology*, 39:289–297.

Venables, P. H. and I. Martin. 1967. *A Manual of Psychophysiological Methods*. Amsterdam: North Holland.

Woodworth, R. S. and H. Schlosberg. 1954. *Experimental Psychology* (rev. ed.). New York: Holt.

1

The Psychophysiology of Anxious
and Depressed Patients

MALCOLM LADER

The Nature of Illness

From its inception the emphasis of this volume has been the *clinical* applications of psychophysiology. Accordingly, I shall concentrate on the physiological changes found in patients studied in the clinical context. However, it is essential to try to clarify the meaning of such terms as "clinical," "abnormal," "disease" and "illness." There is confusion as to the connotations of these words to the extent that some even deny the existence of mental illness (Szasz, 1961). This partly contributes to the widespread differences in diagnostic usage and even in the phenomena noted in patients by psychiatrists in different countries, a problem which has recently been thrown into bold relief by the U.S./U.K. Diagnostic Project (Cooper et al., 1972). The definition of patienthood in general and diagnostic type in particular is not merely an academic exercise but, as will be seen later, dictates the type of experimental strategy, e.g., the use of control groups, adopted by the laboratory scientist.

An attempt at a biologically orientated definition of disease was made by Scadding (1967): "A disease is the sum of the abnormal phenomena displayed by a group of living organisms in

association with a specific common characteristic or set of characteristics by which they differ from the norm for their species
in such a way as to place them at a biological disadvantage."
However, not only does this definition beg the question of what
is meant by abnormal but it includes the vague concept of biological disadvantage.

Another approach is to use subjective, indeed introspective,
criteria. According to this approach patienthood always gives
rise to the attribute of suffering and therefore physicians deal
with patients who suffer. Because many abnormal emotions encountered in the psychiatric clinic such as severe dread and
profound despair undoubtedly have a marked element of suffering, this attribute might seem a suitable defining factor. However, there are psychiatric patients who do not suffer because
they are unconscious or because they have ecstatic delusions,
so that this criterion is unsatisfactory.

An alternative criterion is that of therapeutic concern. In
operational terms it is the patient's concern about his symptoms
such as severe anxiety and his hope of receiving treatment
which brings him to the notice of doctors. This has also been
termed "illness behavior" (Mechanic, 1968). This has the practical advantage of taking into account the usual way in which
suitable patients—i.e., those with specified symptoms—are obtained for laboratory studies. However, not all patients experience therapeutic concern: for example, depressed patients may
welcome their suffering as a well-deserved punishment for
their imagined or real previous misdeeds and peccadilloes.
Nevertheless, therapeutic concern is felt by the social environment of these patients which in practical terms means the close
relatives, friends and colleagues of the affected person. Thus,
we can define patients as human beings whose therapeutic concern for themselves or the therapeutic concern of the social environment for them is so great as to bring them to the notice of
doctors and members of other "caring" professions. This is essentially a social view of patients and it is worth emphasizing
that many of the conceptual problems which clinical scientists
encounter arise out of the dissonance between the ascertain-

ment of patients in social terms, the attribution of certain characteristics of illness in medical terms, and the investigation of the biological mechanisms of that illness using scientific techniques. In essence we deal with that class of people who have as their differentiating characteristic the attribute of diagnosed patienthood, but we can never deal with the total "real" class of patients because of the operational and social nature of the definition (Taylor, 1971).

The concept of abnormality is a complex one. It can be regarded either as an absolute or as a relative attribute. In the first case the deviation is from some criterion of perfection. Thus, a carious tooth is abnormal because it is imperfect. Definitions of mental illness as failures to attain some utopian ideal of perfect mental health have no place in the empirical atmosphere of a clinical research laboratory.

The second type of abnormality is a statistical or actuarial view of a phenomenon as an excessive deviation from some standard or norm. In this case a carious tooth would not be regarded as abnormal because such a feature is so common. However, a mouthful of carious teeth would be regarded as abnormal, as the average amount of caries is much less than that. In fact, there are two types of standard or norm with regard to clinical phenomena. The first type is when the symptoms which cause therapeutic concern are regarded as a change in the status of the patient: The abnormality is according to individual standards and is unusual in comparison with the more or less recent past of that individual. Thus, some patients describe depressive symptoms as a change in their emotional status. They regard themselves and are judged by their relatives as having been relatively free from depression hitherto; they see their present symptoms as a departure from their previous norm (pathological state depression). The symptoms occur as an "attack" and fit the medical or process model of illness (Cohen, 1955). The second criterion for the abnormality is by population standards: the therapeutic concern is for attributes that are unusual in a human population. For example, some patients admit to always having been much more anxious than their peers (pathologically high trait anxiety). Consequently, this condition is a personality abnormality and fits the deviation model of illness.

This leads us back to the careful and justified distinction which many psychologists make between emotional states and emotional traits (Levitt, 1968; Spielberger, Gorsuch, and Lushene, 1968). Emotional state refers to the emotion felt at a moment in time—"I feel miserable now"; "I feel all strung up now." Emotional traits refer to a habitual tendency to experience that emotion in general—"I often feel miserable"; "I often feel all tense." Naturally, an individual with a trait for high levels of a particular emotion may not be experiencing that emotion at any one time but he is more likely to than someone low in that trait. Also, someone with a high trait for an emotion may avoid experiencing it by minimizing situations which might provoke that emotion. In the particular cases of anxiety and depression we can distinguish between the emotional traits such as anxiousness, pessimism, and lugubriousness and the emotional states of anxiety, tension, and depression.

There is, however, a difference between feelings of anxiety and feelings of depression. There have been no substantiated suggestions that clinical anxiety, the morbid emotion complained of by our patients, is *qualitatively* different from normal anxiety although it is quantitatively greater in some respect, either in intensity, duration, or ubiquitousness. If one takes the time to carefully question one's patients on this point, an entirely consistent impression is given that the anxiety complained of is an extension of the anxiety felt at times throughout life and not a new type of feeling.

With depression the situation appears intuitively to be more complicated. Many depressions are undoubtedly an intensification of normal depression. One can envisage a continuum from "feeling blue" to minor depressive reactions. Such a spectrum is found in the most commonly occurring of these conditions, namely, bereavement reactions and mourning (Parkes, 1965a, 1965b, 1969). In patients with this type of depression the affect appears qualitatively similar to although quantitatively greater than the mild depressions which we all experience. In this respect these depressions resemble anxiety reactions out-lined above. However, in many patients with depressive ill-nesses the affect is qualitatively different. It has an all-per-vasive quality, it is more unpleasant and "anhedonic," and it produces much more despair and inability to discern any future through the current gloom. The affect tends to be free-floating and not attached to any object as it is in a reactive depression. This qualitatively abnormal depression need *not* necessarily be intense and indeed mild forms are more common than is gener-ally appreciated. At the other extreme, in its most intense form, the abnormality of affect and mental function is so great that the patient is unable to feel any depression at all and complains of feeling like an empty shell or a dried husk. Again, if one ques-tions one's patients they will in retrospect comment on the dif-ference between depressive episodes in reaction to events and the morbid depression occurring as an illness. For example, a patient of mine, an extremely intelligent and articulate man, said, "In my 'real' depressions I am in a different sphere of exis-tence, an hermetically sealed black box of extreme despair un-like anything else I experience."

To summarize, the term "clinical" refers to the operational behavioral state of an individual who seeks therapeutic help or has therapeutic help sought for him for symptoms or signs of anxiety or depression. There may have been a distinct rise in the levels of anxiety and depression. This may be in response to readily identifiable factors such as marital problems or in-creased responsibilities at work. Sometimes the external factors cannot be identified and the condition is labeled "en-dogenous," a meaningless term. Alternatively, a person who is anxious or depressed may not have experienced an increase in his lifelong symptoms but may realize he can seek help after discussions with sympathetic people or after viewing a relevant television program or reading a newspaper article. However, the two types of condition commonly occur together with in-creased external pressures raising the emotional levels of an al-ready anxiety-prone or depressive individual.

Experimental Strategies

Why deal at length with these rather academic and theoretical ideas? Despite the attempts of philosophers to categorize the scientific approach into the inductive or the hypothetico-deductive models, most experimentalists seem to work by lurching from inspired guess to detailed experiment to deductions and back to further hunches (Medawar, 1969). However, this is carried out within a rough conceptual framework although the scientist may not have explicitly stated or even fully appreciated the implications of his standpoint. Nevertheless, the framework is really very important as it determines the angle of approach to a particular problem. If one believes that anxiety states are only quantitatively different from normal, then the intensive study of a wide range of measures in normal subjects will be regarded as important and potentially fruitful. Thus, anxious patients can be compared with normal subjects; normal subjects can be made anxious; anxious patients can be made less anxious by treatment; and one can combine these approaches. The same models apply for depressive reactions regarded as quantitatively different from normal. However, if one regards some depressive illnesses as qualitatively abnormal then the use of normal subjects as controls is more limited. Essentially, one must search for the abnormal factor which is present in depressive patients and absent in normal subjects. Comparison of depressives with normals with respect to measures which are present in both, or comparison of depressives with themselves when well, can only be expected to give pointers as to where to seek the elusive abnormal factor in depressives.

The use of control groups presents many difficulties, the main problem being that the model requires that one controls for everything except the abnormal emotion. The important variables are age, sex, intelligence, social class, lack of physical illness; but there are many others which might be important in certain conditions. Full control is an unattainable ideal so one can match groups as closely as possible for variables such as age and sex, and console oneself with the supposition that, if other factors are so important that they will obscure the differences between groups of patients or patients and normals, then those differences are probably too small to be of any real significance. But one can be mistaken. Even the alternative model of using the patient as their own control is not ideal, as there are many factors in the patient which will alter with clinical recovery. For example, a depressed patient may be in a poor nutritional state which will improve *pari passu* with the improvement in his mood and appetite.

The relevance of the points made earlier regarding the definition of patienthood and the distinction between trait and state emotion now become apparent with respect to the comparison between patients and normals. In practice, individuals with the operational and usually self-applied label of "patient" are being compared with others not so ascertained. Yet, "normals" may be just as anxious or depressed as "patients." I encountered this problem in a small pilot experiment in which my co-workers and I noted that our "normal" control group contained several individuals with high levels of overt anxiety. Since then, we have selected calm normals as we are interested in the biological attributes of anxiety and not in the social attributes of the label "anxious patient."

A further problem relates to the laboratory situation which is actually so complex that a normally calm subject may develop anxiety while an anxious patient may remain calm, and yet the reasons for this unexpected reversal are obscure. The need for acclimatization to the laboratory situation has been stressed although the lack of such adaptation in some patients could well be studied, thus turning a potential problem to advantage.

Drugs should be useful tools because they induce, in theory at least, reversible states in the patient. However, many psychotropic drugs are delayed in action and others apparently have a "trigger" effect in that they initiate improvement which then continues under its own momentum. Furthermore, there is the very obvious difficulty that the majority of psychotropic

drugs have marked secondary physiological effects which inter-
fere with psychophysiological measures. Some psychotropic
drugs persist for several weeks in the body and with their widespread use in medical practice present very great practical problems. For example, we wished to study acutely ill schizo-

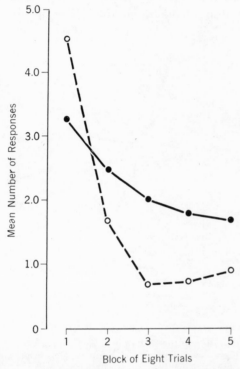

Figure 1.1a *Habituation of the GSR in schizophrenic patients* as compared with
normals. ●——● patients; ○ - - ○ normals. Data from Shakow (1963).

phrenic patients who had not received psychotropic drugs for
four weeks prior to hospital admission. We established a monitoring system for all the admissions from an area of southeast
London with a population of about a million and yet it took over
a year to collect 10 patients who met our criteria.

To recapitulate, there is no universally appropriate model
for psychophysiological research and there is much to commend

the use of several different but complementary approaches. Thus, one can compare patients with emotional abnormalities with normals with respect to the measure of interest, and one can try to induce that particular affect in normal subjects and to reduce it with appropriate treatment in patients. It is also important to show that the physiological changes are *not* found in patients who do not have the morbid affect of interest. One ex-

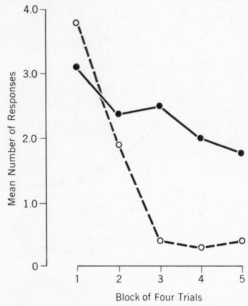

Figure 1.1b *Habituation of the GSR in anxious patients* as compared with normals.●────●patients; o - - o normals. Data from Lader and Wing (1966).

ample concerns habituation of sweat gland responses (GSR-galvanic skin response) which was reported to be impaired in chronic schizophrenic patients and some inferences were drawn about the mechanisms of schizophrenia (Shakow, 1963). However, very similar changes were found in anxious patients (Lader and Wing, 1966) and it is possible that the impaired habituation in chronic schizophrenics reflects increased anxiety levels rather than being a primary consequence of the schizophrenic process itself.

Psychophysiology of Anxiety

STUDIES IN NORMAL SUBJECTS

Considerations of space preclude all but a brief review of psychophysiological studies of anxiety, both in normal subjects and in anxious patients. More detailed accounts are to be found in Martin and Sroufe (1970) and Lader and Marks (1971).

Strong aversive stimuli such as electric shocks usually produce acceleration of the heart, vasoconstriction in skin blood vessels, a burst of increased muscle tone, transient pupillary dilatation, and other autonomic changes including a GSR. The changes form a "startle" reaction (Landis and Hunt, 1939). If anxiety occurs, it follows several seconds after the stimulus. Another situation which induces anxiety is the anticipation of a painful stimulus. The heart accelerates in the half minute before an expected shock except for the last few seconds when it slows. Naive subjects show more tachycardia than experienced subjects (Deane, 1961, 1964). Sweat gland activity rises markedly in the anticipatory period.

Other stimulation procedures have included mirror-drawing tasks, mental arithmetic, and arousing or horrifying films. Real-life situations have consisted of imminent examinations, war situations, and parachute-jumping. The cardiovascular changes during anxiety consist of a rise in blood pressure, chiefly systolic and not sustained at a high level for long, tachycardia, vasoconstriction in the skin and splanchnic regions, vasodilatation in the muscles, with a net drop in peripheral resistance and a consequent rise in stroke volume and cardiac output (Ackner, 1956a; Hickam, Cargill, and Golden, 1948). Palmar sweating increases (rise in skin conductance), the pupil dilates, and salivation diminishes. The changes, in general, are those of increased sympathetic activity.

STUDIES IN ANXIOUS PATIENTS

Many psychophysiological measures have been examined with respect to possible differences between anxious patients and normal subjects. Sometimes the control subjects have been selected because they were judged on interview to be nonanxious; in other studies the controls were merely subjects not known to be receiving medical treatment for anxiety. Similarly, the patients in the various series ranged from groups of psychiatric patients with some anxiety present to patients with unequivocal and sole diagnoses of anxiety state.

Thermal stimulation to the forehead resulted in higher levels of neck muscle electromyograms (EMG) in anxious patients than in normal controls; anxious patients have also been reported to have higher cervical EMG and forearm EMG levels both at rest and during stressful activity (Malmo, Shagass, and Davis, 1951). Simultaneous recording of the EMG from seven recording sites in 21 anxious female patients and 21 controls showed levels to be higher in patients at the masseter and forearm extensor sites (Goldstein, 1964). Other work has been less consistent in showing such differences (Lader and Wing, 1966), and the choice of recording site may be very critical.

Sweating palms are a common accompaniment of anxiety and the degree of sweating can be estimated electrically by measuring the palmar skin conductance. Almost all studies of this measure show an increase in both level of skin conductance and in the number of skin conductance fluctuations. Conductance responses to stimuli are small and show delayed habituation (Lader and Wing, 1966; Lader, 1967).

Other studies using broader patient categories such as "neurotic" or patients with different psychiatric illnesses but the common symptom of anxiety have generally yielded conflicting results, and the usefulness of such studies may be seriously questioned.

Pronounced cardiovascular changes occur in states of high arousal such as anger or fear. A rapid pulse, feelings of palpitations, and pallor are part of the clinical picture of severe anxiety. Altschule (1953) reviewed the literature to that date and concluded that there was no evidence that chronic anxiety, personality disorders or conflict were associated with a sustained rise in arterial pressure. In general, neurotic patients had normal or slightly increased arterial blood pressure, especially systolic.

Pulse rates are usually reported as elevated in anxious patients (Altschule, 1953). White and Gildea (1937), Wenger (1947), and Wishner (1953) all reported such elevations although other studies have not reported such differences between anxious patients and normals. In another study, the mean waking pulse rate in anxious patients and controls were similar but a greater drop in the pulse rate of the anxious patients was observed when they fell asleep (Ackner, 1956b). More recently, both Lader and Wing (1966) and Kelly and Walter (1968) have reported significantly higher pulse rates in patients with anxiety states than in normal controls.

Ackner (1956a) reviewed previous work on the relationship between vasomotor activity and anxiety. In general, anxious patients have vasoconstriction of the blood vessels in the extremities (Neumann, Lhamon, and Cohn, 1944). Vasodilatation occurs during the onset of sleep (Ackner, 1956b). Conversely, muscle blood flow is increased in anxious patients: the mean forearm blood flow for normal controls was 2.2 ml/100 ml arm vol/min, for a mixed group of psychoneurotics, 2.3 ml/100 ml/min, and for a group of anxiety states, 4.8 ml/100 ml/min (Kelly, 1966). Although other studies have been less clear in their results, it does appear that the cardiovascular changes in anxiety states include tachycardia, skin vasoconstriction and muscle vasodilatation.

There have been relatively few studies of the EEG in anxious patients but the results have consistently been that alpha activity is less abundant and that which is present is faster than normal (Brazier, Finesinger, and Cobb, 1945; Lindsley, 1950). This reflects the patients' inability to relax. The well-known excessive distractibility of anxious patients also seems to have a neurophysiological counterpart. The mean contingent negative variation wave (CNV) during acquisition trials was significantly smaller in 40 highly anxious patients than 40 control subjects. When a distracting noise was introduced, the CNV in the normals was only temporarily reduced while in the patients it remained small (McCallum and Walter, 1968).

HORMONAL FUNCTION

The adrenocortical hormone cortisol is increased in the plasma in response to a wide variety of stimuli including venipuncture itself. College examinations, paratroop training, and flying an aircraft are all known to raise plasma cortisol levels and the amount of cortisol metabolites in the urine. However, the increases in steroid level reflect more the subject's emotional involvement in the situation, real-life or laboratory-simulated, than the physical danger, stress involved or affect produced. Release of adrenaline and noradrenaline from the adrenal medulla also occurs during times of stress and the amount in the urine is increased.

In anxious patients plasma cortisol levels are raised; during calm periods the levels drop; during panic states they rise even further. Stressful interviews increase plasma cortisol levels but anxiety, anger, and depression may all be the predominant concomitant affect (Persky et al., 1958). Particularly high levels were found when the anxiety was "disintegrative" in nature such as fear of loss of sanity or of losing self-control.

Adrenomedullary function tends to be increased in anxious patients but there have been relatively few studies of this topic. In one study, various groups of subjects with overt affects of anger and anxiety were studied with respect to their catecholamine excretion in the urine (Silverman et al., 1961). Excretion of adrenaline was highest among the primarily anxious, lowest among the primarily angry; for noradrenaline the reverse pattern was found.

PERSONAL WORK

In some work carried out several years ago, several different groups of subjects all drug-free and with detailed clinical assessments were examined (Lader, 1967; Lader and Sartorius, 1968; Lader and Wing, 1969). The two physiological measures of particular interest were the skin conductance responses to a series of tones and skin conductance fluctuations. The results are tabulated in Table 1.1. It can be seen that the patients diag-

Table 1.1   Rate of Spontaneous Skin Conductance Fluctuations and Rate of GSR Habituation in Various Groups of Patients

Clinical Group	Number in Sample	Spontaneous Fluctuations per Minute	Rate of Habituation *
Normals	75	1.5	72
Specific phobics	19	2.8	68
Social phobics	18	6.2	39
Agoraphobics	19	6.0	39
Anxiety states	16	6.8	29
Anxiety with depression	18	6.9	22
Agitated depressives	17	9.2	10
Retarded depressives	13	0.5	— †
Chronic conversion hysterics	10	11.2	−4

* The higher the value, the more rapid the rate of habituation.

† So few responses were elicited that habituation rates could not be calculated.

nosed as monosymptomatic, specific phobics (circumscribed fears of dogs, spiders, birds, etc.) are close to normal with respect to these measures. A cluster consisting of groups of patients with social phobias (fears of eating in restaurants, public speaking, etc.), agoraphobias (fears of venturing out of doors, of public transport, etc.), anxiety states, and anxiety with depression (both morbid affects without either predominating) have higher fluctuation rates and slower habituation. Agitated depressives and chronic conversion hysterics (with conversion symptoms at the time of testing, such as monoplegia, astasia-abasia, and amnesia) are more active still and habituate slowly, if at all. Significantly less active than normals are a group of depressed patients with marked psychomotor retardation. They had very few fluctuations and too few responses to allow habituation rates to be computed. A close intergroup relationship can be seen between spontaneous fluctuations, a measure of "arousal," and habituation of the GSR, so that the lower the arousal level the more rapid is habituation. No cause and effect relationship can be deduced and, indeed, it is more likely that the two phenomena of arousal and habituation are intimately linked in an interactive manner. The further implications of this interaction and the possibility that at high levels of arousal habituation would be nonexistent, thus perpetuating the high

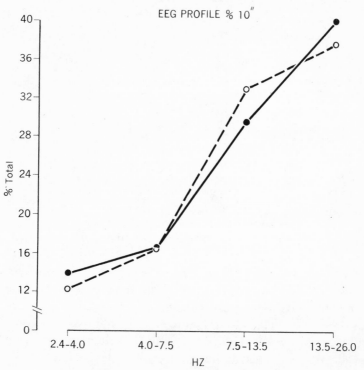

Figure 1.2 *EEG profiles of anxious patients and normal control subjects* during a no-response condition. ●——● patients; o - - - o controls.

levels of arousal, have been explored in more detail (Lader and Mathews, 1969) and have been incorporated into a model of morbid anxiety (Lader, 1972).

In a recent study carried out by Bond and James in my laboratory, 30 patients with unequivocal diagnoses of anxiety state were compared with 30 age- and sex-matched, calm, normal subjects with respect to a range of psychophysiological measures recorded under no-response and simple reaction-time task response conditions to auditory click stimuli.

The EEG recorded under no-response conditions was analyzed into 4 wavebands and the mean integrated voltage for each waveband was expressed as a percentage of the total (Figure 1.2). Only one waveband, 7.5–13.5 Hz, showed significant

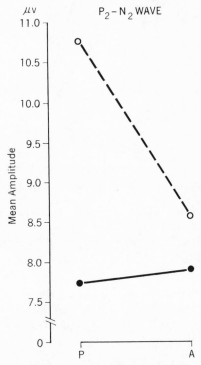

Figure 1.3 *Amplitude of the P_2-N_2 component of the A.E.R. during no-response (P) and response (A) conditions in anxious patients and normal control subjects. Legend as in Figure 1.2.*

differences between the groups, proportionately less energy
being found in the patients' EEGs than in the controls'. Similar
but less marked differences were found between the groups for
the response task condition.

The averaged evoked auditory response to the click stimuli

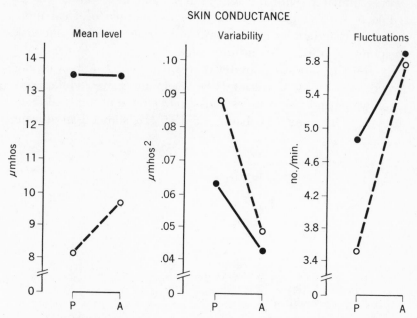

Figure 1.4 *Skin conductance level, variability, and fluctuations* during no-
response (P) and response (A) conditions in anxious patients and
normal control subjects. Legend as in Figure 1.2.

was computed for both no-response and response conditions.
The P_2-N_2 component of the averaged evoked response is a
vertex-negative-going wave between latencies of about 200 and
275 ms after the click. Its amplitude is believed to be inversely
related to the degree of alertness of the subject (Wilkinson,
1967; Bostock and Jarvis, 1970). As such it would be expected to
decrease in size from the no-response to the response condition.
This was indeed found for the normal group (Figure 1.3). The
patients, however, showed no change, the P_2-N_2 wave being
relatively small under both response conditions.

The mean skin conductance level in the patients was considerably higher than that in the controls (Figure 1.4). In the patients, there was no difference between the no-response and response conditions, whereas in the normal subjects the expected rise in conductance during the response situation occurred. Skin conductance variability was lower in the patients especially under no-response conditions. The skin conductance fluctuations were both "spontaneous" and in response to the click stimuli; as the latter were 8 to 12 seconds apart, it was thought impractical to try and separate out the fluctuations. The patients did show an increase in rate under response conditions but this increase was only about half that of the control subjects.

Other autonomic measures were estimated under resting conditions only (Figure 1.5). Pulse rate, as might be expected, was higher in the patients. Pupil size under dim illumination

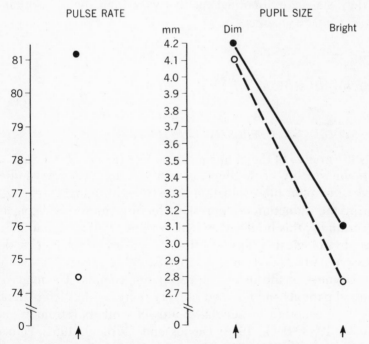

Figure 1.5 *Pulse rate and pupil size in anxious patients and control subjects.* Legend as in Figure 1.2.

was slightly but nonsignificantly greater in patients; with change to bright illumination the patients' pupils constricted significantly less than the controls'.

All in all, the results of this study confirm my long-standing contention that differences between calm normals and anxious patients are maximized by encouraging both groups to relax. Conversely, stimulation procedures actually diminish any differences and the physiological activity of the normal subjects increases toward that of the patients.

The data are all consistent with the hypothesis that anxious patients are "overaroused" chronically (Malmo, 1959, 1972; Lader and Wing, 1966; Lader, 1969, 1972). This hypothesis also implies that anxiety in patients is only quantitatively abnormal and our data, taken as a whole, would support this. I know of no evidence that the physiological changes found in patients with anxiety state are abnormal qualitatively from those in normal subjects made anxious.

Psychophysiology of Depression

STUDIES IN DEPRESSIVE PATIENTS

It is illustrative of the points made earlier regarding the qualitative abnormality of the depressive affect that very few studies have attempted the evaluation of psychophysiological changes during the induction of depressive feelings in normal subjects. Accordingly, this brief review will confine itself to an outline of the physiological differences found consistently between depressive patients and normal subjects.

Dryness of the mouth is a frequent complaint among depressed patients and reduced salivary secretion in such patients has been reported by several groups of workers (Strongin and Hinsie, 1938; Peck, 1959; Davies and Gurland, 1961; Palmai and Blackwell, 1965). Attempts to relate the impairment in salivary flow to the severity of depressive symptoms have produced equivocal reports: Davies and Palmai (1964) claimed such a relationship whereas others found no such progressive diminution in salivation with increase in severity of depressive symptoms (Peck, 1959; Busfield and Wechsler, 1961).

If reduced salivation is associated with depression, then treatment and amelioration of the illness should be accompanied by an increase in salivary flow rate. However, reports have been inconsistent: in two studies the salivation of depressed patients remained unchanged despite clinical improvement (Gottlieb and Paulson, 1961; Hemsie, Whitehead, and Post, 1968); in other studies, a return of diminished salivary flow levels to normal has been claimed (Davies and Palmai, 1964; Palmai and Blackwell, 1965).

Studies of the electromyogram in depressive patients have suggested that muscle activity levels are higher than normal (Whatmore and Ellis, 1959). EMG responses are also greater in depressed patients (Goldstein, 1965). Higher frontalis EMG levels were found in depressed patients than in controls but the forearm muscle activity levels were raised only in the more severely depressed patients (Martin and Davies, 1965). Similarly, in another study, mildly depressed patients had raised masseter EMG levels and severely depressed male patients had elevated forehead and forearm EMG levels (Rimón, Stenbäck, and Huhmar, 1968).

Studies of skin conductance changes in depression are relatively few. In general, sweat-gland activity seems to be depressed (Richter, 1928; Bagg and Crookes, 1966). Twenty depressed patients were rated on a depressive scale derived from the MMPI; those with higher scores showed a reduction in galvanic skin response amplitude to auditory stimuli (Greenfield et al., 1963).

Sleep is often disturbed, patients having fitful, unsatisfying sleep with a tendency to wake early (Hinton, 1963). These clinical observations have been confirmed in EEG studies (Mendels and Hawkins, 1967). Although one study suggested that depressed patients spend more of their time asleep in the deeper stages of sleep (Oswald et al., 1962), other investigators have reported the opposite (Gresham, Agnew, and Williams, 1965; Hawkins and Mendels, 1966). Depressed patients show more EEG reactivity during sleep than normals and than themselves when recovered (Zung, Wilson, and Dodson, 1964).

EEG evoked responses have been used in several ways to investigate cerebral function in depressed patients. In one approach, the "cortical recovery cycle" is evaluated by presenting series of paired stimuli, the interstimulus interval of the pair varying widely. The size of the second response is compared to that of the first, and this ratio is calculated over the range of interstimulus intervals (Shagass, 1972). Abnormalities have been described in depressive patients using somatosensory stimulation with an interstimulus interval of less than 20 ms; such abnormalities were not specific to depressive patients but were found in psychiatric patients in general (Shagass, 1972). Notwithstanding, other studies using visual modality stimulation have suggested that impaired recovery of the second response is to be found in psychotic depressives especially (Speck, Dim, and Mercer, 1966; Vasconetto, Floris, and Morocutti, 1971).

Adrenocortical function is altered in depressed patients. Fairly substantial within-patient correlations have been found between corticosteroid excretion in the urine and intensity of depression; the intensity of anxiety was also a determining factor. Patients who were aware of their mental abnormalities and were actively struggling with their problems had higher steroid levels than those patients who had elaborate psychological defenses and who denied the existence of their illnesses (Bunney, Mason, and Hamburg, 1965).

Plasma cortisol (hydrocortisone) level studies have, in general, supported the findings with urinary steroids. Very high plasma levels were associated with marked emotional anguish and with the onset of progressive personality disintegration (Board, Persky, and Hamburg, 1956). Plasma cortisol levels show a diurnal variation being highest in the morning and the elevation in depressed patients is most marked at this time. Cortisol secretion rate and plasma corticotrophin levels have also been found to be raised (Gibbons, 1966), perhaps due to an insensitivity of the hypothalamus to cortisol with a resulting oversecretion of corticotrophin and cortisol (Carroll, Martin, and Davies, 1968). The cortisol levels in the cerebrospinal fluid of depressives appear to be normal (Coppen et al., 1971).

Catecholamine excretion, reflecting adrenomedullary activity, is reported as low in depressive patients and very high in manic patients (Bergsman, 1959).

PERSONAL WORK

The results of psychophysiological studies of patients with depressive illnesses are even more complex than those of patients with anxiety. The clinical variable to which to relate the psychophysiological measures might at first sight appear to be the depth of depression but an alternative and more heuristic psychophysiological approach has been to examine the patients in terms of agitation and retardation. The clinician cannot help but be impressed by the different type of behavior: the slowed, retarded patient with his tardiness in carrying out commands and his poverty of associated movement and speech, as contrasted with the agitated patient with an abundance of purposeless movements and excess speech whose response to commands is equally ineffective because of interference by other ongoing activity.

In an early study, Dr. Lorna Wing and I made physiological and clinical observations on 35 drug-free patients with the diagnosis of primary depression of moderate or severe degree (Lader and Wing, 1969). Clinically, 17 patients were predominantly agitated, 13 were predominantly retarded, and 5 showed neither feature to any marked extent. The depressed patients were compared with normal subjects matched for age and sex. The palmar skin conductance (sweat-gland activity), the pulse rate and the forearm extensor electromyogram were recorded during the presentation of 20 identical 1 kHz auditory stimuli of 100 dB intensity and 1 second duration occurring at intervals ranging from 45 to 80 seconds. Measures derived included the skin conductance level, the size of the first GSR, the habituation rate of the GSRs, the number of spontaneous skin conductance fluctuations, the pulse rate, and EMG level.

Clear-cut differences were found between the two major groups of depressed patients: the agitated patients had a high mean skin conductance (more sweat-gland activity) and more spontaneous skin conductance fluctuations than the retarded patients. The agitated patients showed little GSR habituation while all but one of the retarded patients displayed so little reactivity that their habituation rate was not calculable. For these measures, the normal values lay between those for the two groups of patients. Pulse rate was increased only in the agitated patients.

Discrimination between the highly agitated and most retarded patients was complete with respect to the GSR habituation rate and spontaneous fluctuations. It should be emphasized, however, that the patients in these categories were severely depressed and could be unequivocally classified as agitated or retarded. It does not necessarily imply that agitation and retardation cannot exist together or that patients do not oscillate from one state to another.

In another study, 34 depressed patients in a drug-free state were assessed before and two weeks subsequent to a course of electroconvulsive therapy (ECT). Psychometric measures were taken and recordings were made of the forearm extensor EMG and forearm blood flow, pulse rate and skin conductance under basal conditions and during a stressful mental arithmetic task. On retesting there was a marked improvement in depressive symptomatology but little change in anxiety levels. Subsequent to ECT, basal EMG levels decreased significantly and EMG reactivity to stress increased significantly as compared to pre-ECT levels (Noble and Lader, 1971a). Mean physiological levels of skin conductance did not alter significantly subsequent to ECT and this might reflect the unchanged anxiety levels (Noble and Lader, 1971b). Forearm blood flow but not pulse rate decreased with remission of the depressive symptoms (Noble and Lader, 1971c). Salivary flow rates were also estimated and did not change after ECT.

There were interesting relationships between symptom ratings (using the Hamilton Depressive Scale) and various physiological measures. Prior to ECT, high basal EMG levels were correlated with the severity of the depression and with high scores for anxiety, gastrointestinal somatic symptoms, loss of libido, and weight loss. Low forearm blood flow correlated with retardation and decline in work and interests. Skin conductance levels and fluctuations correlated negatively with retardation, tending to confirm our earlier work. Salivary secretion was found to be related to retardation: the more retarded patients had low salivary flow rates before ECT which increased subsequently whereas the least retarded patients had high salivary flow rates before ECT which diminished thereafter (Noble and Lader, 1971d).

Using a clinical rating scale we also divided our patients into "endogenous" (16 patients) and "reactive" (18 patients). The only physiological measures to differentiate between the groups were skin conductance and skin conductance fluctuations which were both higher in the reactive groups. We also found a significant correlation (0.41) between ratings of retardation and presence of endogenous depression (Noble and Lader, 1972). As we found more consistent relationships between retardation and the physiological measures we concluded that retardation is a more useful concept from the psychophysiological point of view than is endogenous-reactive.

In general, our results were less clear-cut than in the earlier study which is probably attributable to our patients being selected on the criteria of being drug-free and about to be administered electroconvulsive therapy: such patients are by no means all severely or even moderately depressed.

This study emphasizes a basic problem in this type of research. We focus our attention on one aspect of a patient's mental state, say, depression, but later suspect that other factors were of more relevance to the variables under study. A sort of affective profile can be established which, together with the use of multivariate statistics, could suggest useful studies. However, the classical psychiatric nosologies need not necessarily be discarded but rather amplified and supplemented.

In a third study we concentrated on the central measures

and attempted to find differences between depressed patients and twenty normal controls matched for age and sex. The EEG was analyzed using broad wave-band filters: the depressed patients had significantly less EEG activity in the 2.4–4 Hz wave band and significantly more activity in the 7.5–13.5 and 13.5–26 Hz wave bands than did the normal control subjects. We also measured the evoked responses to clicks in these patients and found that the depressed patients had smaller evoked responses (of components with latencies between about 50 and 250 msec) than did the normal subjects when the interstimulus interval was about 10 secs and the subject was instructed to respond (Julier and Lader, unpublished data).

This work was carried out some time ago but we were concerned because we had been unable to discontinue night sedation in the depressed patients. Practically all received either a moderate dose of a barbiturate or of a nonbarbiturate hypnotic such as nitrazepam (a benzodiazepine derivative). Accordingly, we investigated the effects of such drugs in 10 normal subjects by testing them on a large battery of physiological and psychological tests twelve hours after a hypnotic dose of butobarbitone sodium (100 or 200 mg) or nitrazepam (5 or 10 mg) and compared with a placebo (Bond and Lader, 1972). The subjects received all five treatments in a balanced design. The tests used included self-ratings, the electroencephalogram, the auditory electroencephalographic evoked response, reaction time, tapping, card-sorting, and the digit symbol substitution test. Both drugs were effective hypnotics according to the ratings but butobarbitone had more subjective "hangover" the following morning. The electroencephalogram showed the following effects: both drugs tended to decrease the slow wave bands, 2.4–4 Hz and 4–7.5 Hz, and to increase the fast wave band 13.5–26 Hz. The 7.5–13.5 Hz wave band also tended to decrease with the drugs, especially nitrazepam. Evoked response effects showed some diminution in the amplitude of the various components, especially the N_2 wave and especially with nitrazepam. It would appear that the control of night sedation is yet another factor to be taken into account in psychophysiological research and as this withdrawal of night sedation can lead to problems with the patient and with the nursing staff it is yet another limitation to this type of research.

Conclusions

Psychophysiological research has illuminated several problems in psychiatry as the review of literature has shown. In most cases it has proved more profitable to investigate a clearly observable phenomenon such as overt anxiety, agitation, or retardation rather than deal with broad concepts such as neurotic or psychotic. Problems arise because of the dissonances between the scientific, medical, and social approaches to human illness but it should be remembered that these approaches can be made to complement each other and are not mutually exclusive.

References

Ackner, B. 1956a. Emotions and the peripheral vasomotor system: A review of previous work. *Journal of Psychosomatic Research,* 1:3–20.

—— 1956b. The relationship between anxiety and the level of peripheral vasomotor activity. *Journal of Psychosomatic Research,* 1:21–48.

Altschule, M. D. 1953. *Bodily Physiology in Mental and Emotional Disorders.* New York: Grune and Stratton.

Bagg, C. E. and T. G. Crookes. 1966. Palmar digital sweating in women suffering from depression. *British Journal of Psychiatry,* 112:1251–1255.

Bergsman, A. 1959. The urinary excretion of adrenaline and noradrenaline in some mental diseases: A clinical and experimental study. *Acta Psychiatrica et Neurologica Scandinavia* (Suppl. 133).

Board, F., H. Persky, and D. A. Hamburg. 1956. Psychological stress and endocrine functions: Blood levels of adrenocortical and thyroid hormones in acutely disturbed patients. *Psychosomatic Medicine,* 18:324–333.

Bond, A. J. and M. H. Lader. 1972. Residual effects of hypnotics. *Psychopharmacologia,* 25:117–132.

Bostock, H. and M. J. Jarvis. 1970. Changes in the form of the cerebral evoked response related to the speed of simple reaction time. *Electroencephalography and clinical Neurophysiology*, 29:137–145.

Brazier, Mary A. B., J. E. Finesinger, and S. Cobb. 1945. A contrast between the electroencephalograms of 100 psychoneurotic patients and those of 500 normal adults. *American Journal of Psychiatry*, 101:443–448.

Bunney, W. E., J. W. Mason, and D. A. Hamburg. 1965. Correlations between behavioral variables and urinary 17-hydroxy-corticosteriods in depressed patients. *Psychosomatic Medicine*, 27:299–308.

Busfield, B. L. and H. Wechsler. 1961. Studies of salivation in depression. *Archives of General Psychiatry*, 4:10–15.

Carroll, B. J., F. I. R. Martin, and B. Davies. 1968. Resistance to suppression by dexamethasone of plasma 11-O.H.C.S. levels in severe depressive illness. *British Medical Journal*, 3:285–287.

Cohen, H. 1955. The evolution of the concept of disease. *Proceedings of the Royal Society of Medicine*, 48:155–160.

Cooper, J. E., R. E. Kendell, B. J. Gurland, L. Sharpe, J. R. M. Copeland, and R. Simon. 1972. *Psychiatric Diagnosis in New York and London*. London: Oxford University Press.

Coppen, A., B. W. L. Brooksbank, R. Noguera, and D. A. Wilson. 1971. Cortisol in the cerebrospinal fluid of patients suffering from affective disorders. *Journal of Neurology, Neurosurgery and Psychiatry*, 34:432–435.

Davies, B. M. and J. B. Gurland. 1961. Salivary secretion in depressive illness. *Journal of Psychosomatic Research*, 5:269–271.

Davies, B. M. and G. Palmai. 1964. Salivary and blood pressure responses to methacholine in depressive illness. *British Journal of Psychiatry*, 110:594–598.

Deane, G. E. 1961. Human heart rate responses during experimentally induced anxiety. *Journal of Experimental Psychology*, 61:489–493.

—— 1964. Human heart rate responses during experimentally induced anxiety: A follow up with controlled respiration. *Journal of Experimental Psychology*, 67:193–195.

Gibbons, J. L. 1966. The secretion rate of corticosterone in depressive illness. *Journal of Psychosomatic Research*, 10:263–266.

Goldstein, I. B. 1964. Physiological responses in anxious women patients: A study of autonomic activity and muscle tension. *Archives of General Psychiatry*, 10:382–388.

—— 1965. The relationship of muscle tension and autonomic activity to psychiatric disorders. *Psychosomatic Medicine*, 27:39–52.

Gottlieb, G. and G. Paulson. 1961. Salivation in depressed patients. *Archives of General Psychiatry*, 5:468–471.

Greenfield, N. S., D. Katz, A. A. Alexander, and R. Roessler. 1963. The relationship between physiological and psychological responsivity, depression and galvanic skin response. *Journal of Nervous and Mental Disease*, 136:535–539.

Gresham, S. C., H. W. Agnew, and R. L. Williams. 1965. The sleep of depressed patients: An EEG and eye movement study. *Archives of General Psychiatry*, 13:503–507.

Hawkins, D. R. and J. Mendels. 1966. Sleep disturbance in depressive syndromes. *American Journal of Psychiatry*, 123:682–690.

Hemsi, I. K., A. Whitehead, and F. Post. 1968. Cognitive functioning and cerebral arousal in elderly depressives and dements. *Journal of Psychosomatic Research*, 12:145–156.

Hickam, J. B., W. H. Cargill, and A. Golden. 1948. Cardiovascular reactions to emotional stimuli: Effect on the cardiac output, arteriovenous oxygen difference, arterial pressure, and peripheral resistance. *Journal of Clinical Investigation*, 27:290–298.

Hinton, J. M. 1963. A comparison of the effects of six barbiturates and a placebo on insomnia and motility in psychiatric patients. *British Journal of Pharmacology*, 20:319–325.

Kelly, D. H. W. 1966. Measurement of anxiety by forearm blood flow. *British Journal of Psychiatry*, 112:789–798.

Kelly, D. H. W. and C. J. S. Walter. 1969. A clinical and physiological relationship between anxiety and depression. *British Journal of Psychiatry*, 115:401–406.

Lader, M. H. 1967. Palmar skin conductance measures in anxiety and phobic states. *Journal of Psychosomatic Research*, 11:271–281.

—— 1972. The nature of anxiety. *British Journal of Psychiatry*, 121:481–491.

Lader, M. and I. Marks. 1971. *Clinical Anxiety*. London: Heinemann Medical Books.

Lader, M. and A. Mathews. 1968. Physiological basis of desensitization. *Behaviour Research and Therapy*, 6:411–421.

Lader, M. and G. Sartorious. 1968. Anxiety in patients with hysterical conversion symptoms. *Journal of Neurology, Neurosurgery and Psychiatry*, 31:490–495.

Lader, M. H. and L. Wing. 1966. *Physiological Measures, Sedative Drugs and Morbid Anxiety*. Maudsley Monograph No. 14. London: Oxford University Press.

—— 1969. Physiological measures in agitated and retarded depressed patients. *Journal of Psychiatric Research*, 7:89–100.

Landis, C. and W. A. Hunt. 1939. *The Startle Pattern*. New York: Farrar and Rinehart.

Levitt, E. E. 1968. *The Psychology of Anxiety*. London: Staples Press.

Lindsley, D. B. 1950. Emotions and the electroencephalogram. In M. L. Reymert (ed.), *Feelings and Emotions*. New York: McGraw-Hill.

McCallum, W. C. and W. G. Walter. 1968. The effects of attention and distraction on the contingent negative variation in normal and neurotic subjects. *Electroencephalography and Clinical Neurophysiology*, 25:319–329.

Malmo, R. B. 1959. Activation: A neuropsychological dimension. *Psychological Review*, 66:367–386.

—— 1972. Overview. In N. S. Greenfield and R. A. Sternbach (eds.), *Handbook of Psychophysiology*. New York: Holt, Rinehart and Winston.

Malmo, R. B., C. Shagass, and J. F. Davis. 1951. Electromyographic studies of muscular tension in psychiatric patients under stress. *Journal of Clinical Experimental Psycho-pathology*, 12:45–66.

Martin, B. and L. A. Sroufe. 1970. Anxiety. In C. G. Costello (ed.), *Symptoms of Psychopathology.* New York: Wiley.

Martin, I. and B. M. Davies. 1965. The effect of Na amytal in autonomic and muscle activity of patients with depressive illness. *British Journal of Psychiatry,* 111:168–175.

Mechanic, D. 1968. *Medical Sociology: A Selective View.* New York: Free Press.

Medawar, P. B. 1969. *Induction and Intuition in Scientific Thought.* London: Methuen.

Mendels, J. and D. R. Hawkins. 1967. Sleep and depression: A follow-up study. *Archives of General Psychiatry,* 16:536–542.

Neumann, C., W. T. Lhamon, and A. E. Cohn. 1944. Study of emotional factors responsible for changes in the pattern of rhythmic volume fluctuations of the finger tip. *Journal of Clinical Investigation,* 23:1–9.

Noble, P. J. and M. H. Lader. 1971a. An electromyographic study of depressed patients. *Journal of Psychosomatic Research,* 15:233–239.

—— 1971b. The symptomatic correlates of the skin conductance changes in depression. *Journal of Psychiatric Research,* 9:61–69.

—— 1971c. Depression and forearm blood flow. *British Journal of Psychiatry,* 119:261–266.

—— 1971d. Salivation and depressive illness; a psychometric and physiological study. *Psychological Medicine,* 1:372–376.

—— 1972. A physiological comparison of "endogenous" and "reactive" depression. *British Journal of Psychiatry,* 120:541–542.

Oswald, I., R. J. Berger, R. A. Jaramillo, K. M. G. Keddie, P. C. Olley, and G. B. Plunkett. 1963. Melancholia and barbiturates: A controlled EEG, body and eye movement study of sleep. *British Journal of Psychiatry,* 109:66–78.

Palmai, G. and B. Blackwell. 1965. Diurnal pattern of salivary flow in normal and depressed patients. *British Journal of Psychiatry,* 111:334–338.

Parkes, C. M. 1965a. Bereavement and mental illness. Part 1: A clinical study of the grief of bereaved psychiatric patients. *British Journal of Medical Psychology,* 38:1–12.

—— 1965b. Bereavement and mental illness. Part 2: A classification of bereavement reactions. *British Journal of Medical Psychology,* 38:13–26.

—— 1969. Separation anxiety: An aspect of the search for a lost object. In M. H. Lader (ed.), *Studies of Anxiety.* London: Royal Medico-Psychological Association.

Peck, R. E. 1959. The SHP test: An aid in the detection and measurement of depression. *Archives of General Psychiatry,* 1:35–40.

Persky, H., D. A. Hamburg, H. Basowitz, R. R. Grinker, S. Sabshin, S. J. Korchin, M. Hertz, F. A. Board, and H. A. Heath. 1958. Relation of emotional responses and changes in plasma hydrocortisone level after stressful interview. *Archives of Neurology and Psychiatry,* 79:434–447.

Richter, C. P. 1928. The electrical skin resistance. *Archives of Neurology and Psychiatry,* 19:488–508.

Rimón, R., A. Stenbäck, and E. Huhmar. 1967. Electromyographic findings in depressive patients. *Journal of Psychosomatic Research,* 10:159–170.

Scadding, J. G. 1967. Diagnosis: The clinician and the computer. *Lancet*, 2:877–882.

Shagass, C. 1972. *Evoked Brain Potentials in Psychiatry*. New York: Plenum Press.

Shakow, D. 1963. Psychological deficit in schizophrenia. *Behavioral Science*, 8:275–305.

Silverman, A. J., S. I. Cohen, B. M. Shmavonian, and N. Kirschner. 1961. Catecholamines in psychophysiologic studies. *Recent Advances in Biological Psychiatry*, 3:104–117.

Speck, L. B., B. Dim, and M. Mercer. 1966. Visual evoked responses of psychiatric patients. *Archives of General Psychiatry*, 15:59–63.

Spielberger, C. D., R. L. Gorsuch, and R. E. Lushene. 1968. *Manual for the State-Trait Anxiety Inventory*. Tallahassee: Florida State University.

Strongin, E. I. and L. E. Hinsie. 1938. Parotid gland secretions in manic depressive patients. *American Journal of Psychiatry*, 94:1459–1466.

Szasz, T. S. 1961. *The Myth of Mental Illness—Foundations of a Theory of Personal Conduct*. New York: Hoeber-Harper.

Taylor, F. K. 1971. A logical analysis of the medico-psychological concept of disease. *Psychological Medicine*, 1:356–364.

Vasconetto, C., V. Floris, and C. Morocutti. 1971. Visual evoked responses in normal and psychiatric subjects. *Electroencephalography and Clinical Neurophysiology*, 31:77–83.

Wenger, M. A. 1947. Preliminary study of the significance of measures of autonomic balance. *Psychosomatic Medicine*, 9:301–309.

Whatmore, G. B. and R. M. Ellis. 1959. Some neurophysiological aspects of depressed states. An electromyographic study. *Archives of General Psychiatry*, 1:70–80.

White, B. V. and E. F. Gildea. 1937. "Cold pressor test" in tension and anxiety. A cardiochronographic study. *Archives of Neurology and Psychiatry*, 38:964–984.

Wilkinson, R. T. 1967. Evoked response and reaction time. *Acta Psychologica (Amst.)*, 27:235–245.

Wishner, J. 1953. Neurosis and tension: An exploratory study of the relationship of physiological and Rorschach measures. *Journal of Abnormal and Social Psychology*, 48:253–260.

Zung, W. W. K., W. P. Wilson, and W. E. Dodson. 1964. Effect of depressive disorders on sleep EEG responses. *Archives of General Psychiatry*, 10:439–445.

2

Psychophysiological Studies of Sleep in Depressed Patients: An Overview

J. MENDELS and D. A. CHERNIK

UNTIL RECENTLY, relatively few basic physiological functions had received as little research attention as sleep. Although sleep occupies about one-third of our lives, and although millions of people resort to drugs to achieve it, we do not know what it is. We do not even know what it is to be "tired," except in the most subjective sense. We are not even sure if being awake is the natural state, with sleep some kind of interruption or whether, in fact, sleep is the natural state with wakefulness being the interruption.

The Sleep EEG and Stages of Sleep

The discovery of the electroencephalogram (EEG) by Berger in 1929 and its application in the initial characterization of different levels of sleep by Loomis and associates (Loomis, Harvey, and Hobart, 1937) made it possible to obtain a more detailed understanding of sleep patterns in man.

In the 1950s a group of research workers in Chicago made a

Research for this article was supported in part by NIMH grant #1 R01 MH17551 and research funds from the Veterans Administration.

series of crucial observations. First, Aserinsky, working in Nathaniel Kleitman's laboratory, noticed periodic clusters of horizontal jerky eye movements, observable even though the eyelids were closed. These occurred in a cyclic fashion through the night. There would be four or five bursts of this activity, each lasting from just a few minutes to 45 or 50 minutes (Aserinsky and Kleitman, 1953). It was then noted that these eye movements were accompanied by an activation of the electroencephalogram, producing an EEG pattern close to that of the waking state. There were also changes in heart rate and respira-

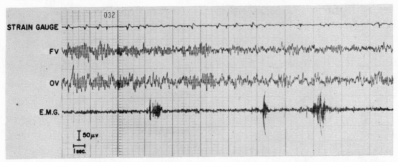

Figure 2.1 *Transition from waking alpha rhythm to Stage 1.* During relaxed wakefulness the EEG is composed of sinusoidal alpha activity (8 to 10 cps) and low voltage activity of mixed frequency, accompanied by eye movements, and high muscle tone. As the subject falls asleep, his EEG gives way to a Stage 1 pattern of relatively low voltage and of mixed frequency.

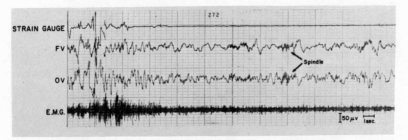

Figure 2.2 *Body movement and Stage 2.* Stage 2 is characterized by 12 to 14 cps sleep spindles, similar in shape to alpha waves but higher in frequency, together with K complexes superimposed on a background of relatively low voltage, mixed frequency electroencephalographic activity.

tory rate. Shortly thereafter, it was found that subjects who were awakened during this phase of sleep usually reported dreaming (Dement and Kleitman, 1957).

Rapid Eye Movement sleep (REM, D-state, or activated sleep) is now widely accepted as being the phase of sleep in which most dreaming occurs. This is not to say that there is no mental activity during other phases of sleep. There is evidence to suggest that there is. However, the material is much more difficult to retrieve and is more fragmented and less meaningful than the material recovered from patients during REM periods.

A night's sleep record is usually divided up into four stages (in addition to REM sleep) according to the system described by Dement and Kleitman (1957) and refined by Rechtschaffen and Kales (1968). Stage 1 sleep (Figure 2.1) consists of a low amplitude high frequency EEG. It is light sleep and occupies a small portion of the night. Stage 2 sleep (Figure 2.2) occupies a major portion of the night and is characterized by the presence

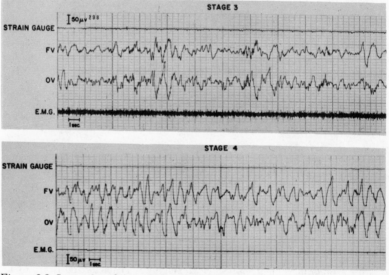

Figure 2.3 *Stages 3 and 4* are defined by high voltage, slow waves of 1 to 2 cps; when more than half the record consists of this slow-wave activity, it is classified as Stage 4, while lesser amounts (but greater than 20 percent) are classified as Stage 3.

of "sleep spindles." These are short bursts of fast EEG activity (12–14 cps). Stages 3 and 4 sleep (Figure 2.3) are periods in which the EEG is dominated by slow (1 to 2 cps) high amplitude delta waves. Stage 1 REM sleep (Figure 2.4) shows an electroencephalographic pattern similar to that of Stage 1 but is accompanied by episodic rapid eye movements and a low amplitude EMG (electromyogram).

There is some evidence that the descending stages of sleep reflect deeper stages of sleep. On the average, Delta Wave sleep (Stages 3 and 4) correlates with the greatest reduction in

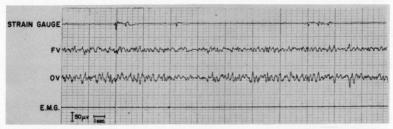

Figure 2.4 *Stage 1 REM sleep* shows an electroencephalographic pattern similar to that of Stage 1 but is accompanied by episodic rapid-eye-movements and low amplitude EMG.

response capacity while REM and Stage 2 are closer to the response capacities of waking (Granda and Hammack, 1961; Mandell, Mandell, and Jacobson, 1965; Snyder, 1971; Zung, Wilson, and Dodson, 1964; Zung and Wilson, 1961).

THE CYCLIC NATURE OF SLEEP

It is possible to map out a typical night of sleep for the average young adult (Figure 2.5). The night is divided into several periods each lasting for approximately 60 to 100 minutes. Each period consists of a cycle in which sleep descends from Stage 1 through to Stage 4, and after some time sleep shifts to a lighter stage, muscle tension decreases, and the person enters Stage 1 REM sleep. Stage 2 follows REM sleep and the cycle begins all over again. There are three to five such cycles in the typical night, with the end of each cycle marked by a period of rapid eye movement sleep, although it is not uncommon to find the first REM period of the night bypassed. REM periods tend to lengthen and periods of Delta Wave sleep shorten as the night progresses so that, in general, Delta Wave sleep dominates the first half of the night while REM sleep dominates the second half of the night.

Delta Wave sleep occupies 15 to 25 percent of the young adult's sleep with Stage 1 REM taking up 20 to 25 percent of

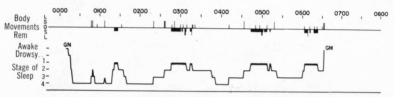

Figure 2.5 *Sleep cycle—adult control subject.* The upper tracing indicates body movements (above the line) and rapid eye movement (below the line). The lower tracing shows the sequence of sleep stages.

the night. With age, there is a change toward a lighter, more disturbed sleep with an increased number of spontaneous awakenings and an appreciable decline in Delta Wave sleep (Feinberg and Carlson, 1968).

TWO PHYSIOLOGICAL STATES OF SLEEP

There is a body of evidence that is consistent with the view that sleep consists of two distinct physiological states: REM and NREM (non-rapid eye movement). These phases not only have the obvious differences in EEG characteristics but also differ in most physiological parameters, and they probably serve different functions. Delta Wave sleep most closely approximates the popular concept of rest. During this phase of sleep, most autonomic functions are slowed down and the organism is usually at its lowest level of activity. During Stage 1 REM sleep there is a general physiological activation and most autonomic systems show an increased level of activity, often of an extremely irregular nature.

There appears to be a biological *need* for both REM and

Delta Wave sleep, as deprivation of either phase leads to a selective rebound on subsequent nights (Agnew, Webb, and Williams, 1964; Berger and Oswald, 1962; Dement, 1960; Hartmann, 1967; Jouvet, 1965). The normal occurrence of Delta Wave sleep at the beginning of the night suggests that it may have an important biological priority. Following total sleep deprivation, moreover, human subjects show an increase in Delta Wave sleep on the first night as if they were "making up" for what was lost. The REM rebound is generally delayed until the second recovery night (Berger and Oswald, 1962; Williams et al., 1964).

The Sleep of the Depressed

Sleep disturbance is a frequent and major complaint of the depressed patient. Patients complain of shortened, broken sleep, difficulty in falling asleep, a tendency to early morning wakening, or feeling very tired even though they may have slept their normal number of hours, suggesting that the quality of their sleep is in some way impaired. Clinicians have attributed a variety of implications to these changes in sleep, suggesting for example, associations with taxonomy (sleep onset difficulty may be associated with reactive depression, while early morning wakening may be a feature of endogenous depression), or that a significant sleep disturbance (especially early morning wakening) is associated with an improved response to electroconvulsive therapy.

While electroencephalographic studies of the sleep of depressed patients have, in large part, confirmed the patient's contention of sleep disturbance, the subjective report of disturbance may be greater than that found in the EEG recording. It is not unusual for a patient to indicate that he has not slept at all for several nights, while the polygraph recordings indicate that he slept for four or five hours per night—however, the quality of the sleep is usually different from that of a control subject.

It must be noted that when we talk of depression we are referring to a clinical syndrome characterized by a number of signs and symptoms. There is considerable evidence that this syndrome arises from different sources; that we are probably dealing with several separate clinical states, with distinct (although perhaps overlapping) genetic, psychophysiological, biochemical, and clinical characteristics (Mendels, 1970; Mendels, 1973). It is likely that the considerable intersubject variability seen in the sleep of depressed patients studied in the sleep laboratory may be because we are really studying (but sometimes failing to recognize and separate) several different clinical conditions. We will return to this problem below and indicate the results of some initial attempts to make some discriminations.

Diaz-Guerrero and his colleagues were the first investigators to study the sleep of depressed patients (Diaz-Guerrero, Gottlieb, and Knott, 1946). They studied patients with a diagnosis of manic-depressed, depressed. Under standardized conditions and allowing for an adaptation to the sleep laboratory (they did not utilize the first night) they found that their patients had difficulty in falling asleep with frequent awakening during the night. The patients often woke early in the morning, their sleep was lighter, and there were more frequent fluctuations from one level of sleep to another in comparison with normal subjects. No differentiation between the various stages of sleep were made at that time.

METHODOLOGICAL DIFFICULTIES

In the past few years there have been a number of studies of the sleep of depressed patients from several laboratories (Green & Stajduhar, 1966; Gresham, Agnew, and Williams, 1965; Hartmann, 1968; Hawkins and Mendels, 1966; Hawkins et al., 1967; Lowy, 1971; Mendels and Chernik, 1972; Mendels and Hawkins, 1967a, 1967b, 1967c, 1968, 1971b, 1972; Oswald et al., 1963; Snyder, 1968, 1969a, 1969b; Vaughan, Wyatt, and Green, 1972; Vogel, 1968; Vogel et al., 1968; Zung, Wilson, and Dodson, 1964). One major difficulty with these studies has been the need (not clearly recognized until relatively recently) to study patients only when they were free of all medications. Not only do the drugs used in the treatment of depression or of the sleep difficulty associated with depression alter the sleep electroencephalographic pattern when they are being taken by the patient, but they have a residual effect on the EEG which may persist for several weeks, resulting in a distortion of the findings (Lewis and Oswald, 1969).

This is clearly illustrated in the two series of studies which are summarized in this report. The first, conducted at the University of North Carolina in collaboration with David R. Hawkins, included a number of depressed patients who had received a variety of drugs up to several days prior to initiation of the sleep studies. We had recognized at the time that this might cause some problems but thought that a few days off drugs would be sufficient to eliminate most of the drug effects. As will be shown, we were only partly correct, and we were probably wrong insofar as the measurement of Stage 1 REM sleep was concerned.

In the second series of studies, which are still in progress in our laboratory in Philadelphia, we have been able to study a number of patients who had received no medication for several weeks. Several important differences have emerged between these studies and the earlier series.

Another important methodological lesson involved the duration of the study: the number of nights each subject spent in the sleep laboratory. In many studies, including part of our Chapel Hill series, patients spent only three or four nights in the laboratory. We assumed, on the basis of studies of normal subjects, that it would be sufficient to allow one adaptation night for the subject to adjust to the laboratory situation, and that we would then have a reliable index of sleep. Two difficulties have become apparent. First, it seems likely that the depressed patient takes longer to adapt to the laboratory than do control subjects. Second, the intrasubject variability, the fluctuations in sleep from night to night, are so marked in some patients that one can easily be misled by looking at the results from a brief cross-sectional study. More careful longitudinal studies of individual patients are needed if one is to obtain a reasonably complete and reliable picture of the sleep of these individuals.

One other important problem should be noted. This applies to the difficulties involved in comparing results from different laboratories. Initially there were important differences in the methods of scoring the records. The introduction of a standardized convention for the scoring of sleep records (Rechtschaffen and Kales, 1968) has resulted in considerable improvement in this. However, there is still variability in the application of this manual and in the way in which individuals will actually score a particular segment of recording. This is especially true of records obtained from depressed patients where it is not uncommon to find unusual wave forms, or the juxtaposition of wave forms not usually seen together. This inevitably results in occasional arbitrary decisions being made. The practice of scoring a record without knowledge of the subject and his clinical state will eliminate some of these biases. There is the need to continually establish interscorer reliability.

INITIAL CROSS-SECTIONAL STUDY

In the initial study in Chapel Hill, the sleep patterns of 21 depressed inpatients were compared with the sleep patterns of 15 age- and sex-matched control subjects. The patients were studied in an air-conditioned, sound-attenuated, electrically shielded subject room connected to an observation room. The EEG tracings, from the occipital and frontal regions referred to the vertex, were recorded on a Grass Model 6, 16-channel electroencephalograph. Electromyographic (EMG) monitoring of the submental muscles was routine. Eye movements were monitored in most cases by a ceramic strain gauge attached over the eyelid, a technique somewhat different from the usual one of using electrodes placed around the orbit. Body movements were measured as artifacts appearing in the EEG and EMG tracings. Records were analyzed in 1-minute epochs, using the

Dement-Kleitman system (1957). We also introduced the practice of scoring the stage Drowsy, which consists of slow alpha waves, intermediate between Awake and Stage 1 sleep, where the alpha frequency is 2 to 4 cps (cycles per second) slower than in waking. The alpha is intermittent, but the slower rate dominates the 1-minute epochs scored in this manner. During the Drowsy periods patients are behaviorally asleep. Details of this study have been reported (Hawkins and Mendels, 1966; Mendels and Hawkins, 1967a, 1967b, 1967c, 1968).

Initial Comparisons

The initial comparisons were based on the findings of the second night in the sleep laboratory. The patients spent significantly less time in the "Total" sleep period (time from the first minute of Drowsy to the last minute of sleep), the Actual sleep period ("Total" sleep period minus the time Awake and Drowsy), Stage 1 REM, and Stage 4; they spent significantly more time Awake and Drowsy. The findings were the same whether the data were expressed as actual minutes in these stages or as a percentage of the Total or Actual sleep periods. More specific analysis of the time awake indicated that the patients took longer to fall asleep, awoke significantly earlier in the morning, and had significantly more spontaneous awakenings from Stage 2 and Stage 1 REM than did the controls.

In an effort to define more precisely the nature of sleep *through* the night, the percentage of sleep spent in each third of the night (Figure 2.6) and the percentage of each third of the night occupied by each stage of sleep (Figure 2.7) were determined. The depressed patients spent a larger percentage of the last third of the night Awake or Drowsy than did the controls (depressives 24.9 percent and controls 3.8 percent); and they had no Stage 4 sleep in the last third of the night, whereas the controls had 12.2 percent of their Stage 4 sleep in this part of the night. These findings probably account for the frequent complaint of "early morning awakening."

We noted a very high variance among the depressed pa-

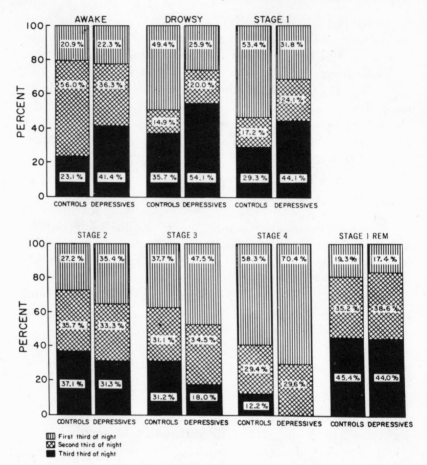

Figure 2.6 *Percent of each stage which occurred within each third of the night.*
Reprinted by permission from J. Mendels and D. R. Hawkins
(1967c). The psychophysiology of sleep in depression. *Mental
Hygiene*, 51: 501–11.

tients. This could be due to such factors as differences in severity of the depression, age, psychotic or neurotic features, treatment effects (before hospitalization), varying adaptation to the
experimental situation, different stages of the illness, different
"types" of depression, etc. We have analyzed our data to determine what effect some of these variables might have had on the
sleep pattern.

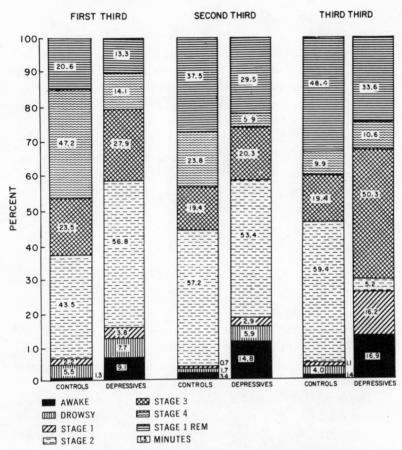

Figure 2.7 *Composition of each third of the night.* Reprinted by permission from J. Mendels and D. R. Hawkins (1967c). The psychophysiology of sleep in depression. *Mental Hygiene,* 51: 501–11.

Age. The subjects were divided into two groups: under and over 50 years. The controls somewhat surprisingly showed no changes related to age (one would have expected them to have less Delta Wave sleep), but the depressives over 50 showed more wakefulness than the younger depressives, and only about one-fourth as much Stage 4 sleep. There was no age difference for Stage 1 REM. This suggests that age and depression interact to lower the amount of Stage 4 sleep.

Severity. Nineteen of the patients were divided into two groups according to scores on the Depression Inventory (Beck et al., 1961): 9 patients with a score of 25 or more (severe), and 10 with a score of 24 or less (mild-moderate). There were no significant differences between the two groups, although there was a *trend* toward more wakefulness and less Delta Wave and REM sleep in the more severely depressed.

Psychotic-Neurotic Dimensions. Seventeen patients were diagnosed as neurotic depressives and 4 as psychotic depressives, a distinction made independently of knowledge of the sleep pattern. The psychotic depressives had significantly more time Awake, more time in Stage 1, less time in Stage 1 REM, and a great deal less in Stage 4 (mean of less than 1 minute per night).

Follow-Up

Thirteen of the 21 patients were restudied a mean of 47.1 (range: 15–69) days after the initial investigation and just prior to discharge from hospital, after significant clinical improvement had occurred (Mendels and Hawkins, 1967b).

These findings must be interpreted with caution in view of the small number of patients and the varying degree of illness and recovery. Also, the patients had received (and in some cases were still receiving) electroconvulsive therapy, imipramine, and barbiturates, all of which have been reported to affect sleep parameters, especially REM time (Cohen and Dement, 1966; Oswald et al., 1963; Whitman et al., 1961).

Actual sleep time, Stage 1 REM sleep, and early morning wakefulness returned to control values while Stage 4 sleep continued to be low (mean value was 37.8 minutes, $p < .05$). The patients still had significantly more Awake ($p < .05$) and Drowsy ($p < .005$) time, and took longer to fall asleep ($p < .01$).

In summary, this initial investigation suggested a relatively consistent sleep pattern in spite of the heterogeneity of the patients, a pattern which agreed with most other studies (Green and Stajduhar, 1966; Gresham, Agnew, and Williams, 1965; Lowy, 1971; Oswald et al., 1963, Snyder, 1969a, 1969b, 1972; Zung, Wilson, and Dodson, 1964). While the patients had some difficulty in falling asleep, the major abnormality seemed to be an increasing tendency to wakefulness as the night progressed. A reduction in Delta Wave sleep was particularly striking, especially in view of the initial observation that it often did not return to control values after clinical recovery when many other parameters of sleep were back to normal. In this sample we found an overall reduction in Stage 1 REM sleep, although the occasional patient had an increase in this stage. As we will see later, we now believe that the elevation in REM sleep may be more typical of the depressed patient, and the lower values found in this study may have been an experimental artifact: insufficient adaptation to the sleep laboratory and only one night of actual recording being used for data analysis.

We also found that sleep disturbances tended to be worse in older, more severely depressed patients, particularly in those with psychotic features. There did seem to be a striking interaction between age and disease in adversely affecting sleep. The inability to establish a positive relationship between sleep abnormality and severity of the depression may be due to the limited reliability or sensitivity of the rating scale used (Mendels, Weinstein, and Cochrane, 1972).

By this time it was clear to us that the only way in which we would be able to further unravel the complex changes in the sleep of the depressive, and to advance our understanding of the relationships between these changes and a number of important clinical and personal variables was to conduct a series of longitudinal studies in which carefully selected patients were studied for a large number of nights, prior to and during controlled treatment. In our initial series, 8 patients were studied in this way (Mendels and Hawkins, 1971b, 1972); an additional 14 have been studied in our second series.

Longitudinal Depression-Sleep Studies

INITIAL SERIES

Our first patient (HJ) serves as an illustrative example. He was a 51-year-old married male with a severe psychotic depression of approximately three months' duration. We were able to study him for thirty-one out of thirty-six hospital nights and again for two nights three weeks after discharge from the hospital (Hawkins et al., 1967). He was successfully treated with nine electroconvulsive treatments. The course of his treatment and related sleep findings are illustrated in Figures 2.8, 2.9. While depressed his sleep was markedly abnormal, characterized by an erratic EEG pattern with rapid shifts of wave forms and an intermingling of patterns not ordinarily seen together.

He had difficulty in falling asleep, awoke frequently during the night, and terminated sleep early in the morning, with a significantly reduced actual sleep time. Likewise, REM and Stage 4 sleep were significantly diminished. His sleep pattern changed abruptly after six ECTs when actual sleep and time awake approached normal values. REM sleep showed a rebound or compensatory increase but Stage 4 sleep showed a very sluggish and incomplete return to normal values. His appetite improved and a severe constipation ended coincidentally with an improvement in his sleep. Behavior and mood improvement were clearly detectable just two days later.

One of the most striking observations in this study was the abrupt simultaneous normalization of almost all the somatic abnormalities. Improvement in mood and behavior seemed to lag slightly behind. Although Stage 4 sleep showed a considerable improvement at the same time that other somatic aspects of the depression improved, it remained low at follow-up.

The other 7 patients studied in this series showed similar changes. However, while a few also had a reduction in REM sleep while depressed, with a rebound above normal levels in association with successful treatment, others had a normal or

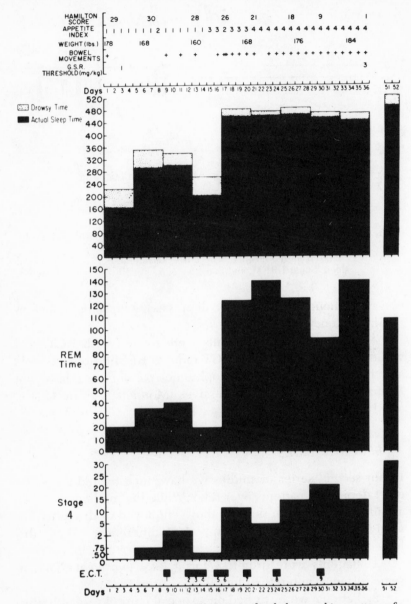

Figure 2.8 *Overall course—Patient HJ.* Longitudinal sleep-waking pattern of a severe, psychotic depressed patient throughout hospitalization and again on two nights, three weeks following discharge. During the first sixteen hospital days his sleep was impoverished. Abruptly on night 17, following his sixth ECT, his total sleep time rose to normal values and continued in this range for the rest of the study.

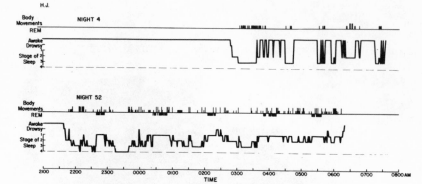

Figure 2.9 *All-night sleep pattern of Patient HJ* during period of severe, depression (night 4) and his sleep on night 52, three weeks after discharge from the hospital. There is a considerable increase in Actual sleep, Stage 1 REM, and Stage 4 sleep with clinical improvement.

elevated amount of REM while depressed, with some reduction in REM latency.

A number of these patients were treated with ECT, and while there are reports that ECT reduces REM time in animals and in some (probably schizophrenic) patients, we have not found this to be true of depressives (Mendels, Van de Castle, and Hawkins, 1973).

SECOND SERIES

In our second series of studies we have investigated the sleep of 14 depressed patients over time. While the methods of study are in many ways the same as those employed in the initial investigation, there are some important differences. These differences include:

1. Patients were drug-free for at least two weeks (and in some instances more than four weeks) prior to study.

2. Patients were studied on a special clinical research ward for the investigation of affective disorders, rather than in a general clinical ward. Closer observation of the patients, exclusion of medications, and better control of daytime napping were

therefore possible. Also, daily depression ratings could be obtained by a specially trained staff.

3. The patients slept in their own rooms on the ward. These were connected by cable to the monitoring equipment. This allows for much less disruption of the patients (they do not have to be moved to a sleep laboratory which may be some distance away from the ward) and, we believe, provides a more reliable record.

4. Additional electrodes were placed at the outer canthus of each eye for a bipolar recording of phasic integrated potentials (PIPs).[1] Conventional disc electrodes were used to record these spikes which have a rather uniform amplitude of 100 to 200 μV and a predominantly monophasic shape. Initial skin-electrode resistances of both the spike and EMG electrodes was less than 3 K ohms. The initial resistance obtained on all other electrodes never exceeded 5 K ohms. A special coupler (2852SLi) with a built-in amplifier was used to record the spike (PIP) potential. The integration "spread" individual EMG spike potentials out in time so that they fall within the frequency response of the galvanometers (see Rechtschaffen et al., 1971; Rechtschaffen, Michel, and Metz, 1972).

5. The recordings were scored according to the procedures outlined by Rechtschaffen and Kales (1968) which involve a slight modification and expansion of the Dement-Kleitman criteria used in the initial study.

The patients were carefully screened before being admitted to our research unit and carefully evaluated during an adaptation period on the ward before a decision was made whether or not to include them in the sleep studies. All medication was discontinued.

Depressed patients were divided into two groups: (1)

---

[1] PIP activity is highly correlated with REM sleep, REM sleep mentation, and PGO (pontine-geniculate-occipital) activity in the cat, but may represent a more fundamental mechanism than REM sleep as presently defined (Dement, 1969; Rechtschaffen and Chernik, 1972; Rechtschaffen, Michel, and Metz, 1972; Watson, 1972).

manic-depressives—those who had at least one clearly documented manic episode in the past as well as the clinical features of depression outlined below, and (2) unipolar, recurrent depressive—those patients who did not have a history of a previous episode of mania. There is an extensive literature which points to the importance of separating these two groups of patients. The depressed patients had moderate to severe depression as determined by the Depression Inventory (Beck et al., 1961) with a minimum of six of the following features (determined independently by two psychiatrists): previous episodes, family history, lack of precipitating causes, nonreactive, inevitability, blame, poor concentration, loss of interest, sleep disturbances, and suicidal thoughts or attempts. These items best characterize the syndrome of endogenous depression (see Mendels and Cochrane, 1968), a term which we use descriptively but without subscription to its etiological implications. Manic patients were those who had (a) at least one well-documented manic episode in the past and (b) at least three of the following symptoms: elevated mood, distractability, pressure of speech, flight of ideas, overactivity, increased sex drive, and racing thoughts.

The control subjects were paid volunteers. Each control was screened by a research psychiatrist for evidence of significant previous or present psychopathology. In addition, the control subjects completed the Minnesota Multiphasic Personality Inventory (MMPI). All subjects who scored two standard deviations from the mean for any MMPI scale were rejected. Control subjects spent three to six nights in the sleep laboratory.

Many of the observations made in this second study confirm our initial findings. Several important differences and additional features have been noted and these will be highlighted (see Table 2.1).

Instead of reduced REM sleep (as we had previously reported), we found that these patients had normal or elevated amounts of Stage 1 REM sleep (Mendels and Chernik, 1972). As a group the patients spent an average of 103.0 minutes or 27.7 percent of the actual sleep period (total time in bed minus

Table 2.1 Pretreatment Baseline Sleep of 14 Hospitalized Depressed Patients Compared with 12 Controls

	Patients (183 Nights) Mean Age 47.4 Years		Controls (42 Nights) Mean Age 48.6 Years		
Minutes of	Mean	S.D.	Mean	S.D.	t
Actual sleep	371.4	29.9	361.5	42.5	0.695
Wakefulness	59.8	35.6	57.3	47.7	0.153
Delta (stages 3 and 4)	15.0	18.5	25.6	27.7	1.163
Stage 1 REM	103.0	21.6	81.1	22.6	2.523 *
Movement time	6.0	4.6	5.4	6.8	0.267
% of Actual Sleep					
Stage 1	11.4	7.8	9.5	6.2	0.679
Stage 2	58.5	6.5	60.6	7.8	0.749
Delta (stages 3 and 4)	4.0	5.0	7.1	7.4	1.227
Stage 1 REM	27.7	5.7	22.5	5.7	2.319 †
Phasic Activities					
Phasic REM (% REM epochs with eye movements)	71.2	10.2	56.0	16.8	2.835 ‡
Phasic integrated activity:					
% REM PIPs	54.1	18.0	51.7	20.6	0.317
% NREM PIPs	4.3	2.9	5.0	4.7	0.464
REM latency (min. to first REM period)	42.8	13.3	72.0	33.5	3.005 ‡
Other Parameters					
Sleep latency (min to first spindle)	26.8	14.1	20.6	17.7	0.994
Sleep cycle (min.)	94.3	8.5	90.6	14.6	0.804
Actual sleep (% of TSP)	85.5	6.7	85.2	10.5	0.088
Movement time (% of TSP)	1.3	1.0	1.2	1.5	0.203
Early morning awakening (min. awake before 6:00 A.M.)	20.4	37.9	9.6	19.9	0.886

† p <.05, two-tailed t test.

* p <.02, two-tailed t test.

‡ p <.01, two-tailed t test.

wakefulness) in REM sleep compared with 81.1 minutes or 22.5 percent for the control group (p < .02 and p < .05, respectively, two-tailed *t* test). The depressed patients also had an increase in several phasic events:

1. For the patients 71.2 percent of all REM epochs had one or more eye movements, compared with 56.0 percent in the control group (*t* p < .01).[2]

2. The patients had a significantly (p < .01) shorter latency to the first REM period, averaging 42.8 minutes vs 72.0 minutes in the control group.

The increase in REM sleep, increased eye movements per REM epoch, and reduced time to REM sleep onset are all indications of an increased pressure or need for REM sleep. The number of REM PIPs, another possible indicator of REM pressure, was higher in the patient group but the increase was directly proportional to the increased amount of REM sleep. Thus the percentage of REM PIPs was similar in the patient and control groups.

Elevation of REM Sleep in Depressed Patients

Since our finding of increased REM sleep in depression differs from our earlier findings at Chapel Hill as well as from reports from other laboratories (Gresham, Agnew, and Williams, 1965; Snyder, 1968; Vogel, 1968; Vogel et al., 1968), we questioned whether the abnormally high amounts of REM sleep found in these patients might be due to a delayed rebound due to prior medication. While all patients in this study had been drug free for a minimum of fourteen days, Lewis and Oswald (1969) have demonstrated a delayed rebound from various antidepressant medications with a peak effect (major increase) oc-

---

[2] Stage 1 REM sleep is determined on the basis of three indicators: EEG, EOG, and EMG activity which may or may not occur simultaneously (Rechtschaffen and Kales, 1968). Since Stage 1 REM sleep can occur without rapid eye movements, percent REM epochs (epochs represent 30-second recordings) with one or more eye movements is one measure of the intensity of phasic activity.

curring between the eleventh and the thirteenth day, and with some elevation in REM sleep up to six weeks later. Thus, the elevation in REM sleep might represent a compensatory increase due to previous drug induced suppression.

We therefore analyzed the sleep record of 6 patients who had been drug-free for at least two months. These 6 patients were studied for a total of eighty-four sleep nights and averaged 29.1 percent and 108.1 minutes of REM sleep during the pretreatment period. Minutes of REM sleep ranged from an individual mean of 25.8 percent and 96.5 minutes to 32.1 percent or 124.3 minutes. These values are similar to that of the total group of 14 depressives. Thus, previous medication does not explain the elevated REM sleep found during the pretreatment period.

We also investigated the possibility that the elevation in REM sleep might be due to studying different diagnostic groups. We compared the REM sleep of 5 manic-depressed, depressed patients with that of 6 unipolar depressed patients. The former group averaged 26.0 percent and 101.2 minutes of REM sleep as compared with 30.7 percent and 110.6 minutes in the unipolar group. The differences were not significant ($t = 1.31$ and .64, respectively). In both groups, REM sleep was somewhat elevated.

Thus, the increased REM sleep found in this study could not be attributed to a delayed rebound or diagnostic condition. We conclude, therefore, that the high REM percentages and increased phasic activity observed in depressed patients in our laboratory probably reflects a real phenomenon and that the understanding of the meaning of this increased "need" for REM sleep may be of importance in unraveling the neurochemical disturbances in depressed patients.

The reduced REM sleep found in our first study as well as by other investigators may be due to such variables as drugs, laboratory setting, adaptation effect, or an insufficient number of nights studied.

We have found significant fluctuations in Stage 1 REM sleep in the depressed patients. In some instances, the number of minutes of REM sleep more than doubled from one night to the next, e.g., patient FM had 133 minutes of REM sleep on night 2, 68 minutes on night 3, 142 minutes on night 4, and 119 minutes on night 5. Such extreme fluctuations from night to night are not unusual; rather, they typify the sleep of the depressed patient. If the sleep of the depressed is not studied for a sufficient number of consecutive nights (a minimum of five nights), the results obtained may be misleading. This may account for the apparently erroneous earlier conclusion that all depressed patients have reduced levels of Stage 1 REM sleep.

Preliminary evidence suggests that the fluctuations in Stage 1 REM sleep are related to the psychiatric condition of the patient (Bunney, Goodwin, and Murphy, 1972; Hauri and Hawkins, 1971; Snyder, 1969a, 1969b, 1972). If further research verifies this, the amount of REM sleep obtained on any one night could provide us with valuable information about the patient.

A FOLLOW-UP STUDY OF PATIENTS IN REMISSION

We are studying the sleep of ten recovered patients after discharge from hospital. Four of these outpatients are drug-free and six are taking lithium carbonate. This study is still in progress. Several initial evaluations of the data lead to the following *preliminary* observations (subject to reevaluation when the study is completed).

The pretreatment baseline sleep of the four drug-free outpatients has been compared with their sleep after discharge from the hospital (Table 2.2). Clinical improvement and discharge from hospital were associated with an improvement in some parameters of sleep. There was a significant decrease ($p < 0.05$, two-tailed t test) in minutes of REM sleep (previously elevated) and a significant increase ($p < 0.05$) in the percentage of Delta Wave sleep. In both instances, values tended toward normal levels. There was no significant difference between the sleep of these four recovered drug-free patients and that of the older controls with the exception of the amount of Actual sleep time, which was reduced (averaging 304.1 minutes vs 361.5

Table 2.2 Sleep of Four Depressed Patients (Drug-Free) Compared with Their Sleep After Discharge from the Hospital (Drug-Free)

	Treatment (Hospitalized) (32 Nights)		After Discharge (20 Nights)		
Minutes of	*Mean*	*S.D.*	*Mean*	*S.D.*	*t*
Actual sleep	359.8	25.1	304.1	40.9	2.170
Wakefulness	48.2	18.5	53.2	43.4	0.229
Delta (stages 3 and 4)	12.6	13.3	17.8	12.8	1.674
Stage 1 REM	105.7	11.3	82.5	5.4	3.362 *
Movement time	5.2	5.4	3.8	2.3	0.463
% of Actual Sleep					
Stage 1	10.5	4.0	10.5	5.3	0.013
Stage 2	57.2	2.2	55.1	11.2	0.366
Delta (stages 3 and 4)	3.2	3.8	6.3	5.3	3.130 *
Stage 1 REM	29.2	2.3	27.8	4.5	0.689
Phasic Activities					
Phasic REM (% REM epochs with eye movements)	69.6	8.8	67.0	11.1	0.474
Phasic Integrated Activity:					
% REM PIPs	49.2	9.5	50.9	11.9	0.248
% NREM PIPs	3.5	3.6	2.4	1.1	0.688
REM latency (min. to first REM period)	44.6	12.7	49.4	20.8	0.612
Other Parameters					
Sleep latency (min. to first spindle)	29.3	17.6	27.1	20.1	0.226
Sleep cycle (min.)	93.5	5.4	96.6	16.5	0.357
Actual sleep (% of TSP)	87.3	3.9	84.3	11.6	0.557
Movement time (% of TSP)	1.2	1.2	1.1	0.7	0.093
Early morning awakening (min. awake before 6:00 A.M.)	49.1	67.5	47.2	60.9	0.042

* $p = .05$, two-tailed t test.

minutes for controls).[3] The recovered patients continued to show some elevation in percentage of REM and in the amount of eye movements during REM sleep (Phasic REM).

Two of the four patients relapsed during the two years of follow-up, one of whom (JD) was sufficiently depressed to require rehospitalization. There appear to be some differences between the sleep of the two patients who relapsed and the other two outpatients which may indicate a greater vulnerability for a recurrence of symptoms in those subjects who continue to have abnormal sleep patterns. The rehospitalized patient (JD) had substantially greater amounts of PIP activity, both during REM and NREM sleep. He averaged 61.6 percent REM PIPs and 8.8 percent NREM PIPs whereas the rest of the group averaged 50.9 percent REM PIPs and 2.4 percent NREM PIPs. This patient also had a greatly reduced latency to REM sleep averaging 25.9 minutes to REM onset vs 49.4 minutes for the other recovered patients and 72.0 minutes in the control group.

JD as well as the second patient (OH), who suffered a relapse but was not hospitalized, had increased amounts of Stage 1 sleep, increased Phasic REM and increased latency to Stage 2 (35.6 and 49.9 minutes, respectively). In only one respect did either of the two patients have "improved" sleep patterns when compared with the other two. They both had substantially greater amounts of Delta Wave sleep (15.4 and 30.2 minutes, respectively). The other two subjects averaged 2.0 and 2.5 minutes per night.

We have some additional preliminary evidence that the development of abnormal features in the sleep pattern of patients during follow-up studies may indicate an imminent clinical relapse. In the course of our quarterly follow-up of ten former patients (including six outpatients undergoing lithium treatment) we found a significant change in the sleep of four of these subjects. Three of the four subjects subsequently had a clinical

---

[3] $p < .005$ one-tailed t test. All previous t values were evaluated using a two-tailed t test, even though we could have justified the use of a one-tailed test due to our prior hypothesis.

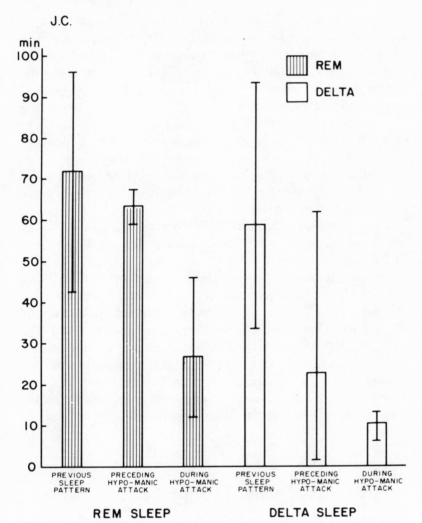

Figure 2.10 *Change in mean levels of REM and Delta Wave sleep* prior to and during a hypomanic attack.

relapse. The change in sleep preceded the change in clinical state by two to eight weeks. The three subjects who relapsed had a *prior* reduction in REM sleep ranging from 15 to 30 percent. There was also a change in the amount of Delta Wave sleep prior to clinical relapse. However, the results were not

consistent across subjects. Two of the three patients who relapsed had a marked reduction in Delta Wave sleep (64 and 90
percent reduction, respectively) whereas the third had a three-
fold increase in Delta Wave sleep. Figure 2.10 illustrates the
change which occurred in one of these patients.

If a disturbance in sleep consistently precedes overt psychopathological symptoms, this would constitute the first evidence for neurophysiological changes *prior* to depression and
we would be in a position to predict future relapses and plan
clinical intervention. Further, it would be of interest to try to
"normalize" the sleep pattern in patients and see if we could
prevent recurrence of the illness.

We have found that recovered depressed patients who are
maintained on long-term lithium carbonate treatment have generally improved sleep (Chernik and Mendels, 1972a). They
have *more* Actual sleep, more Delta Wave sleep and less Stage
1 REM sleep than the recovered depressives who were not
maintained on lithium carbonate (see Table 2.3). Minutes of
Stage 1 REM and Delta Wave sleep, latency to the first REM,
and sleep latency were not significantly different in the lithium
and control groups. In many ways, prophylactic lithium appeared to "normalize" the sleep of the lithium group. It would
be important to determine if the improvement in sleep is in any
way linked with the reported prophylactic effects of lithium carbonate.

Sleep Studies of Manic Patients

The sleep of manic patients has not been adequately studied. This is probably due to the relative infrequency of this condition and to the difficulty in obtaining the necessary cooperation from manic patients.

Mendels and Hawkins (1971a) studied the sleep of a hypomanic patient for seventeen nights out of a twenty-five-night
period. Their findings were similar to observations made by

Table 2.3   Effect of Lithium Carbonate on Sleep

	OUTPATIENTS (N = 7) Mean Age 47.0 Years		CONTROLS (N = 12) Mean Age 48.6 Years		
Minutes of	Mean	S.D.	Mean	S.D.	t
Actual sleep	356.2	50.1	361.5	42.5	0.246
Wakefulness	56.4	51.4	57.3	47.7	0.038
Delta (stages 3 and 4)	37.4	36.8	25.6	27.7	0.795
Stage 1 REM	72.6	27.5	81.1	22.6	0.731
Movement time	6.4	6.7	5.4	6.8	0.311
% of Actual Sleep					
Stage 1	6.2	4.0	9.5	6.2	1.256
Stage 2	62.5	9.7	60.6	7.8	0.469
Delta (stages 3 and 4)	10.8	12.2	7.0	7.4	0.852
Stage 1 REM	20.0	5.5	22.5	5.7	0.934
Phasic Activities					
Phasic REM (% REM epochs with eye movements)	56.0	13.1	56.0	16.8	0.000
Phasic integrated activity:					
% REM PIPs	42.6	24.6	51.7	20.6	0.866
% NREM PIPs	5.3	4.6	5.0	4.7	0.135
REM latency (min. to first REM period)	66.4	15.3	72.0	33.5	0.414
Other Parameters					
Sleep latency (min. to first spindle)	8.5	3.9	20.6	17.7	1.764
Sleep cycle (min.)	86.3	12.7	90.6	14.6	0.648
Actual sleep (% of TSP)	84.4	10.7	85.2	10.5	0.159
Movement time (% of TSP)	1.1	0.55	1.2	1.5	0.168
Early morning awakening (min. awake before 6:00 A.M.)	24.8	28.6	9.6	19.9	1.369

NOTE: There are no significant differences in sleep between the lithium patients in remission and the older controls on any of the parameters studied.

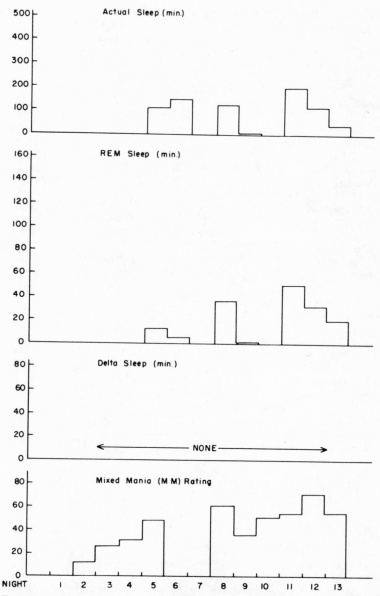

Figure 2.11 *Sleep of manic (Patient AR) while drug free.* (The "mixed mania" rating refers to a scale which rates symptoms of both mania and depression and is used to provide a global rating of psychopathology.) Note: Sleep recordings were not possible on nights 7 and 10.

Hartmann (1968). They found a mean of 256 and 282 minutes of actual sleep; 63.6 and 60.4 minutes of REM sleep; and 100.8 and 102.6 minutes latency to REM onset in the two studies, respectively. The studies differ in the amount of Stage 4 sleep reported. Hartmann (1968) reported a mean of 37.4 minutes of Stage 4 sleep, whereas Mendels and Hawkins (1971a) found a mean of 2.9 minutes of Stage 4 sleep.

More recently, we have been able to study the sleep of three manic patients (Chernik and Mendels, 1972b). All of the subjects were drug-free during the study. One patient was severely manic and the other two were hypomanic. Actual sleep time was significantly reduced in the psychotic manic patient (see Fig. 2.11) whose Sleep time ranged from 0 to 199 minutes per night (mean of 105 minutes for seven nights). This patient exhibited extreme fluctuations in REM sleep ranging from 2 to 54 minutes per night with an average of 22.6 minutes of REM sleep or 21.6 percent of Actual sleep. Thus while there was a reduction in the number of minutes of REM sleep, all had normal to high REM percentages similar to that seen in depressed patients studied in our laboratory.

We have compared the sleep of a psychotic, agitated depressed patient with the manic patient (AR) described above. The manic had significantly less Actual sleep (105.4 minutes vs 223.3 minutes in the depressed patient). However, there was no significant difference in the *percentage* of REM or Delta Wave sleep or in any of the phasic events (eye movements, PIPs, etc.) studied.

Summary

Depressed patients as a group have an extremely variable sleep pattern. This is to be expected in view of the considerable heterogeneity of this nosology group. In general they may have less of a disturbance in the quantity of sleep (actual time asleep) than in its quality. Indeed their frequent complaints of severe

sleep disturbance are in part at least a reflection of this disturbance in quality.

They have substantially less Delta Wave sleep. This is particularly low in older, more severely depressed patients, especially those with psychotic features. The depressed patient appears to have a pressure for REM sleep as evidenced by
significantly elevated amounts of REM sleep, increase in eye
movement activity (Phasic REM), and a significant decrease in
the latency to REM onset.

Their sleep tends to normalize with clinical improvement,
although some patients continue to manifest sleep disturbance:
a need for increased REM or a reduction in Delta Wave sleep.
This finding of a persistent abnormality in the sleep electroencephalogram of recovered depressed patients is compatible
with the hypothesis that there is a persistent abnormality in
aspects of neurophysiological and biochemical functioning in
some depressed patients after clinical recovery (Whybrow and
Mendels, 1969). There is indeed mounting clinical evidence
that, for many patients, depression is not an acute, self-limited
disorder but a relatively chronic condition. For example, we
have found that over 40 percent of depressed patients are rehospitalized within two years (in preparation). An additional significant percentage require further outpatient treatment. A number
of other abnormalities have been noted to persist after clinical
recovery in some depressed patients. These include (1) a persistence in low cerebrospinal fluid 5-hydroxyindoleacetic acid
concentration (Coppen et al., 1972; Mendels et al., 1972); (2) a
continued abnormal response to dexamethasone (Carroll et al.,
1968); (3) a continued abnormal growth hormone release (Sachar, Finkelstein, and Hellman, 1971); (4) the presence of hyperponesis (a heightened residual motor activity) in patients
while depressed and after remission (Whatmore and Ellis,
1962).

References

Agnew, H. W., Jr., W. B. Webb, and R. L. Williams. 1964. The effect of stage four sleep deprivation. *Electroencephalography and Clinical Neurophysiology*, 17:68–70.

Aserinsky, E. and N. Kleitman. 1953. Regularly occurring periods of eye motility and concurrent phenomena during sleep. *Science*, 118:273–274.

Beck, A. T., C. H. Ward, M. Mendelson, J. Mock, and J. K. Erbaugh. 1961. An inventory for measuring depression. *Archives of General Psychiatry*, 4:561–571.

Berger, R. J. and I. Oswald. 1962. Effect of sleep deprivation on behaviour, subsequent sleep and dreaming. *Journal of Mental Science*, 108:457–465.

Bunney, W. E., Jr., F. K. Goodwin, and D. L. Murphy. 1972. The "switch process" in manic-depressive illness. II: Relationship to catecholamines, REM sleep and drugs. *Archives of General Psychiatry*, 27:304–309.

Carroll, B. J., F. I. R. Martin, and B. M. Davies. 1968. Resistance to suppression by dexamethasone of plasma 11-OHCS levels in severe depressive illnesses. *British Medical Journal*, 3:285–287.

Chernik, D. A. and J. Mendels. 1972a. The effect of lithium carbonate on sleep. Paper presented to the Association for the Psychophysiological Study of Sleep, New York.

—— 1972b. The sleep of the manic. Paper presented to the Association for the Psychophysiological Study of Sleep, New York.

Cohen, H. B. and W. C. Dement. 1966. Sleep: Suppression of rapid eye movement phase in the cat after electroconvulsive shock. *Science*, 154:396–398.

Coppen, A., A. J. Prange, Jr., P. C. Whybrow, and R. Noguera. 1972. Abnormalities of indoleamines in affective disorders. *Archives of General Psychiatry*, 26:474–478.

Dement, W. C. 1960. Effect of dream deprivation. *Science*, 131:1705–1707.

—— 1969. The biological role of REM sleep (circa 1968). In A. Kales (ed.), *Sleep: Physiology and Pathology: A Symposium*. Philadelphia: Lippincott.

Dement, W. C. and N. Kleitman. 1957. Cyclic variations in EEG during sleep and their relation to eye movements, body motility and dreaming. *Electroencephalography and Clinical Neurophysiology*, 9:673–690.

Diaz-Guerrero, R., J. S. Gottlieb, and J. R. Knott. 1946. The sleep of patients with manic-depressive psychosis, depressive type. *Psychosomatic Medicine*, 8:399–404.

Feinberg, I. and V. R. Carlson. 1968. Sleep variables as a function of age in man. *Archives of General Psychiatry*, 18:239–250.

Granda, A. M. and J. T. Hammack. 1961. Operant behavior during sleep. *Science*, 133:1485–1486.

Green, W. J. and P. P. Stajduhar. 1966. The effect of ECT on the sleep-dream cycle in a psychotic depression. *Journal of Nervous and Mental Disease*, 143:123–134.

Gresham, S., H. Agnew, and R. Williams. 1965. The sleep of depressed patients: An EEG and eye movement study. *Archives of General Psychiatry*, 12:503–507.

Hartmann, E. 1968. Longitudinal studies of sleep and dream patterns in manic-depressive patients. *Archives of General Psychiatry,* 19: 312–329.

Hauri, P. and D. R. Hawkins. 1971. Phasic REM, depression, and the relationship between sleeping and waking. *Archives of General Psychiatry,* 25: 56–63.

Hawkins, D. R. and J. Mendels. 1966. Sleep disturbance in depressive syndromes. *American Journal of Psychiatry,* 123:682–690.

Hawkins, D. R., J. Mendels, J. Scott, G. Bensch, and W. Teachey. 1967. The psychophysiology of sleep in psychotic depression: A longitudinal study. *Psychosomatic Medicine,* 29:329–344.

Jouvet, M. 1965. Paradoxical sleep—a study of its nature and mechanism. In K. Akert, C. Bally, and J. P. Schade (eds.), *Sleep Mechanism: Progress in Brain Research.* Vol. 18. New York: Elsevier.

Lewis, S. A. and I. Oswald. 1969. Overdose of tricyclic anti-depressants and deductions concerning their cerebral action. *British Journal of Psychiatry,* 115:1403–1410.

Loomis, A. L., E. N. Harvey, and G. A. Hobart. 1937. Cerebral states during sleep as studied by human brain potentials. *Journal of Experimental Psychology,* 21:127–144.

Lowy, F. H., J. M. Cleghorn, and D. J. McClure. 1971. Sleep patterns in depression: Longitudinal study of six patients and brief review of literature. *Journal of Nervous and Mental Disease,* 153:10–26.

Mandell, M. P., A. J. Mandell, and A. Jacobson. 1965. Biochemical and neurophysiological studies of paradoxical sleep. *Recent Advances in Biological Psychiatry,* 7:115–122.

Mendels, J. 1970. *Concepts of Depression.* New York: Wiley.

—— 1974. Biological aspects of affective illness. In S. Arieti (ed.), *American Handbook of Psychiatry,* Vol. 3. 2d ed. New York: Basic Books.

Mendels, J. and D. A. Chernik. 1972. REM sleep and depression. Paper presented to the Association for the Psychophysiological Study of Sleep, New York, May 1972.

Mendels, J. and C. Cochrane. 1968. The nosology of depression: The endogenous-reactive concept. *American Journal of Psychiatry,* 124:1–11 (suppl.).

Mendels, J., A. Frazer, R. G. Fitzgerald, T. A. Ramsey, and J. W. Stokes. 1972. Biogenic amine metabolites in cerebrospinal fluid of depressed and manic patients. *Science,* 175:1380–1382.

Mendels, J. and D. R. Hawkins. 1967a. Sleep and depression: A controlled EEG study. *Archives of General Psychiatry,* 16:344–354.

—— 1967b. Sleep and depression: A follow-up study. *Archives of General Psychiatry,* 16:536–542.

—— 1967c. Studies of psychophysiology of sleep in depression. *Mental Hygiene,* 51:501–510.

—— 1968. Sleep and depression: Further considerations. *Archives of General Psychiatry,* 19:445–452.

—— 1971a. Longitudinal sleep study in hypomania. *Archives of General Psychiatry,* 25:274–277.

—— 1971b. Sleep and depression: Longitudinal studies. *Journal of Nervous and Mental Disease,* 153:251–272.

—— 1972. Sleep studies in depression. In T. A. Williams, M. Katz, and J. A. Shield (eds.), *Recent Advances in the Psychobiology of the Depressive Illnesses.* Washington, D.C.: Government Printing Office.

Mendels, J., R. L. Van de Castle, and D. R. Hawkins. 1974. Electroconvulsive therapy and sleep. In M. Fink, S. Kety, J. McGaugh, and T. A. Williams (eds.), *Psychobiology of Convulsive Therapy.* New York: Halsted-Wiley.

Mendels, J., N. Weinstein, and C. Cochrane. 1972. The relationship between depression and anxiety. *Archives of General Psychiatry,* 27:649–653.

Oswald, I., R. J. Berger, R. A. Jarmillo, K. M. G. Keddie, P. C. Olley, and H. G. B. Plunkett. 1963. Melancholia and barbiturates: Controlled EEG, body and eye movement study of sleep. *British Journal of Psychiatry,* 109:66–78.

Rechtschaffen, A. and D. A. Chernik. 1972. The effect of REM deprivation on periorbital spike activity in NREM sleep. *Psycophysiology,* 9:128. (Abstract)

Rechtschaffen, A. and A. Kales. 1968. *A Manual of Standardized Terminology Techniques and Scoring System for Sleep Stages of Human Subjects.* Public Health Service, Washington, D.C.: U.S. Government Printing Office.

Rechtschaffen, A., F. Michel, and J. T. Metz. 1972. Relationship between extraocular and PGO activity in the cat. *Psychophysiology,* 9:128. (Abstract)

Rechtschaffen, A., S. Molinari, R. Watson, and M. Z. Wincor. 1971. Extraocular potentials: A possible indication of PGO activity in the human. *Psychophysiology,* 7:336. (Abstract)

Sachar, E. J., J. Finkelstein, and L. Hellman. 1971. Growth hormone responses in depressive illness. I: Reponse to insulin tolerance test. *Archives of General Psychiatry,* 25:263–269.

Snyder, F. 1968. Electrographic studies of sleep in depression. In N. S. Kline and E. Laske (eds.), *Computers and Electronic Devices in Psychiatry.* New York: Grune and Stratton.

—— 1969a. Dynamic aspects of sleep disturbance in relation to mental illness. *Biological Psychiatry,* 1 (2):119–130.

—— 1969b. Sleep disturbance in relation to acute psychosis. In A. Kales (ed.), *Sleep: Physiology and Pathology.* Philadelphia: Lippincott.

—— 1971. Psychophysiology of human sleep. *Clinical Neurosurgery,* 18:503–536.

—— 1972. NIH studies of EEG sleep in affective illness. In T. A. Williams, M. M. Katz, and J. A. Shield (eds.), *Recent Advances in the Psychobiology of the Depressive Illnesses.* Washington, D.C.: U.S. Government Printing Office.

Vaughan, T., R. J. Wyatt, and R. Green. 1972. Changes in REM sleep of chronically anxious depressed patients given alphamethylparatyrosine (AMPT). *Psychophysiology,* 9:96. (Abstract)

Vogel, G. W. 1968. REM deprivation. III: Dreaming and psychosis. *Archives of General Psychiatry,* 18:312–329.

Vogel, G. W., A. C. Traub, P. Ben-Horin, and G. M. Myers. 1968. REM deprivation. II: The effects on depressed patients. *Archives of General Psychiatry,* 18:301–312.

Watson, R. 1972. Mental correlates of periorbital PIPs during REM sleep. In

M. H. Chase, W. C. Stern, P. L. Walter (eds.), *Sleep Research*, Vol. 1. Los Angeles: Brain Information Service/Brain Research Institute, UCLA.

Whatmore, G. B. and R. M. Ellis, Jr. 1962. Further neurophysiologic aspects of depressed states: An electromyographic study. *Archives of General Psychiatry*, 6:243–253.

Whitman, R. M., C. M. Pierce, J. W. Mass, and B. Baldridge. 1961. Drugs and dreams. II: Imipramine and prochlorperazine. *Comprehensive Psychiatry*, 2:219–226.

Whybrow, P. C. and J. Mendels. 1969. Toward a biology of depression: Some suggestions from neurophysiology. *American Journal of Psychiatry*, 125:1491–1500.

Williams, R., H. Agnew, and W. Webb. 1967. *Effects of prolonged stage 4 and 1-REM sleep deprivation*. Washington, D.C.: U.S. Government Printing Office.

Zung, W. W. K. and W. P. Wilson. 1961. Response to auditory stimulation during sleep: Discrimination and arousal as studied with electroencephalography. *Archives of General Psychiatry*, 4:548–552.

Zung, W. W. K., W. P. Wilson, and W. E. Dodson. 1964. Effect of depressive disorders on sleep EEG responses. *Archives of General Psychiatry*, 10:439–445.

3

Psychophysiological Studies of Psychopathy

ROBERT D. HARE

SINCE SEVERAL GENERAL REVIEWS of the research on psychopathy are available elsewhere (Hare, 1968, 1970a, 1971), emphasis in the present discussion will be upon recent (some as yet unpublished) research and upon some issues that arise from this research. Perhaps the best way of beginning would be to explain what I mean by psychopathy and how we go about selecting subjects (Ss) for our research.

The Concept of Psychopathy

One of the many difficulties with doing research in this area is that the term "psychopathy" has long had a variety of meanings. As a result, every discussion of psychopathy has to be preceded by a description of the way the term is being used. Although the problem is not as bad as it was nine or ten years ago, largely because of the continually increasing interest of behavioral scientists, the time when such preliminary discussions

Preparation of this article and some of the research reported were supported by the Canadian Mental Health Association, Public Health Research Grant 609-7-163 from the National Health Grants Program (Canada), and by Grant MA-4511 from the Medical Research Council of Canada.

will no longer be necessary is still some time away. And even after the concept has been defined there often remains the problem of convincing others that it represents something more than a convenient abstraction.

The concept of psychopathy (or sociopathy) being used by many North American investigators is related to the detailed clinical descriptions and case histories provided by the four editions of Cleckley's *The Mask of Sanity*. The disorder described by Cleckley is listed in the World Health Organization's *International Classification of Diseases* (1968) and in the American Psychiatric Association's *Diagnostic and Statistical Manual of Mental Disorders* (1968) as category 301.7, *antisocial personality*. To quote the American Psychiatric Association:

This term is reserved for individuals who are basically unsocialized and whose behavior pattern brings them repeatedly into conflict with society. They are incapable of significant loyalty to individuals, irresponsible, impulsive, and unable to feel guilt or to learn from experience and punishment. Frustration tolerance is low. They tend to blame others or offer plausible rationalizations for their behavior. A mere history of repeated legal or social offences is not sufficient to justify this diagnosis . . . . [p. 43]

To elaborate somewhat, the psychopath tends to treat others as objects rather than as persons with feelings of their own, and experiences little guilt or remorse for having done so and for having used them to satisfy his own selfish needs. His judgment is poor, and his behavior reflects a sort of "short-term hedonism" in which current, momentary needs are satisfied in spite of the possibility of more temporally remote punishments or unpleasant consequences to himself or to others. Although his asocial behavior (which can be parasitically demanding as well as aggressive) frequently gets him into trouble, he is often sufficiently charming and skilled at manipulation, lying, and rationalization to convince others that he is not really to blame or that he sincerely intends to mend his ways. The apparent inability to empathize with others and to form genuine emotional relationships with them, plus a lack of appropriate emotional response (anxiety, guilt, remorse) for his social depredations, leads to the suggestion that the psychopath is a "two-dimensional" or "hollow" person—a person with apparently normal intellectual and physical attributes but one whose personal and interpersonal behavior lacks essential emotional concomitants.

Not everyone sees psychopathy in such a negative light. Halleck (1966), for example, considers the psychopath's behavior to be the logical result of persistent attempts to be free of meaningful involvements with others and to worry only about self-gratification. Others have noted that some of the psychopath's characteristics—his hedonism and his tendency to avoid social contracts, to live by his own set of rules, and to engage in impersonal sexual relationships, etc.—are often associated with a life-style that is both envied and admired by others. Several writers (e.g., Mailer, 1957) have suggested that psychopathy is the forerunner of a new expression of human nature in which violence, self-assertion, lack of commitments and emotional ties with others, and complete satisfaction of needs and impulses will be the norm. Others (e.g., Harrington, 1972) feel that psychopaths are the only ones equipped to survive the pressures of our society, and that these pressures will be responsible for a tremendous upsurge in the incidence of psychopathy. While these latter views are rather extreme, it is probably true that the increasing tolerance of diverse forms of behavior and life-style in our society is making it easier for clinical psychopaths to "blend in." Similarly, it is becoming easier for people to adopt a style of life that includes some of the features of psychopathy. Although it is possible that in doing so their lives are made more tolerable and enjoyable, it is often at the expense of others.

Selection of Subjects

Anyone trying to do research in this area soon realizes that there are real problems associated with the selection of subjects that fit his conception of psychopathy. Part of the difficulty is

that some of the relevant clinical characteristics are quite subjective and, in some cases, based upon inferences about underlying motivations and processes. In spite of this, several investigators have been reasonably successful in selecting
subjects on the basis of criteria outlined by Cleckley (1964)—
successful in the sense that meaningful and replicable results
have been obtained. It is obvious, though, that there is a great
deal of room for improvement, particularly in the direction of
objectivity and inter-rater reliability.

In my own research program we usually begin a study by
discussing Cleckley's concept of psychopathy with the institu-
tion's psychologist, psychiatrist, counselors, and classification
officers, and asking them to submit the names of inmates whom
they could roughly categorize as psychopaths or nonpsychopaths. Two or three research associates and I then read each
potential subject's file and make a global assessment (on a seven-
point scale) of the extent to which we are confident that the inmate is or is not a psychopath. In some studies, this global rating is preceded by a fifteen-item checklist of criteria derived
from Cleckley (and orginally used by Lykken, 1955). We have
found, however, that the use of this checklist is not always that
useful, since independent ratings of inmates with and without it
usually lead to the same result. Part of the reason for this is that
there seems to be a large halo effect associated with filling out
the checklist, so that each item is not really independent of the
others. The main use of the checklist seems to be in helping us
to keep the concept of psychopathy clearly in mind while the
global rating is being made. So far we have found that the inter-
rater agreement using the seven-point global rating of psychopathy is generally rather good. For example, in one study (Hare
and Quinn, 1971), two raters agreed exactly on 70 percent of the
subjects and were only one step apart on 26 percent. Recently
Dengerink and Bertilson (1972, research in progress) used some
of our subjects, and although the extent of the agreement in our
categorization of subjects has not been quantified yet, it appeared to be substantial.

Using this procedure we usually end up with two or three
groups of subjects. One group (Group P) consists of those in-

mates who consistently receive a 1 or 2 on the seven-point scale, while another group (Group NP) consists of those who receive a 6 or 7. Sometimes a third group (Group M) is used, consisting of those who may be psychopaths but about whom we do not have enough information to be certain. In several of our studies (Hare, 1968, 1972a; Hare and Quinn, 1971) Groups P and M were physiologically similar, leading us to believe that the proportion of misclassified psychopaths in Group M was generally rather large. The remaining subjects probably included those that others would consider secondary (Karpman, 1961) or pseudo (Arieti, 1967) psychopaths.

It should be noted that our Group NP may even be more heterogeneous than Group M, and that many of the subjects contained therein could hardly be considered normal. In some of our research we have attempted to subdivide this group into various categories, e.g., subcultural criminal, neurotic, normal, etc., but the number of subjects in some of the subgroups has generally been too small for meaningful analyses to be carried out. However, it is obvious that a better procedure would be to obtain enough subjects so that the psychopaths in Group P could be compared with a number of more homogeneous non-psychopathic subgroups.

This suggestion is related to the problem of what really constitutes appropriate comparison groups, a problem that extends to much of the research in psychopathology in which the subjects of interest are institutionalized or otherwise separated from the general population. Further, with respect to psychopathy, it is evident that we generally deal only with those psychopaths who manage to end up in prison. Even if they differ in important ways from other criminals, it doesn't necessarily mean that they would differ in the same ways from appropriate segments of the normal population. What is badly needed is research with those psychopaths who manage to remain out of prisons. Such research will obviously be difficult to do.

Incidentally, even though we assume that our Group P is relatively homogeneous with respect to the core attributes of psychopathy, we recognize that appreciable diversity in behavior patterns and personality structure exists. It is quite likely

that future research will find a common set of psychophysiological processes associated with psychopathy in general, as well as
other processes that are specific to the various subtypes of psychopathy that may exist, including Karpman's (1961) aggressive
and passive types, and Arieti's (1967) simple and complex
types.

Several attempts have been made to make the selections of
subjects more objective by using various psychometric invento-
ries, most notably the MMPI (Dahlstrom and Welsh, 1960), the
Behavior Problem Checklist (Quay and Peterson, 1967) and the
Activity Preference Questionnaire (Lykken, 1955; Lykken, Tel-
legan, and Katzenmeyer, 1973). While each investigator is of
course free to choose his own operational definition of psychopathy, he should be reasonably sure that the definition is related to the conception of psychopathy that underlies his research. I have the feeling, however, that this is not always the
case, particularly where the Activity Preference Questionnaire
(APQ) is concerned. The APQ is generally assumed to be a
measure of anxiety reactivity, and although psychopaths should
theoretically receive relatively low scores on it, several studies
have found that they do not (e.g., Fenz, 1971; Hare, 1972a; Hare
and Craigen, 1974). What this suggests, among other things, is
that studies in which the APQ is the sole criterion of psychopathy may not be directly relevant to the clinical concept of
psychopathy. The most recent revision of the APQ (Lykken,
Tellegen, and Katzenmeyer, 1973) does in fact caution against
this use of the scale for selection of psychopathic Ss.

There may be similar problems associated with the MMPI,
especially where selection is based upon only the Psychopathic
Deviate (Pd) scale, or upon the Pd and the Hypomania (Ma)
scales. As some data presented below indicate, many inmates
with very high Pd and Ma scores are clearly not psychopathic.
Perhaps a better procedure would be to use MMPI profiles as
the basis for selection, although here again it may be difficult
(though probably not as difficult as with the APQ) to know to
what extent subjects so selected fit clinical conceptions of the
psychopath.

The Behavior Problem Checklist (Quay and Parsons, 1971)

would seem to be a promising instrument for the selection of young subjects, particularly since it relies upon ratings of observed behavior (as opposed to the self-report responses involved in the MMPI and the APQ), and permits the identification of various forms of antisocial behavior—psychopathic, neurotic, and subcultural.

Amount of Research

Before discussing some of our recent research, I would like to make a few comments about the relatively small amount of empirical research being done on psychopathy. A quick survey of the number of articles on schizophrenia and psychopathy reported in *Psychological Abstracts* and *Index Medicus* during the last ten years revealed that research on schizophrenia outweighed that on psychopathy by almost 20 to 1, a ratio that has not improved much during recent years. Although the incidence of schizophrenia may be higher than that of psychopathy, I suspect that psychopaths generate proportionately more social disruption and personal distress than does any other form of behavior abnormality. Part of the reason for this is that the psychopath spreads himself around, affecting a very large number of people—family, friends, and strangers—during his lifetime. Any psychiatrist, social worker, probation officer, family counselor, etc., can certainly attest to the great social damage and mental anguish produced by psychopathic individuals. It is hoped that the problem will begin to receive more attention from professional organizations, government, and researchers.

Some Recent Research and Issues

Although the number of studies concerned with learning in psychopaths is still relatively small, the available evidence indicates that under the usual laboratory conditions they are "de-

ficient" in the acquisition of classically conditioned electrodermal responses (Hare, 1965a, 1965b; Hare and Quinn, 1971;
Lykken, 1957), and the learning and performance of responses
mediated by fear or anxiety (Lykken, 1957; Rosen and Schalling, 1971; Schachter and Latane, 1964; Schoenherr, 1964;
Schmauk, 1970). As Lykken (1957) recognized some time ago,
these two learning deficiencies are conceptually related. Thus,
learning to avoid punishment can be viewed as a two-stage process (Mowrer, 1947) involving the classical conditioning of fear
to cues associated with punishment, and the subsequent reinforcement, by fear reduction, of behavior that removes the individual from the fear-producing cues. The psychopath's apparent
disregard for the future consequences of his behavior may
therefore be seen as reflecting the failure of cues (visual, kinesthetic, verbal, symbolic, etc.) associated with punishment to
elicit sufficient anticipatory fear for the instigation and subsequent reinforcement of avoidance behavior. Moreover, it appears that the psychopath's relative inability to experience anticipatory fear may be especially marked when the expected
punishment is temporally remote, a reflection, perhaps, of an
unusually steep "temporal gradient of fear arousal" (Hare,
1965a, 1965c).

Although it is evident that the concept of anticipatory fear
is a useful one, it is important to note that conclusions about the
psychopath's capacity for experiencing anticipatory fear are
largely based upon the assumption that electrodermal activity is
an adequate indicant of such fear. Since most of the relevant experiments involved painful electric shock, the assumption
seems reasonable enough. Some difficulties arise, however,
when other physiological responses are involved.

Consider for example, a recent study (Hare and Quinn,
1971) involving a delayed, differential conditioning paradigm in
which three noticeably different conditioned stimuli (tones)
were each presented 16 times in random order. Each tone was
10 seconds long; termination of two of the tones was accompanied by either a strong electric shock (CS^s) or a 2-second slide
of a nude female (CS^p). No UCS followed the third tone (CS$^-$).

The Ss included 18 psychopathic criminals (Group P), 18 non-psychopathic criminals (Group NP), and 18 criminals about whom there was some doubt (Group M); the Ss in this latter group probably represented a heterogeneous mixture of misclassified psychopaths and nonpsychopaths. Dependent variables were electrodermal, cardiac, and both peripheral and cephalic vasomotor responses. Electrodermal responses with a latency of 4 to 11 seconds after CS onset were defined as anticipatory responses (AR). The results clearly showed that the main difference between groups lay in the size of the AR to the CS^s and, to a lesser extent, to the CS^p, with Group NP giving large responses and the other groups very small responses. In addition, Group NP was the only group to show clear-cut differentiation between CS^s and CS^-. This can be illustrated by plotting differential ARs, obtained by subtracting the mean amplitude of the AR elicited by the CS^-, on a trial-by-trial basis, from the mean amplitude of the ARs elicited by the CS^s and by the CS^p. The resulting differential ARs are plotted in Figure 3.1 where it can be seen that only Group NP showed any evidence of differential conditioning, particularly with shock as the UCS. Since there is some evidence that the electrodermal OR is also capable of being conditioned (e.g., Gale and Stern, 1967), the differential amplitude of EDRs occurring from 1 to 4 seconds after CS onset were computed for each group. The results, shown in Figure 3.2, indicate that only Group NP acquired conditioned differential electrodermal ORs to the CS^s and the CS^p.

It is thus quite clear that the nonpsychopaths were superior to the psychopaths in the conditioning of differential electrodermal ORs and ARs—the psychopaths, in fact, showed virtually no evidence of differential electrodermal conditioning, with the result that the differences between groups were rather dramatic, particularly where shock was involved as the UCS. Moreover, the responses given by the psychopaths were very small in an absolute sense. With shock as the UCS, the results are consistent with earlier research (Hare, 1965b; Lykken, 1955) and with the hypothesis that psychopaths do not acquire conditioned fear responses readily.

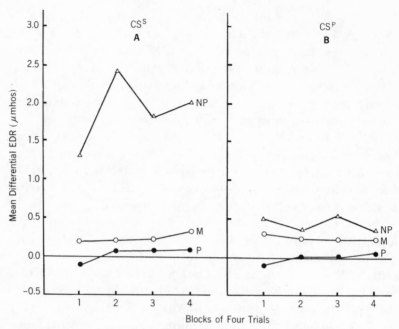

Figure 3.1 *Mean differential anticipatory SC responses* given by each group to the CS^s (A) and the CS^P (B) (Hare and Quinn, 1971).

However, the differences between groups in electrodermal conditioning did not extend to cardiac and vasomotor conditioning. The differential cardiac (decelerative) and digital vasomotor (constrictive) conditioning of the psychopaths was at least as good as that of the other Ss, and was similar to the results of other research with normal Ss (e.g., Gale and Stern, 1968; Obrist, 1968). Moreover, the failure of either psychopaths or nonpsychopaths to show any evidence of differential cephalic vasomotor conditioning is consistent with a study by Brotsky (1969), in which normal Ss showed no evidence of cephalic vasomotor conditioning in spite of the fact that electrodermal conditioning took place.

What these results suggest is that the psychopath may be a poor electrodermal conditioner but a good cardiovascular one. Before discussing some of the possible implications of these findings, let me tell you about another study in which a dissoci-

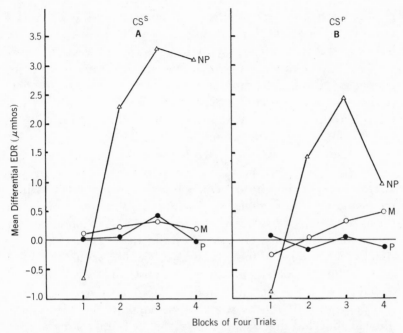

Figure 3.2 *Mean differential electrodermal orienting responses* given by each group to the CS[s] (A) and the CS[p] (B) (Hare and Quinn, 1971).

ation between electrodermal and cardiac conditioning occurred. In this study (Hare and Craigen, 1974) we wished to investigate the behavioral and physiological responses of psychopaths in a situation involving interactions with another individual. The design was perhaps a bit more complex than it need have been, though it did manage to result in a good deal of usable data. Briefly, pairs of subjects (A and B) were required to take turns in deciding how much shock to administer to one another. On each of eight trials A had to determined how much shock he himself was to receive and how much B, sitting on the other side of a screen, was to receive. The choices available to A were arranged so that the smaller the shock selected for himself, the larger the shock received by B. After making his choice a tone sounded for 10 seconds, and with its termination A received his shock. Another tone then sounded for 10 seconds, following which B received his shock. It was then B's turn to choose the shock intensities. Following B's choice, 10-second tones sounded prior to shock to B himself and shock to A. Although both A and B were inmates, only the behavior of A was of interest to the experimenters—B had electrodes attached but not connected to the polygraph, and his shock choices were overridden by the experimenter. Of the A subjects, 17 were psychopaths (Group P) and 17 were not (Group NP).

We found that both groups chose to give slightly less intense shocks to themselves than to the other subjects (i.e., B); however, there was no difference between groups in the choices made. The clinical characteristics of psychopaths notwithstanding, the fact that Group P's choices were similar to those of Group NP is not really surprising. The most rational course of action for each subject would be to chose moderate shocks for himself and the other subject, and hope that the other subject did the same. And no doubt most subjects were influenced by what they felt the experimenter considered to be normal and rational, and by what might happen after the experiment if they did give very intense shocks to the other subject (who was, after all, a fellow inmate who could retaliate outside of the experiment if he wished to). The physiological data were more revealing. Group P gave significantly smaller skin conductance (SC) responses to shock (no matter who the recipient was) than did Group NP. Both groups gave larger responses when they themselves received the shock than when the other subject was the recipient. There were no differences between groups in the type or size of heart rate (HR) response to shock—acceleration to direct shock, and very slight deceleration when the other S was shocked. The findings presented thus far support the hypotheses that psychopaths are electrodermally hyporesponsive to noxious stimuli (Hare and Quinn, 1971; Lykken, 1955), but that their cardiac responses are normal (Hare, 1972a; Hare and Quinn, 1971).

It is possible to view the experimental procedure as a delayed, discrimination conditioning paradigm involving two different conditioned stimuli (CSs), i.e., tones, two different unconditioned stimuli (UCSs), i.e., shock to self or to the other subject, and the use of instructions to establish the CS-UCS contingencies beforehand. Responses occurring prior to reception of shock may then be considered to be anticipatory responses, with those preceding shock to the other subject perhaps being vicariously instigated (cf. Berger, 1962). In each case, an anticipatory response (AR) was defined as an increase in SC beginning between 4 and 11 seconds after CS onset. The results, plotted in Figure 3.3, indicate that the largest anticipatory SC responses were given by Group NP to shock they themselves received during the early trials. The relatively small responses given by Group P are consistent with the results of several other studies (Hare, 1965a; Hare and Quinn, 1971; Lippert and Senter, 1966; Lykken, 1957; Schalling and Levander, 1967) and provide further support for the hypothesis that psychopaths are electrodermally hyporesponsive to cues associated with impending pain or punishment to themselves. It is interesting that although Group NP gave larger anticipatory re-

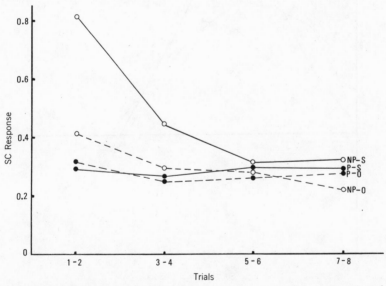

Figure 3.3 *Mean anticipatory SC responses* given by psychopaths (P) and
nonpsychopaths (NP) to tones preceding shock to themselves (S)
and to the other subjects (O) (Hare and Craigen, 1974).

sponses when they themselves were about to receive shock
than when the other subject was going to receive it, Group P
failed to show the same discrimination; presumably this reflects
a general hyporesponsivity to cues signaling pain, whether to
themselves or to others.

Besides these anticipatory responses, the design of the experiment permitted the identification of electrodermal orienting
responses (ORs), defined as increases in SC beginning between
1 and 4 seconds after CS onset. The results were similar to
those obtained for the AR. That is, the CS preceding shock to
self elicited much larger ORs in Group NP than in Group P, a
finding that is consistent with results from a previous study
(Hare and Quinn, 1971). It is noteworthy here that both groups
gave small electrodermal ORs to the CS preceding shock to the

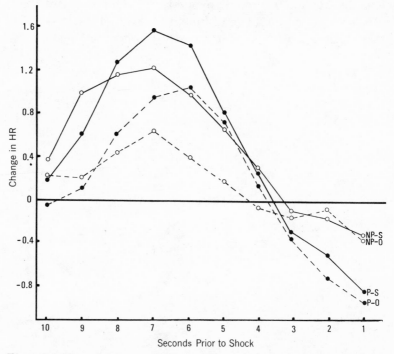

Figure 3.4 *Mean anticipatory HR responses* given by each group to tones pre-
        ceding shock to themselves (S) and to the other subjects (O).
        Averaged over eight trials (Hare and Craigen, 1974).

other subjects. As far as Group P is concerned this probably reflects electrodermal hyporesponsivity to warning cues in general. With Group NP it is possible that the small ORs to the tone preceding shock to the other subjects is related to the use of a within-subjects design. That is, the subject may have been so attentive to stimuli warning of shock to himself that the significance of stimuli preceding shock to another was more to indicate that he himself would not be shocked, rather than that another person was about to be shocked. The same explanation could perhaps be applied to the AR data already discussed.

Turning now to cardiac activity, Figure 3.4 shows the mean second-by-second changes in heart rate (HR) following onset of each CS, averaged over all eight trials. The anticipatory HR response was generally biphasic—acceleration during the first 5 or 6 seconds after CS onset, followed by deceleration just prior to the time when shock was expected. The size and form of the response was the same whether shock was about to be received directly or when the other S was the recipient. However, both the accelerative and decelerative components were significantly larger in Group P than in Group NP. The most dramatic difference between groups, a difference partially obscured through the averaging of data across trials, occurred on the very first trial. As Figure 3.5 indicates, the anticipatory HR responses of Group P on Trial 1 consisted primarily of marked acceleration during the first 5 or 6 seconds after CS onset, while those of Group NP were small and slightly decelerative. On the second trial, Group P developed a secondary decelerative component, while Group NP's responses were similar to those given by Group P on the first trial. On subsequent trials, the response patterns of each group became more and more similar to one another.

These findings, when considered along with those from a previous study (Hare and Quinn, 1971), again suggest that psychopaths may be poor electrodermal conditioners but good cardiovascular ones. It appears that much the same can be said for "vicariously" conditioned responses, since the anticipatory electrodermal and HR responses of Group P were more or less

Robert D. Hare

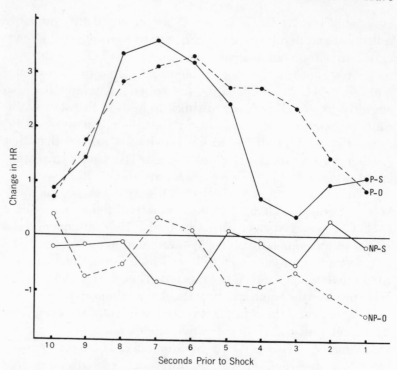

Figure 3.5 *Mean anticipatory HR responses* given by each group to tones pre-
    ceding shock to themselves (S) and to the other subjects (O) on the
    first trial (Hare and Craigen, 1974).

the same when others were about to receive shock as when it
was about to be directly experienced. In some respects this is
surprising, since psychopaths are generally considered to lack
empathy and concern for the welfare of others.

However, a discrepancy arises only if anticipatory HR activity is assumed to be primarily related to some form of emotional arousal. While such may be the case, there is increasing
evidence that cardiovascular activity also either influences or at
least is associated with the modulation of sensory input and
with transactions with the environment. For example, it has
been suggested (Graham and Clifton, 1966; Lacey, 1967) that
HR deceleration is related to sensory intake, increased cortical
arousal, and is part of an orienting response (OR) to novel stim-

uli, while HR acceleration is related to sensory rejection, decreased cortical arousal, and is one component of a defensive response (DR) to very intense or noxious stimuli. Although most of the supporting evidence has involved the use of auditory stimuli and electric shock (e.g., see Graham and Clifton, 1966; Raskin, Kotses and Bever, 1969), there is some evidence that such visual stimuli as slides of homicide victims and spiders can produce HR deceleration in those Ss who find the slides interesting, and HR acceleration in those who fear the contents of the slide (Hare, 1972b, 1973).

What all this suggests is the possibility that the anticipatory HR responses of the Ss in the present study may have been more related to defensive behavior than to emotional arousal in the usual sense. Since the tones preceding shock functioned as warning signals, it is quite possible that the initial period of HR acceleration was part of a defensive response to cues that had acquired aversive properties. Presumably this DR served to reduce the aversiveness of the situation and helped the Ss to cope with it (Lacey, 1967; Lykken, 1968; Sokolov, 1963). There is some evidence (Obrist, Wood, and Perez-Reyes, 1965) that the HR acceleration observed during the first few seconds after CS onset is due more to a reduction in vagal (parasympathetic) activity than to an increase in sympathetic activity. The deceleration component that followed this intial period of acceleration may therefore have been partly due to "vagal rebound." Dronsejko (1972) has suggested that this decelerative phase also reflects the operation of a mechanism for coping with the forthcoming stressor.

If anticipatory HR responses are related to the efficiency with which Ss modulate aversive cues and cope with an impending stressor, the present results, along with clinical data, suggest that psychopaths may be relatively adept at the process. Both the accelerative and decelerative components were generally larger in Group P than in Group NP. The fact that Group P gave large accelerative responses on the first trial while Group NP did not is of special interest here. It appears that, whereas Group NP required a considerable amount of actual experience with the stimuli and contingencies involved in the experiment before conditioned HR responses appeared, the pre-experimental instructions were largely sufficient for Group P. Presumably these instructions were able to activate previously established cognitive associations between classes of warning signals and aversive stimuli, with the result that the cardiac acceleratory response appeared very early in the experiment.

Incidentally, although the preceding evidence and arguments are based upon the study of psychopathy, it is possible that they could be extended to the general population. For example, it could be hypothesized that in some cases an inverse relationship exists between electrodermal and cardiac conditioning, such that some individuals who develop large anticipatory HR response readily will give relatively small anticipatory electrodermal responses, and vice versa. Further, the former should tend to be individuals who are comparatively proficient at tuning out cues related to impending aversive stimulation. It could also be suggested that defensive behavior of this sort would be adaptive only when the individual cannot engage in appropriate avoidance behavior.

I would like to turn now to a study of autonomic responses to simple stimuli which George Blevings and I have just completed. The study is of interest for two reasons. First, previous studies of the psychopath's physiological responsivity to simple stimuli (usually tones or shock) generally used only one or two stimulus intensities; the different selection procedures and experimental conditions used therefore make it difficult to draw any conclusions about responsivity over a range of stimulus intensities. Second, although the subjects were initially selected in our usual way, i.e., on the basis of clinical criteria, we later used the MMPI to reclassify them, thus permitting us to compare the results obtained with one selection procedure with those obtained with another.

Each subject was presented with a random series of 80, 90, 100, 110, and 120 dB tones; each tone was presented five times, with an average intertrial interval of about 30 seconds. The subjects (inmates) for the study were selected on the basis of the

Cleckley criteria, and were assigned to psychopathic (P) and nonpsychopathic (NP) groups, with 15 subjects in each group. The variables of interest were heart rate, respiration, digital and cephalic vasomotor activity, and palmar and dorsal skin conductance (SC). There was no difference between groups in tonic HR during an initial "rest" period. The resting levels of tonic palmar and dorsal skin conductance of Group P were lower than those of Group NP; similarly the palmar and dorsal SC responses of Group P to the tones, particularly the 120 dB tone, were smaller than were those of Group NP. However, in each case, the group differences did not reach statistical significance. There was a tendency, not quite significant, for the two groups to differ in the tone intensity at which HR deceleration gave way to HR acceleration—110 dB for Group NP and 120 dB for Group P. There were no significant differences between groups in the digital vasomotor response to tones below 120 dB. However, the 120 dB tone elicited a significantly larger vasoconstrictive response in Group P (a 30 percent reduction in pulse amplitude) than in Group NP (a 15 percent reduction in pulse amplitude).

Although the direction of the group differences was more or less consistent with expectation and previous research, the results were not very impressive. It is possible, of course, to provide all sorts of after-the-fact explanations of negative findings. Rather than doing so here, let me outline what happened when the Ss were reclassified on the basis of their MMPI profiles rather than on the basis of clinical judgments. The 28 MMPI profiles available (13 from Group P and 15 from Group NP) were grouped according to their similarity to one another, using the hierarchical group (H Group) program described by Veldman (1967). (This program uses a clustering technique to organize individual profiles into natural clusters or groups, such that the average intragroup distance between profiles is minimized, while the average intergroup distance is maximized.) The three groups or types of profile that emerged from the analysis are plotted in Figure 3.6. Although my experience with the MMPI is very limited, some interpretation of these profiles can be attempted. The Type I profile is similar to that frequently associated with psychopathy. Of the 11 inmates in this group, 7 had orginally been clinically diagnosed by us as psychopaths. The Type II profile has both neurotic and psychopathic features, and may be similar to what has variously been called neurotic sociopathy (Lykken, 1955), secondary psychopathy (Karpman, 1961), or neurotic delinquency (Hare, 1970b). Four of the

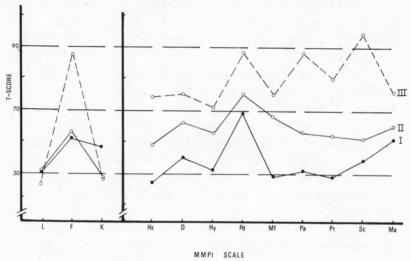

MMPI SCALE

Figure 3.6 *The three types of MMPI profile* generated by H-Group analysis of individual profiles.

11 subjects in this group had earlier been diagnosed as psychopaths. The Type III profile reflects the greatest amount of disturbance, and is similar to the schizophrenic reaction, paranoid type of profile described by Gilberstadt and Duker (1965) and to the paranoid-aggressive type described by Blackburn (1971). We had earlier diagnosed 2 of the 6 subjects in this group as psychopaths.

However one interprets these profile types, it is apparent that they provide a system of classification that is not entirely concordant with our clinical classifications. Before commenting on this discrepancy, I would like to illustrate how these three types of profiles were related to physiological activity. Type I

Ss had the lowest tonic palmar SC during the rest period while Type II Ss had the highest, the difference between types being significant (p < .01). A similar pattern was obtained for tonic dorsal SC, but the differences were not significant. Although the tonic HR of Type III during the rest period (67.9 bpm) was lower than that of either Type I (70.7) or Type II (75.2), none of the differences was significant.

Figure 3.7 shows the mean electrodermal responses given

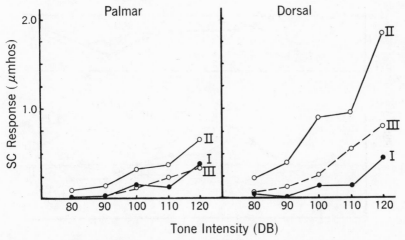

Figure 3.7 *Mean palmer and dorsal SC responses of three MMPI types* as a function of stimulus intensity.

by each type to the five tone intensities; plotted are palmar and dorsal SC responses. Although Type II Ss generally gave the largest palmar SC responses, the differences were not quite significant. More clear-cut (and highly significant) differences were obtained with the dorsal SC response, with the difference between groups increasing with increases in stimulus intensity. These results could be interpreted to mean that intense stimuli elicit relatively small orienting or alerting responses in Type I subjects, since Edelberg and his associates (Edelberg and Wright, 1964; Mordkoff, Edelberg, and Ustick, 1967) have argued that palmar SC responses reflect both eccrine and epidermal activity and are associated with both orienting and affec-

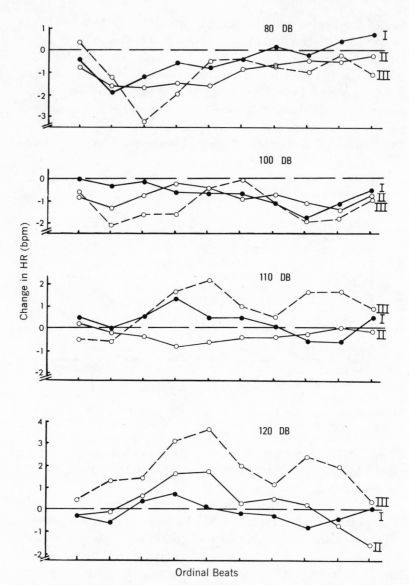

Figure 3.8 *Mean beat-by-beat changes in HR* as a function of stimulus intensity. Deviations below baseline represent deceleration.

tive behavior, whereas dorsal SC responses reflect epidermal activity and are associated only with orienting behavior.

The mean HR responses of each type are plotted in Figure 3.8. Although there is a great deal of variability in the data, it is clear that the three types differed in the pattern of their responses across stimulus intensity. The 80 dB tone elicited the largest decelerative response from the Type III subjects; by the time stimulus intensity had increased to 110 dB the response of these subjects had shifted to acceleration. Such a shift did not occur for Type II subjects until 120 dB, and not even then for the Type I subjects. These results should be considered along with the cephalic vasomotor data, presented in Figure 3.9. The data are second-by-second changes in pulse amplitude (PA) following stimulus onset—deviations below the baseline are decreases in PA, and represent vasoconstriction. As was the case with heart rate, the responses of the Type III subjects stood out from those of the other subjects—as stimulus intensity increased a large constrictive component appeared, whereas the responses of the other two types changed relatively little.

To put these findings in some sort of context, recent integrations of Western and Soviet theory and research (e.g., Graham and Clifton, 1966; Sokolov, 1963) indicate that the orienting response (OR) to novel, moderately intense stimulation should include simultaneous HR deceleration and cephalic vasoconstriction. However, while there is evidence that the predicted HR changes occur, several studies have found that the pattern of cephalic vasomotor activity is not related to stimulus intensity (e.g., Brotsky, 1969; Cohen and Johnson, 1971; Raskin, Kotses, and Bever, 1969). Elsewhere (Hare, 1972b) I have argued that this failure to find the patterns of cardiovascular activity presumed to be associated with the OR and DR partly reflects the common practice of presenting undifferentiated group data, thus obscuring any individual response patterns that may be consistent with the OR–DR concept, that is, not all subjects in any given situation would be expected to respond with complete or even partial orienting or defensive response patterns.

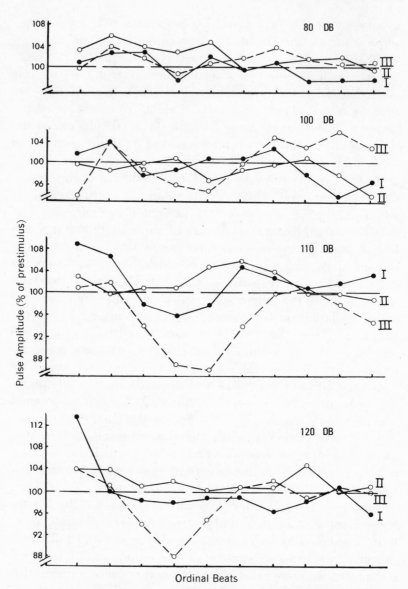

Figure 3.9 *Mean beat-by-beat changes in cephalic pulse amplitude* (PA) *as a function of stimulus intensity. Deviations below baseline represent constriction.*

With respect to the present paper, it appears that the subjects with Type III profiles showed a shift from an OR to a DR pattern as stimulus intensity increased, whereas the other types did not. To the extent that Type I subjects can be considered more psychopathic than the other Ss, their failure to show this shift is consistent with an earlier speculation (Hare and Quinn, 1971) that the shift might not occur in psychopaths until stimulus intensity is very great. We cannot make too much of this finding, however, since Type II Ss gave similar responses and since the groups to which Type I Ss were compared could hardly be considered normal. More reasonable conclusions could have been drawn had subjects with normal MMPI profiles been available for comparison. As it stands, the study may tell us as much about severely disturbed inmates (Type III profile) as it does about psychopathic ones.

Actually, a good argument could be made for routinely including more normal, as well as various neurotic and psychotic, groups in studies of psychopathy. There would, of course, be real difficulties in doing so, but the results may be worth it, particularly since some of the psychophysiological concepts and inferred mechanisms used to account for psychopathy and some forms of psychoticism (especially schizophrenia, cf. Broen, 1968; Venables, 1972) seem to be closely related.

One of the disconcerting things about the study I have just discussed is that the clinically based procedures used to select psychopathic subjects failed to screen out two subjects with MMPI profiles suggestive of severe psychological disturbance. Although it is often difficult to know what deviant test scores mean, especially when dealing with testwise inmate populations, there may be some merit in using devices like the MMPI to assist in the selection of psychopathic subjects. Thus, a psychopath could be defined as a subject who met the Cleckley criteria and who had an MMPI profile similar to that traditionally associated with the disorder. To what extent such a selection procedure would improve upon current methods is a matter for research to determine.

I should mention that this procedure was in fact used in the study just described. That is, Group P and NP, defined in accordance with clinical considerations, were each divided into three subgroups on the basis of the MMPI profiles of the subjects in these groups. The Ns in some of the subgroups were so small that statistical analysis of the physiological data was not attempted. However, inspection of the data indicated that those subjects in Group P with Type I profiles responded the way we had predicted psychopaths would, i.e., they gave generally smaller electrodermal responses and showed a shift from cardiac deceleration and cephalic vasodilation to cardiac acceleration and cephalic vasoconstriction at a higher stimulus intensity than did other subgroups. In future research we will attempt to obtain sufficient subjects to form subgroups that are large enough to make more meaningful comparisons.

I should note here that the three types of MMPI profiles just described were also obtained when we subjected MMPI data from two other studies (Hare, 1972a; Hare and Craigen, 1974) to hierarchical grouping analysis. However, in each study physiological activity was related to clinical diagnosis but not to MMPI profile type. It is difficult to determine, therefore, whether the MMPI-physiology relationships described above are chance findings or whether they are specific to the experimental situation involved.

Finally, I might note that our current research plans include placing some emphasis on the study of noncriminal populations. How we are going to go about it is a matter of some discussion at this point. Obviously it will be difficult to detect psychopaths who are functioning reasonably well in society and who are willing to participate in our research. Until we solve this problem we plan to look at some of the dimensions that seem crucial to the concept of psychopathy (such as impulsivity, lack of anxiety and empathy, etc.), with our subjects being obtained from normal populations.

References

American Psychiatric Association. 1968. *Diagnostic and Statistical Manual: Mental Disorders.* Washington, D.C., 1968.

Arieti, S. 1967. *The Intrapsychic Self.* New York: Basic Books.

Berger, S. M. 1962. Conditioning through vicarious instigation. *Psychological Review,* 69:450–466.

Blackburn, R. 1971. Personality types among abnormal homicides. *British Journal of Criminology,* 11:14–31.

Broen, W. E., Jr. 1968. *Schizophrenia: Research and Theory.* New York: Academic Press.

Brotsky, S. 1969. Cephalic vasomotor responses as indices of the orienting reflex, the defensive reflex, and semantic conditioning and generalization: A failure to replicate Soviet research. *Psychonomic Science,* 17:228–229.

Cleckley, H. 1964. *The Mask of Sanity.* 4th ed. St. Louis: Mosby.

Cohen, M. J. and H. J. Johnson. 1971. Effects of intensity and the signal value of stimuli on the orienting and defensive responses. *Journal of Experimental Psychology,* 88:286–288.

Dahlstrom, W. G. and G. S. Welsh. 1960. *An MMPI Handbook.* Minneapolis: University of Minnesota Press.

Dronsejko, K. 1972. Effects of CS duration and instructional set on cardiac anticipatory responses to stress in field dependent and independent subjects. *Psychophysiology,* 9:1–13.

Edelberg, R. and D. J. Wright. 1964. Two galvanic skin response effector organs and their stimulus specificity. *Psychophysiology,* 1:39–47.

Fenz, W. 1971. Heart rate responses to a stressor: A comparison between primary and secondary psychopaths and normal controls. *Journal of Experimental Research in Personality,* 5:7–13.

Gale, E. and J. Stern. 1967. Conditioning of the electrodermal orienting response. *Psychophysiology,* 3:291–301.

Gantt, W. Horsley. 1970. Mechanisms of behavior. *Conditional Reflex,* 5:171–179.

Gilberstadt, H. and J. Duker. 1965. *A Handbook for Clinical and Actuarial MMPI Interpretation.* Philadelphia: W. B. Saunders.

Graham, F. and R. Clifton. 1966. Heart rate change as a component of the orienting response. *Psychological Bulletin,* 65:305–320.

Hare, R. D. 1965a. Temporal gradient of fear arousal in psychopaths. *Journal of Abnormal Psychology,* 70:442–445.

—— 1965b. Acquisition and generalization of a conditioned fear response in psychopathic and nonpsychopathic criminals. *Journal of Psychology,* 59:357–370.

—— 1965c. A conflict and learning theory analysis of psychopathic behavior. *Journal of Research in Crime and Delinquency,* 2:12–19.

—— 1968. Psychopathy, autonomic functioning, and the orienting response. *Journal of Abnormal Psychology,* Monograph Supplement, 73:(3, Pt. 2).

—— 1970a. *Psychopathy: Theory and Research.* New York: Wiley.

—— 1970b. Autonomic activity and conditioning in psychopaths. Paper pre-

sented at Society for Psychophysiological Research, Symposium on Sociopathy, New Orleans.

—— 1971. Psychopathic behavior: Some recent theory and research. In
H. Adams and W. Boardman (eds.), *Advances in Experimental Clinical Psychology.* New York: Pergamon.

—— 1972a. Psychopathy and sensitivity to adrenalin. *Journal of Abnormal Psychology,* 79:138–147.

—— 1972b. Cardiovascular components of orienting and defensive responses.
Psychophysiology, 9:606–614.

—— 1973. Orienting and defensive responses to visual stimuli. *Psychophysiology,* 10:453–464.

Hare, R. D. and D. Craigen. 1974. Psychopathy and physiological activity in a
mixed-motive game situation. *Psychophysiology,* 11:197–206.

Hare, R. D. and M. Quinn. 1971. Psychopathy and autonomic conditioning.
Journal of Abnormal Psychology, 77:223–239.

Harrington, A. 1972. *Psychopaths.* New York: Simon and Schuster.

Karpman, B. 1961. The structure of neurosis: With special differentials between
neurosis, psychosis, homosexuality, alcoholism, psychopathy, and criminality.
Archives of Criminal Psychodynamics, 4:599–646.

Lacey, J. I. 1967. Somatic response patterning and stress: Some revisions of activation theory. In M. H. Appley and R. Trumbell (eds.), *Psychological Stress:
Issues in Research.* New York: Appleton-Century-Crofts.

Lippert, W. W. and R. J. Senter. 1966. Electrodermal responses in the sociopath.
Psychonomic Science, 4:25–26.

Lykken, D. T. 1955. *A Study of Anxiety in the Sociopathic Personality.* (Doctoral dissertation, University of Minnesota.) Ann Arbor, Mich.: University
Microfilms, 1955. No. 55-944.

—— 1957. A study of anxiety in the sociopathic personality. *Journal of Abnormal and Clinical Psychology,* 55:6–10.

—— 1968. Neuropsychology and psychophysiology in personality research. In
E. Borgotta and W. Lambert (eds.), *Handbook of Personality Theory and
Research.* Chicago: Rand McNally.

Lykken, D. T., A. Tellegen, and G. Katzenmeyer. 1973. *Manual for the Activity
Preference Questionnaire (APQ).* Research Report No. PR-73-4, Department
of Psychiatry, University of Minnesota.

Mailer, N. 1957. The white Negro. *Dissent,* 4:276–293.

Mordkoff, A. M. 1968. Palmar-dorsal skin conductance differences during classical conditioning. *Psychophysiology,* 5:61–66.

Mordkoff, A. M., R. Edelberg, and M. Ustick. 1967. The differential condi-
tionability of two components of the skin conductance response. *Psychophysiology,* 4:40–47.

Mowrer, O. H. 1947. On the dual nature of learning—a reinterpretation of "conditioning" and "problem-solving." *Harvard Educational Review,* 17:102–148.

Obrist, P. A. 1968. Heart rate and somatic-motor coupling during classical aversive conditioning in humans. *Journal of Experimental Psychology,*
77:189–193.

Obrist, P. A., D. M. Wood, and M. Perez-Reyes. 1965. Heart-rate conditioning in

humans: Effects of UCS intensity, vagal blockade, and adrenergic block of vasomotor activity. *Journal of Experimental Psychology,* 70:32–42.
Quay, H. C. and L. B. Parsons. 1971. *The Differential Behavioral Classification of the Juvenile Offender.* Washington, D.C.: Bureau of Prisons.
Quay, H. C. and D. R. Peterson. 1967. Manual for the Behavior Problem Checklist. Unpublished manuscript.
Raskin, D., H. Kotses, and J. Bever. 1969. Cephalic vasomotor and heart rate measures of orienting and defensive reflexes. *Psychophysiology,* 6:149–159.
Rosen, A. and D. Schalling. 1971. Probability learning in psychopathic and nonpsychopathic criminals. *Journal of Experimental Research in Personality,* 5:191–198.
Schachter, S. and B. Latane. 1964. Crime, cognition and the autonomic nervous system. In M. R. Jones (ed.), *Nebraska Symposium on Motivation.* Lincoln: University of Nebraska Press.
Schalling, D. and S. Levander. 1967. Spontaneous fluctuations in EDA during anticipation of pain in two delinquent groups differing in anxiety-proneness. Report No. 238 from the Psychological Laboratory, University of Stockholm.
Schmauk, F. J. 1970. A study of the relationship between kinds of punishment, autonomic arousal, subjective anxiety and avoidance learning in the primary sociopath. *Journal of Abnormal Psychology,* 76:325–355.
Schoenherr, J. C. 1964. *Avoidance of noxious stimulation in psychopathic personality.* (Doctoral dissertation, University of California, Los Angeles.) Ann Arbor: University Microfilms. No. 64-8334.
Sokolov, E. N. 1963. *Perception and the Conditioned Reflex.* New York: Macmillan.
Veldman, D. 1967. *Fortran Programming for the Behavioral Sciences.* New York: Holt, Rinehart and Winston.
Venables, P. H. 1972. Psychophysiological research in schizophrenia. Paper presented at Ninth Annual Conference on Current Concerns in Clinical Psychology, University of Iowa.
World Health Organization. 1968. *International Classification of Diseases* (eighth revision). Geneva.

4

A Psychophysiological Approach to Research in Schizophrenia

P. H. VENABLES

IT IS NOW traditional to start a review of work on schizophrenia by discussing the subgrouping of the disease. On occasions the classical Kraepelinian quadripartite subclassification has been used, and on others the relatively more recent dichotomy into process and reactive. To a very large extent, these kinds of division have grown out of clinical observation, in contrast to other divisions which have arisen from an experimental approach where the experimenter has seen in his data that the performance of his group of patients naturally divides in some fashion which does not necessarily accord with the established subgroupings.

Such was the case in an early experiment by Tizard and Venables (1957), where it was found that in response to changes in background noise in a visual reaction time experiment, some patients speeded up while others slowed down. A clinical impression given by the patient's behavior was that those whose performance improved in noisy conditions were the more withdrawn and those who slowed down had more florid symptoms. Use of a rating scale to measure this behavioral dimension

This work was carried out while in receipt of a grant from the Mental Health Trust and Research Fund. The Medical Director, Dr. M. Markowe, and staff of Springfield Hospital are thanked for their cooperation in these studies.

showed that the results were replicable and capable of extension (e.g., Venables, 1960). The point that is made here is that the data sometimes force subdivision of the patients upon the experimenter and result in classifications that have not necessarily arisen from a theoretical basis.

There are, of course, other examples of this sort of approach in the literature; in many it would be difficult to say that the particular worker did not start with some ideas of subgrouping, or did not have some theoretical basis for his approach. The outcome is, however, often the same, where it is the data which force the issue. Examples of being pushed by the data are the division used by Cromwell (1968) into "high and low redundant" groups, and Silverman (1964) into groups best described as "poor premorbid, non-paranoid; and the rest," a classification closely allied to Langfeldt's (1953) "nuclear" and "schizophreniform."

The data which are the particular concern of this paper, and the subgrouping which they bring about, arise, however, from a more indirect approach, where the theory produced a search for existing data, and where the evidence which was available in the literature was conflicting. The point of departure is that several not entirely similar approaches have produced the idea that what may be at least a partial feature of schizophrenic pathology is a disturbance of limbic system function, and that if this is so, then certain disturbances of autonomic function can be predicted and investigated by phychophysiological techniques.

There are three groups of ideas leading to the notion of disturbance of limbic function. First, there are data on the role of obstetric and perinatal birth complications as factors giving rise to schizophrenia in genetically predisposed persons. Second, the occurrence of schizophrenic-like symptoms in patients with organic brain pathology in limbic structures. Third, data will be considered on disturbances of attention in schizophrenic patients that accord with theoretical ideas of limbic system dysfunction which derive from lesion and stimulation experiments on animals.

First, data on birth complications. Stabenau and Pollin

(1967) studied twins discordant for schizophrenia and found that the schizophrenic member of the pair tended to be characterized by a lower birth weight and a higher degree of anoxia at birth. Pollack and Woerner (1966), and Pollack, Woerner, and Klein (1972) have shown that the member of a family who became schizophrenic had shown a greater number of pregnancy and birth complications than his siblings. Lane and Albee (1966) also reported a lower birth weight for schizophrenics when compared to controls. In 1970, Mednick reported that of those children at high genetic risk for schizophrenia by virtue of having a parent who was schizophrenic (Mednick and Schulsinger, 1968) and who subsequently suffered a psychiatric breakdown, 70 percent had had pregnancy and/or birth complications. Of those at genetic risk who did not become schizophrenic 15 percent had perinatal complications, whereas of those not at genetic risk, none of whom became psychiatrically disturbed, 33 percent had perinatal birth complications. Work on perinatal complications suggests that anoxia may be a factor of major importance in the determination of pathology. It has been suggested that certain brain structures are selectively vulnerable to the effects of anoxia. These areas include the hippocampus and cerebellum (Blackwood et al., 1967). Spector (1965), Friedes (1966), and MacLean (1968) suggest that the hippocampus is particularly vulnerable.

The second type of evidence is concerned with the occurrence of psychotic symptoms in association with demonstrable organic brain pathology. The data from work on temporal lobe epilepsy are important because of the involvement of parts of the limbic system (the amygdala and the hippocampus and septum) in this psychomotor disturbance. Slater and Beard (1963) and Flor-Henry (1969) describe an association of temporal lobe epilepsy with psychosis. This association tends to be of a reciprocal kind in that psychotic symptoms tend to be shown in the absence of psychomotor discharge and vice versa. Of particular importance in relation to data which will be presented later is the suggestion from Flor-Henry of an association between schizophrenic symptoms and epilepsy resulting from foci in the dominant temporal lobe, and between depressive symptoms and foci in the nondominant lobe. This accords with a well-recognized, but not documented, belief that "strokes" of right hemisphere location tend to be associated with depressive symptoms.

Data from Malamud (1967) reinforces the association of schizophrenic symptomatology with disturbances of the temporal/limbic system. He describes several cases in which tumors located in temporal regions were only discovered by post-mortem examination in patients in whom the presenting symptoms had been those of schizophrenia. Additional data are from the work of Heath (1964) who, recording from implanted electrodes in the septal area of schizophrenic patients, reported abnormal spiking concomitant with the exacerbation of psychotic behavior.

The third approach, which leads to the same sort of end, is that which suggests that one of the main features of schizophrenic behavior is a dysfunction of attentional processes (McGhie and Chapman, 1961; McGhie, 1969; Silverman, 1964, 1967; Orzack and Kornetsky, 1966; Kornetsky, 1972; Venables, 1964, 1971, 1973). It is beyond the scope of this paper to attempt a definition of attention or resolution of input filter versus output selection theories. However, recent work by Rothblat and Pribram (1972) suggest that both an input filter system (Broadbent, 1958; Triesman and Geffen, 1967) and an output selection system (Deutsch and Deutsch, 1963) are appropriate at different stages in the process of learning to attend to particular stimuli, and that both the striate and temporal cortex are involved in the process. Nevertheless, there is adequate evidence to suggest that the limbic system is involved in the attentional process (Douglas and Pribram, 1966; Douglas, 1967; Kimble, 1968). Two slightly different mechanisms are suggested by Douglas and Pribram, on the one hand, and Kimble on the other. The former view—of the role of the hippocampus—is that it "is postulated to exclude stimulus patterns from attention through a process of efferent control of sensory reception known as 'gating'." The latter view is that "the neural output of this structure (the hippocampus) in response to the occurrence of novelty or mismatch may act to inhibit certain excitatory systems . . . and reduce their effectiveness, thus allowing the animal to disengage its attentional processes and facilitate an attention shift to the novel or unexpected event."

It is possible to make the suggestion that a malfunction of the hippocampal system thus described could lead to the experience of the acute schizophrenic patient who is reported by McGhie and Chapman (1961) as saying, "everything seems to grip my attention, although I am not particularly interested in anything. I am speaking to you now, but I can hear noises going on next door, and in the corridor. I find it difficult to shut these out, and it makes it more difficult to concentrate on what I am saying to you." The patient appears to be describing difficulty in both gating and switching.

On the basis of work on size estimation, Cromwell (1968, 1972) has put forward a view which also derives its basis from work in Pribram's laboratory (Pribram and Melges, 1969) where it is proposed that "the input may be blocked out to produce a highly redundant field or contrarily that the input may be admitted in intermediate or high amounts thus reducing the redundancy of the field." This is a view stated epigrammatically by Douglas (1967), who says, "the amygdaloid system makes stimuli more figural while the hippocampal system converts figure into ground." Cromwell goes on to suggest that two groups of schizophrenics are to be found; a high redundancy group who "reject high amounts and variability of stimulus input," and a low redundancy group who have "a distaste for stimulus deprivation and . . . are likely to accommodate to, and even improve, performance as a function of high stimulus surroundings." According to Cromwell (1972) the "high redundancy" type is fairly similar to the process-poor premorbid-nonparanoid type of patient, while the low redundancy type has more affinity with the good premorbid-reactive-paranoid. The important point is that behavioral and clinical data seen in relation to work on limbic function in animals also points to the possibility of limbic dysfunction being involved in schizophrenia.

Three lines of work, thus, all converge to suggest that further investigation of limbic function in schizophrenic patients is a worthwhile undertaking. This is a point of view which has the substantial backing of MacLean (1970), who discusses the possibility "that rumblings in the hippocampal portion of the limbic brain may cause certain types of upheaval in the endogeneous and toxic psychoses" and that it is worthwhile exploring the possibility "that eruptions in this part of the brain may give rise to: (a) disturbances of emotion and mood, (b) feelings of depersonalization, (c) distortions of perception, and (d) paranoid symptoms" (p. 129). Reviewing the area from a slightly different viewpoint, Smythies (1969) suggests "that many so-called bizarre symptoms of schizophrenia may be accounted for if we regard the disease as a disturbance in those biochemical mechanisms that are utilised in synaptic transmission in the crucial areas of the limbic system, including its important component in the temporal lobe."

One obscurity arises from what has been said so far, insofar as it has been emphasized that it is hippocampal function which would seem to be implicated by perinatal anoxic damage, and a similar emphasis on the hippocampus has been given by Mac-Lean. The behavioral and clinical data, however, would rather tend to suggest a bi-directional departure from normal balanced functioning in schizophrenia. In any reciprocally acting excitatory and inhibitory system it is fairly obvious that resultant excitation may be achieved either by an excess of excitation, or a diminution of inhibition, and vice versa. Thus the "low redundancy," poor gating, flooding of stimulation situation could be achieved by either diminution of hippocampal function or excess of amygdaloid function if, following Pribram and his colleagues, we may see these as reciprocal. With the data so far discussed it is not possible to resolve this issue. However, reverting to the points made at the beginning of the paper, what does seem to be available is a theoretical basis for suggesting a dichotomous subgrouping of schizophrenics.

How, then, should limbic dysfunction in schizophrenia be further investigated? Clearly, approaches such as recording from indwelling electrodes is in general ethically undesirable. Psychophysiological techniques would seem more acceptable and to offer promise of investigation of processes in patients where poor performance of a voluntary task can never be fully established as resulting from defect of function or lack of cooperation.

The use of psychophysiological techniques in the investigation of schizophrenia has a long and useful history. What is, however, being put forward here is an illustration, if no more, of their use to push forward work on a particular theoretical position. Three factors are seen as important in this exercise. First, the correct use of techniques, so that the electrical event recorded on the polygraph is the most faithful representation which can be achieved of the physiological event which gives rise to it. Second, the use of psychophysiological data from work on animals with known disturbances of nervous system function, or from data on man in whom there are organic structural changes of known extent due to disease or accident. The hope is that this will give rise to a greater understanding of the relation of the psychophysiological measures to the aspects of central nervous system function which they reflect. Third, it is suggested that initially, at any rate, the nature of the "psychological" part of the experiment should be as simple as possible so that the results obtained should be most easily interpretable.

In the context of the work reviewed, where the aim is to investigate the activity of the limbic system particularly in relation to attentional and stimulus-processing functions, the orienting response is perhaps the potentially most fruitful and objectively the most simple type of system that may be studied. The advocacy of investigation of the orienting response in schizophrenia has already been extensively made (Venables, 1973). Pavlov (1927) described the orientation reaction as "the reflex which brings about the immediate response in man and animals to the slightest change in the world around them so that they immediately orient their appropriate receptor organ in accordance with the perceptible quality of this agent bringing about change making full investigation of it." The closeness of this early definition to some present ideas of attention is evident. Coupled closely to the notion of the orientation response is its habituation; without habituation there would be continued arousal and uncontrolled attention to all stimuli. Jasper (1958) suggests that "indiscriminate arousal reaction to all stimuli could only result in chaotic behaviour as may be the case in certain mental disorders." Russell (1966) describes the situation as "the most primitive and fundamental form of learning," and in a pertinent review Epstein (1967) suggests that "the stimulus acquires cue value through the process of habituation." That is, that the organism learns the characteristics of the stimuli to which he need not attend when they are all the same, but to which he will orient when they are different. In another passage Epstein suggests that "to the simple process of habituation is assigned the magical property of being able to transmute stimulus energy into meaning." Later, Epstein says, "the schizophrenic is defective in ability to attend to, to establish expectancies for, and assign meaning to cues," or by retranslation, if a person orients to stimuli but does not show habituation of the orientation reaction, then he does not "assign meaning" to those cue stimuli or, on the other hand, if he does not adequately orient to stimuli, then he is defective in his ability to attend to cues.

A brief description of the orientation reaction is perhaps pertinent at this point. Graham and Clifton (1966) define it as "a system of unconditioned motor, autonomic, and central responses elicited by any change in the stimulation and independent of stimulus quality." In general, it may be said that it results from stimulation of moderate intensity and has among its autonomic concomitants phasic increase in skin conductance, a pattern of heart rate change which is of initial deceleration followed by acceleration, vasodilatation of the vascular system at the head, and vasoconstriction of the limbs. Lacey (e.g., 1967) has suggested that the decelerative heart rate change is part of the system which functionally "opens the gate" for the intake of environmental stimulation, in contrast to an accelerative change which is the accompaniment of "environmental rejection," and is, in Russian terminology, a defensive reaction. According to work from Pribram's laboratory, on the other hand, the skin conductance response (SCR) is an indication of the registration of the stimulus which gave rise to the OR in order to form a "neural model" (Sokolov, 1963). Repeated registration completes the formation of the neural model so that there is decreasing mismatch between the perceptual representation of the external stimulus and the neural model in memory, and the decreasing error signal results in decreased orientation. This view of the SCR as an index of registration is derived from a series of experiments by Pribram and his colleagues which form an essential background to the work on schizophrenics to be described.

Bagshaw, Kimble, and Pribram (1965) showed that amygdalectomy in monkeys produced a marked diminution of the SCR to tone stimuli (a finding replicated by Bagshaw and Benzies, 1968), while ablation of the hippocampus and inferotemporal cortex had no effect on either the appearance of the SCR or its habituation. In a parallel series of experiments Kimble, Bagshaw, and Pribram (1965) showed that lateral, frontal cortical lesions depressed SCR while medial frontal and anterior cingulate lesions did not. The indication from these experiments, that the amygdala is an excitatory area for electrodermal activity, is supported by data from other laboratories. Lang, Tuovinen, and Valleala (1964) showed that stimulation of the amygdala produced a skin potential response (SPR), a finding which accords with reports by Yokota, Sato and Fujimori (1963). These latter authors were also able to show that stimulation of the hippocampus and fornix produces inhibition of the SPR. These results would in general support the idea of reciprocity of action of the hippocampus and amygdala as suggested by Douglas and Pribram (1966).

The idea that the SCR is an index of "registration" is put forward by Pribram and his group (e.g., Koepke and Pribram 1966) in the following argument. Lesions of the amygdala produce an animal exhibiting the Kluver-Bucy syndrome (Goddard,

1964a) in which behavioral orientation does not habituate. The same lesions virtually eliminate skin conductance responses (Bagshaw, Kimble, and Pribram, 1965). Thus, if registration of perceptual impressions to form a neural model (Sokolov, 1963) does not occur, as suggested by the absence of SCRs, the amygdalectomized animal will continue to act toward identical stimuli as though they are continually novel. A not dissimilar viewpoint is put forward by Goddard (1964b), where he suggests that low intensity stimulation of the amygdala "acting as a functional lesion by scrambling the otherwise orderly traffic of impulses . . . disrupts the consolidation of association of a stimulus with a noxious event."

What is available, then, is reasonably firm data which suggest that if the orienting response and its habituation to simple stimuli in schizophrenic patients is examined this may throw light on suggestions which have already been made concerning the role of the limbic system in schizophrenic pathology.

Two major sets of studies exist in the literature which might have helped in this direction. Unfortunately, they present conflicting results. Zahn, Rosenthal, and Lawlor (1968) showed that schizophrenics had larger SCRs and habituated less than normals, a finding supported by Dykman et al. (1968). This finding is also in accord with that of Mednick and Schulsinger (1968) that one of the major features which distinguished children of schizophrenic mothers who were to continue without evidence of pathology from those who later became psychiatrically disturbed was that the latter had larger SCRs which did not readily habituate.

On the other hand, studies by Bernstein in which patients were divided into remitted versus regressed (1964) or clear versus confused (1970) observed faster habituation than controls for both groups. His data tend to be in accord with the general findings of Russian workers reported by Lynn (1963) where diminished, or even absence of, electrodermal activity is reported from schizophrenic patients. Empirical backing for the theoretical position put forward in the earlier part of the paper was thus ambiguous. Attempts to investigate this position have resulted in a series of papers (Gruzelier, 1973a, 1973b; Gruzelier and Venables, 1972, 1973, 1974a).

With the conflict between the Zahn-Dykman and the Russo-Bernstein results in mind, we tested a large unselected group of schizophrenic patients. They were, in the opinion of the psychiatrist at the hospital where the work was carried out, all undoubtedly schizophrenic. Bearing in mind the less British than U.S. willingness to diagnose schizophrenia (Cooper et al., 1969), we see that these diagnoses were probably on the conservative side.

Eighty schizophrenics were tested. Fifty, termed noninstitutionalized, had been currently hospitalized for an average of 0.8 years (SD 1.1 years). In terms of previously used terminology they would thus largely be classified as acute if the acute/chronic dichotomy is at two years. However, as they had up to six previous admissions they did not clearly fall into an acute category. In contrast to the pre-1955, pre-tranquilizer period it is very difficult to label patients seen in a general psychiatric hospital as acute, insofar as it is likely that the truly acute phase of their illness may have occurred while under the care of a general practitioner or in a general hospital. In contrast, the 30 remaining patients who were tested had all been in hospital over eight years (mean 17.1 years) and were justifiably termed "institutionalized." The mean ages of the two groups were respectively, 33.6 (SD 9.5 years) and 48.1 (SD 8.0 years). The attempt was made to include as heterogenous a sample of schizophrenics as possible with regard to psychiatric subgrouping. No patient was lobotomized or had brain damage. Nonpsychotic patient controls and normal control subjects were also tested.

Skin conductance was measured from bipolar placements on the distal phalanges of the first and second fingers of the right hand using 30 mm diameter Silver/silver chloride electrodes and 0.5 percent potassium chloride/Agar-agar electrolyte Skin conductance was measured directly with a constant voltage system (Lykken and Venables, 1971; Venables and Christie,

1973). The orienting stimulus was a 1000 Hz, 1 second, 85 dB tone presented fifteen times at irregular intervals, pseudo-randomized between 30 and 60 seconds, and delivered binaurally through headphones. A skin conductance orienting response was defined as an increase in conductance greater than .05 μmho and occurring between 1 and 5 seconds after the stimulus.

The results show that both Zahn and Bernstein were partially correct. No responses at all were elicited from 43 of the 80 schizophrenics. Of the remaining 37 who responded, 34 did not habituate to the criterion of three successive failures to respond. The controls all responded and habituated. From now on those schizophrenics who respond, but do not habituate, will be termed "responders," and those who do not respond "nonresponders." Of the responders, 23 were noninstitutionalized out of 50, and 14 out of 30 were institutionalized. The pattern of roughly 50 percent responders and nonresponders is thus preserved across patients dichotomized on length of stay.

The pattern of percentage of subjects responding by trials in the control group and the group of schizophrenics who respond is shown in Figure 4.1. The data from the schizophrenic group who do not respond are not shown on this figure. The data in the form of change of amplitude of *nonzero* responses over trials are shown in Figure 4.2. Here, a similar pattern is seen, with the control subjects reaching a position where no responses are elicited while both schizophrenic groups continue to give responses up to the presentation of the fifteenth stimulus. It will be seen from this figure that the pattern of habituation tends to follow that suggested by Groves and Thompson (1970). That is, that the data fall into two segments; the first is of exponential slope and represents habituation of phasic responses until an asymptote is reached. From this point the second segment starts and is dependent on tonic arousal level. Individual curves were examined and the point of inflection between segments 1 and 2 judged by eye. The mean amplitude for segment 1 was 0.80, 0.47, and 0.27 μmho for the noninstitutionalized schizophrenic, institutionalized schizophrenic,

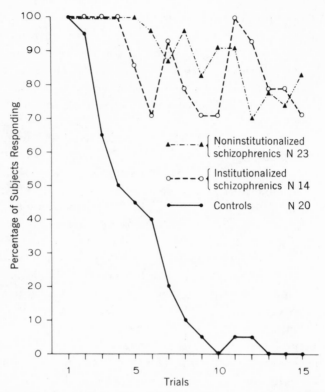

Figure 4.1 *Percentage of subjects with skin conductance responses to orienting
     tones* in the control and noninstitutionalized and institutionalized
     responder groups.

and control groups, respectively; and for segment 2 similar figures were 0.39, 0.15, and 0.01 μmho. As can be seen from Figure 4.2, the rates of habituation in segment 1 for the three
groups appear different. However, when these rates were calculated as a function of the amplitude of the initial response then
no group differences in rate were found. In summary at this
point, about 50 percent of schizophrenics do not respond at all;
of those who do respond, there is a tendency for them to have
higher than normal initial amplitudes of response and for them
to continue to respond at an asymptotic value greater than zero
when normal subjects have habituated to zero and ceased to
respond.

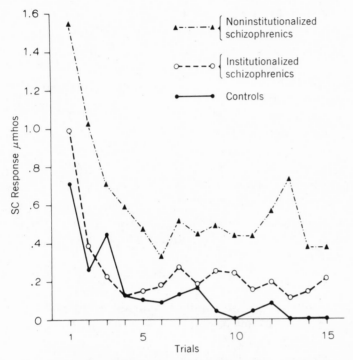

Figure 4.2 *Mean amplitude of nonzero skin conductance responses* for control and noninstitutionalized and institutionalized schizophrenic responder groups.

Given this dichotomy of patients on the basis of their orientation and habituation to simple tones, a finding which would seem to accord with theoretical expectations of excitatory or inhibitory imbalance of limbic systems, it becomes important to ask whether there are other differences between the responding and nonresponding groups. It has already been stated that the 50/50 pattern extends over the institutionalized/noninstitutionalized dichotomy. The average length of hospitalization for the noninstitutionalized responders was 41.7 weeks, and for the nonresponders was 38.9 weeks. For the institutionalized responders the average length of hospitalization was 16.7 years, and for the nonresponders 17.5 years.

As far as subdiagnostic groupings was concerned there is almost a complete coverage of all categories in the responder and nonresponder groups. It is only the case of defect or residual schizophrenic state that there are slightly more to be found among the nonresponders than the responders. There was no difference in age between the responding and nonresponding groups; they differed only by 0.3 years, with a standard deviation of about 8.0 years. All patients were on phenothiazines, but there were no differences either in the type of drug or the size of the daily dosage between the responders and nonresponders.

The possibility that there might be some aspects of the testing conditions which would give rise to the condition of nonresponding was examined. One of the possibilities was that the nonresponders' skin temperature was lower than that of the responders; when the hands of nonresponders were warmed to temperature levels matched to those of responders, responses were not, however, capable of being elicited. Another possibility was that because of the functioning of the "law of initial value," the nonresponders might be unable to respond because they already had high skin conductance levels. Examination of Figure 4.3 shows that this is not the case. It is the responders who have the higher levels of skin conductance than the nonresponders, with the control subjects occupying an intermediate position. The possibility that the stimulation was of inadequate intensity to elicit responses was examined. When stimuli of 100 dB or over were presented there were still no responses. The point of particular importance concerns instructions given to the subjects. The patients were very carefully instructed that the tone that they would hear had no particular significance. They were questioned afterwards as to whether they had counted the numbers of tones, or made any other attempt to particularly attend to them. If they had, their records were discarded. In an experiment which will be described later, tones were given signal value by being included in a discrimination task. Under these conditions responses were elicited from those patients who performed as nonresponders in the orientation and habituation experiment.

The conditions for the appearance of the bimodal distribu-

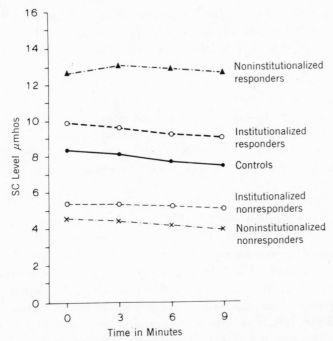

Figure 4.3 *Mean skin conductance level* during the tone series for controls and schizophrenic responders and nonresponders.

tion that was achieved would thus seem to be that great care should be taken that the tones should not have signal value. Given this, it has been shown that the results are replicable. Approximately the same proportion of responders and nonresponders in a group of schizophrenics had been reported by another worker (T. Lobstein, Birkbeck College, University of London; personal communication).

Why, then, have other workers not reported similar findings? It may be that those who report all, or nearly all, patients as responders have, by their instructions, invested their tones with signal value, or it may be that those who achieved no responses thought their apparatus or technique at fault and disposed of the data. Certainly, now that these results have been seen in schizophrenics there has been a greater alertness to look out for them in normal subjects. A small proportion of genuine nonresponders (about 7 percent) are found amongst normals, and this has been particularly reported by G. W. De Marchi (Birkbeck College, University of London; personal communication) as occurring during certain phases of the menstrual cycle. One feasible explanation for the finding of a greater number of responders and nonhabituators in their schizophrenic population by Zahn and his colleagues (1968) is that they used a constant 30-second interstimulus interval which by the process of temporal conditioning and the consequent investing of the stimuli with signal value would maintain responsivity.

From the work which was reviewed earlier there is, in the light of the findings described, the possibility of suggesting that the usual fine balance which we see between excitatory and inhibitory processes or, following Pribram and Kimble, between amygdaloid and hippocampal function, is destroyed in schizophrenic patients. The patient is either tipped toward dominance of amygdaloid or dominance of hippocampal function. Here, then, to return to the introduction to the paper, there is a subgrouping of schizophrenics that has arisen from investigating a theoretical position, and that has very much been forced on us by the data.

Having found the dichotomy, several questions must be asked: (1) are there other characteristics of the patients which we can discover? (2) is the dichotomy ephemeral, or do patients change in their classification? (3) is the classification useful? and (4) is there any suggestion in the literature that other workers have found similar divisions?

In an attempt to answer the first question, it is suggested that in the case of the nonresponders there is something which approaches a functional amygdalectomy, and in the case of the responders an overstimulation of the amygdala, and we should, therefore, expect that the nonresponders might be more placid and less aggressive than the responders (Goddard, 1964a). Behavioral ratings on subscales of the Wittenborn Psychiatric Rating Scale have shown that among the noninstitutionalized patients the responders are significantly more reactive, belligerent, attention-demanding, and anxious than the nonresponders. Other autonomic characteristics on which the two groups have been shown to differ significantly are heart rate, where the responders have the higher rate, and systolic blood pressure, where again the responders have the higher values. Further evidence can be elicited by the use of the two-flash threshold technique (Gruzelier and Venables, 1974b). Spinelli and Pribram (1966) have shown that after stimulation of the amygdala, cortical recovery cycles were shorter and that after stimulation of the hippocampus there was a lengthening or recovery. Vaughan and Costa (1964) produced evidence of a parallelism between cortical events and perceptual experience when examining two-flash thresholds. This evidence has recently been amply confirmed by Peck and Lindsley (1972) in a study in which "changes in averaged evoked potentials were determined which paralleled the behavioural response to pairs of flashes as a function of IFI." It could, therefore, be predicted that two-flash thresholds of the responders would be lower than that of the nonresponders. This been shown to be the case although the two-flash threshold of controls was not significantly different from that of the responding group. Perhaps more interesting is that the false positive rates of report shown by the responding and nonresponding schizophrenic groups differed from that of the control group, although they did not differ between the schizophrenic groups. This indicates that the schizophrenics often give reports of double flashes when single ones are present. This is a risky mode of responding, for it acts to maximize hit rate, but at the cost of false positives. Riskiness could be said to be akin to impulsivity, and impulsivity is said to be a characteristic of hippocampal rats.

These few pieces of data probably serve to indicate that there are sufficient other aspects on which responding and nonresponding patients are differentiated to make it clear that there is a fairly substantial body of data backing up the dichotomy. It will have been noticed that the experiment which has been so far described, on which the dichotomous division of schizophrenics was based, used as stimuli to elicit an orientation response tones of 85 dB intensity. It could be argued on the basis of other results in the literature that 85 dB is rather intense as an orienting stimulus, and therefore that the results are concerned not so much with orientation as forms of defense. A replication study on a fresh set of subjects was therefore carried out with tones of 75 dB intensity and with a different and shorter range of interstimulus intervals. Forty of these subjects were schizophrenic. Patients were selected from admission or long-stay wards according to the previous criteria. They were tested until two equal groups of responders and nonresponders were obtained, with 10 patients in each group having had more than five years continuous hospitalization. There were thus equal groups of institutionalized and noninstitutionalized responding and nonresponding schizophrenic patients. Ten other subjects with disorders of affect were tested having depression as the sole or primary feature at the time of testing, and another 10 patients were tested having disorders of personality as the primary diagnosis. With minor exceptions the results which have so far been reported were replicated in this study. Similar results were obtained with 75 dB as the intensity of the orienting stimulus as were obtained in the major study with an 85 dB tone stimulus (Gruzelier and Venables, 1974a).

The orientation data described so far have arisen from measures of skin conductance. It was considered to be important to examine how far patients classed as skin conductance responders or nonresponders would also be responders or nonresponders in other modalities. Heart-rate orienting activity has been examined in two as yet unpublished experiments. Gruzelier (1973b) showed that those schizophrenic patients who were skin conductance responders, gave an essentially acceleratory response to 85 dB tones while those classed as skin conductance nonresponders showed no response after a minor initial deceleration over the first two post-stimulus beats. In this study, Gruzelier used 85 dB tones having a sharp onset and interprets his data as showing some aspects of the startle response. In contrast to these findings, Lobstein (personal communication) has reported data using tones of 70, 85, and 100 dB

having a 25 msec rise time to peak intensity. With schizophrenics defined as skin conductance responders, Lobstein reports uniphasic deceleration to 70 dB tones and biphasic deceleration and acceleration to 85 and 100 dB tones. More
strikingly, however, he reports marked deceleration to all intensities of tones in his skin conductance nonresponder group. Either on a Lacey (e.g., Lacey, 1967) or an Obrist (e.g., Obrist et
al., 1970) type of hypothesis, this is the type of cardiovascular
response that often accompanies conditions of "openness to the
environment" and thus is in accord with the clinical reports of
McGhie and Chapman (1961) already cited, and also the notion
of Silverman (1967) that some schizophrenics, particularly the
process nonparanoid type, might display "sensory input
processing/ideational gating" types of activity. Whatever the interpretation of this work it is apparent that importance must be
attached to the fine characteristics of the stimuli used in these
sorts of experiments.

The work reported shows that at any one time we appear to
be able to find groups of responding and nonresponding schizophrenics defined as having, or not having, skin conductance
orienting responses. The question must be asked, how far is this
a continuing characteristic of a single patient? So far, not a great
deal of work has been done on this question. However, a little
knowledge has been gained with individual patients. One patient described as having an "acute schizophrenic episode" was
tested on three occasions within three weeks during a sequence
of excitement, inactivity, and excitement. During both periods
of excitement skin conductance responses were present and did
not habituate. During the period of inactivity no skin conductance responses occurred. The impression has also been gained,
although unsystematically, that patients who, in the most severe
phases of their illness, may be nonresponders become nonha-
bituating responders as they are clinically approaching a period
when they may be discharged. They do not, however, appear to
achieve a pattern of responses akin to that of a normal subject in
showing both orientation and habituation.

One of the underlying fears about the use of a dichotomy

such as that of responders versus nonresponders, which does not readily correspond to any familiar clinical subgrouping, is that it may be interesting, but virtually useless. From what has been said so far there does seem to be some indication that the features which exemplify the patients in each category do hang together to form meaningful wholes, and it is a hope that in the not too distant future it may be possible to use the categorization to enable a more rational use of medication to be adopted, however, at this moment it is too early to do more than speculate in this area. Nevertheless, if this were to be a feasible operation it would be one of the first demonstrations of the direct use of psychophysiological techniques in pharmacological treatment procedures in clinical psychology.

What has been discussed so far is the extent to which the subgrouping of responders versus nonresponders is a useful classificatory procedure, and the attempt has been made to answer this in terms of external criteria. It is perhaps now most useful to answer the question in terms of the extent to which the subclassification and the theory can be extended. The concern is with the extent to which psychophysiological techniques in clinical psychology can be seen as part of a process interacting between neurology, physiological psychology, experimental psychology, and clinical psychology.

Earlier in this paper, the idea that schizophrenic symptoms were the accompaniment of disturbances of the dominant temporal lobe, and depressive symptoms were the accompaniment of disturbances of the nondominant lobe was discussed. Bearing these ideas in mind, researchers have extended the techniques used in examining orientation in schizophrenics. Instead of being recorded from the right hand only, skin conductance is now routinely recorded from both the left and the right hands. In a study (Gruzelier, 1973a) looking at the orienting responses to 85 dB tones, 60 schizophrenics and 15 healthy subjects were tested. Schizophrenics were selected at random from the total hospital population and tested until equal numbers of responders or nonresponders were obtained. The patients were also divided equally into institutionalized and noninstitutionalized groups.

Bilateral orienting response frequency in blocks of five trials for groups of noninstitutionalized and institutionalized schizophrenic responders, and a control group, are shown in Figure 4.4. The most striking result here is the bilateral difference in responsivity for the institutionalized schizophrenic

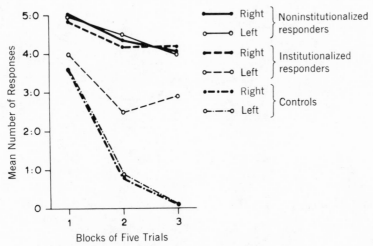

Figure 4.4 *Bilateral mean skin conductance response frequency* in blocks of 5 trials for noninstitutionalized and institutionalized schizophrenics and control groups.

group. These data show that the number of responses from the right hand is significantly larger than the number of responses from the left hand in this group of patients. This figure does not contain data from 3 schizophrenic patients whose responses on the left hand were minimal, or absent, where responses on the right hand failed to habituate, or were slow to do so. Thus, at one and the same time a patient may be a "responder" on his right hand, and a "nonresponder" on his left hand.

In Figure 4.5, skin conductance response amplitude over trials is presented. Here is seen the same sort of pattern previously reported, with the schizophrenic responder groups ha-

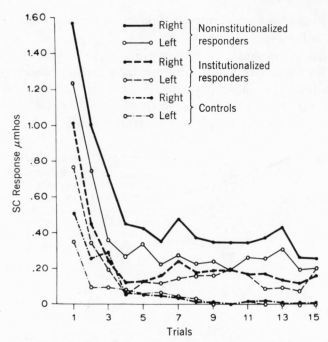

Figure 4.5 *Bilateral mean skin conductance response amplitudes* during the
tone habituation sequence for noninstitutionalized and institutionalized schizophrenic and control groups.

bituating to an asymptote which is significantly different from
zero, while the control groups habituate to a criterion of three
successive zero responses. The data are quite complicated to
describe statistically, but in summary it can be said that in the
asymptotic segment the noninstitutionalized patients show
greater responding on the right hand than on the left hand,
while this does not reach significance in the institutionalized
group.

Figure 4.6 shows the skin conductance levels for the patient groups and controls. Here it will be seen, as reported elsewhere in the literature, there is no significant difference between the skin conductance level from the right and left hands
in normal control subjects. Otherwise, it will be seen that skin
conductance levels are higher on the right hand for the responder subjects, and higher on the left hand for nonresponding

subjects. These data have been essentially replicated in further groups using 75 dB tone for orientation.

One interesting feature in the data is shown in Figure 4.7 where the depressive group, who largely otherwise behaved like normals, insofar as they showed orientation and habitua-

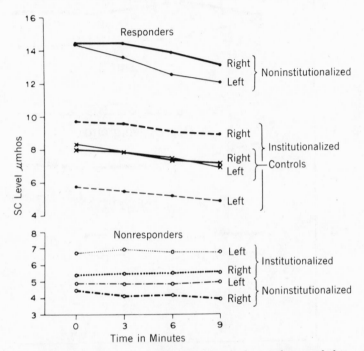

Figure 4.6 *Bilateral mean skin conductance levels* during the tone habituation sequence for the schizophrenic responder and control groups (top) and the schizophrenic nonresponder groups (bottom).

tion, were, as far as their skin conductance levels were concerned, showing bilateral differences in the opposite direction to the responding schizophrenic group, by having a higher level of activity on the left hand than on the right. This reversal is what might have been predicted from the statements of Flor-Henry's theory cited earlier. A direct interpretation of these bilateral results is, of course, not easy. We need to know the extent to which lateral brain dysfunction expresses itself as contra-

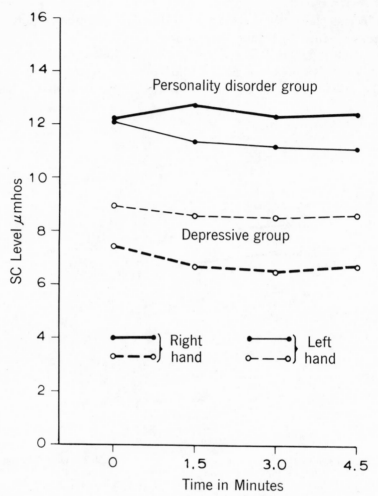

Figure 4.7 *Bilateral mean skin conductance levels* during tone habituation sequence for the personality disorder and depressive groups.

lateral or ipsilateral disturbance at the palm. The data are rather few. Luria and Homskaya (1963) report an absence of responses on the left hand in a patient with a tumour of the left frontal lobe, and Sourek (1965), when comparing skin potential response amplitudes bilaterally in patients with unilateral surgical removal of the medial and basal parts of the frontal lobe, or medial parts of the temporal lobe, found that amplitudes were smaller on the hand homolateral to the lesion. What appears to be a deficiency in responding on the left side in schizophrenics, therefore, would suggest left hemispheric dysfunction in these patients.

One other finding which has already been hinted at also serves to illustrate the interaction between neurology and psychophysiology which can be fruitful in this area. It has been suggested that the important feature which must be preserved to obtain the dichotomy of nonresponding and responding already described is that the tones used to elicit orientation should have no signal value. An experiment (Gruzelier and Venables, 1974a) has been carried out which follows directly from one reported by Luria and Homskaya (1970). These investigators examined electrodermal and vascular responses to repeated acoustic stimuli, with or without attentional significance, in subjects free from pathology, and in patients with brain damage localized in either the frontal lobes or the temporal, parietal, and occipital lobes. They found that in normal subjects orienting responses to the neutral stimuli, that is, those that did not require the subject's attention, habituated within ten to fifteen stimulus presentations. Patients in all groups showed atypical orienting or habituation, that is, responses were irregular or failed to occur, or responses failed to habituate. In normal subjects responses were restored when stimuli acquired signal values, as was the case in all groups of patients except with those with frontal pathology. These patients failed to respond or responded irregularly.

In the present experiment using schizophrenic subjects and also patients diagnosed as personality disorders and depressives, tones of 75 dB of either 1000 Hz or 2000 Hz were presented in a randomized sequence at intervals between 30 and 60 seconds. The subject was instructed to press a button in response to the 1000 Hz tone. This was, therefore, designated the signal tone, and the 2000 Hz tone was designated as the neutral tone to which no response was required. Figure 4.8 shows the responses of four groups. It will be seen that to the neutral tone the schizophrenic nonresponders, defined from a previous habituation sequence, showed only minimal responding, while to the signal tone they showed quite extensive responses. In the case of the schizophrenic responders the responses to the signal tone were larger than to the neutral tone. Similar findings are indicated for personality disorders and de-

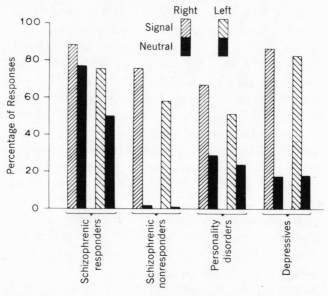

Figure 4.8 *Percentage of skin conductance responses bilaterally to the signal and neutral tones* for the responder and nonresponder schizophrenic groups and the personality disorder and depressive groups.

pressives. It will also be noted that there are marked differences bilaterally, with the right hand generally showing a larger responding than the left hand. The point which is suggested at this stage is that these data indicate that attention should be confined to the temporal lobes where schizophrenic disturbance is concerned, insofar as the data appear to indicate a preservation of response to signal tones which would not be found if there were disturbance of a frontal function. In summary, therefore, what these data have so far suggested is that in schizophrenic patients there would appear to be some form of functional disturbance which is to be found maximally in the left temporal lobe. Clearly, this is a very bold statement that needs much more support before it can be considered established, but the data do at least point the way to what would be a fruitful line of investigation.

The final point which must be made is concerned with an attempt to answer the question: What surprise should be felt about the dichotomy of responders and nonresponders elicited by this series of investigations? Silverman, in 1967, pointed out that it was quite usual to find schizophrenics' performance scores defining the limits of a response range falling outside normal values in both directions. We have already mentioned the work of Cromwell in 1968 resulting in the idea of two dissimilar groups of schizophrenics having characteristics of high or low redundancy methods of dealing with stimulus input. In a very similar way to the results which have been reported, Epstein (1970) describes the work of two of his students, which showed two very different kinds of skin conductance reactivity and habituation. This was used to back up the suggestion that schizophrenics suffer from a poorly modulated inhibitory system so that there can either be an excess or a deficit of inhibition resulting in two different kinds of response patterns. Some Russian work which supports this sort of idea is that of Popova, described by Stern and Mcdonald (1965). Popova showed that the orienting responses of paranoid schizophrenic patients were either absent when the patients were acutely confused or, when the patients had stable systematic illusions, clear-cut responses were evident. Orzack and Kornetsky (1966) report schizophrenics' performance on the continuous performance test, where it was found that there was significant overall impairment in comparison to a normal group. This, however, was due to the fact that the performance of 7 of the schizophrenic subjects was severely impaired, and that of the other 9 fell within the normal range. It is reported that no difference could be discerned between the two groups with respect to subdiagnosis, sex, or length of hospitalization, a finding very similar to ours with the responding and nonresponding groups. However, Or-

134   *P. H. Venables*

zack (personal communication) has reported that the poor per-
formers are in fact distinguished from the rest by having a genetic background for their disease. In summary, then, the
results which we have reported are to be seen as further evidence for a major differentiation within the schizophrenic group
at any one time, and within a particular patient, possibly, from
time to time in his illness. The bimodality of distribution of
scores has evidently been reported in various ways from other
sources and is therefore not a wholly new finding. Rather, it is
hoped that it is one that will aid movement toward a sounder
theoretical basis for the disease.

References

Bagshaw, M. H. and S. Benzies. 1968. Multiple measures of the orienting reaction and their dissociation after amygdalectomy in monkeys. *Experimental
Neurology*, 20:175–187.
Bagshaw, M. H., D. P. Kimble, and K. H. Pribram. 1965. The GSR of monkeys
during orienting and habituation and after ablation of the amygdala, hippocampus, and inferotemporal cortex. *Neuropsychologia*, 3:111–119.
Bernstein, A. S. 1964. The galvanic skin response orienting reflex among
chronic schizophrenics. *Psychonomic Science*, 1:391–392.
—— 1970. The phasic electrodermal orienting response in chronic schizophrenics. II: Response to auditory signals of varying intensity. *Journal of Abnormal Psychology*, 75:146–156.
Blackwood, W., W. H. McMenemey, A. Meyer, R. M. Norman, and D. S. Russell. 1967. *Greenfield's Neuropathology*. Baltimore: Williams and Wilkins.
Broadbent, D. E. 1958. *Perception and Communication*. New York: Pergamon
Press.
Cooper, J. E., R. E. Kendell, B. J. Gurland, N. Sartorius, and T. Farkas. 1969.
Cross-national study of diagnosis of the mental disorders: Some results from
the first comparative investigation. *American Journal of Psychiatry*,
125:21–29. (Supp.)
Cromwell, R. L. 1968. Stimulus redundancy and schizophrenia. *Journal of Nervous and Mental Disease*, 146:360–375.
—— 1972. Strategies for studying schizophrenic behaviour. *Psychopharmacologia* (Berlin), 24:121–146.
Deutsch, J. A. and D. Deutsch. 1963. Attention: Some theoretical considerations. *Psychological Review*, 70:80–90.
Douglas, R. J. 1967. The hippocampus and behavior. *Psychological Bulletin*,
67:416–442.

Douglas, R. J. and K. H. Pribram. 1966. Learning and limbic lesions. *Neuropsychologia*, 4:197–220.

Dykman, R. A., W. G. Reese, C. R. Galbrecht, P. T. Ackerman, and R. S. Sunderman. 1968. Autonomic responses in psychiatric patients. *Annals of the New York Academy of Sciences*, 147:237–303.

Epstein, S. 1967. Toward a unified theory of anxiety. In B. A. Maher (ed.), *Progress in Experimental Personality Research.* New York: Academic Press.

—— 1970. Anxiety, reality and schizophrenia. *Schizophrenia*, 2:11–35.

Flor-Henry, P. 1969. Psychosis and temporal lobe epilepsy: A controlled investigation. *Epilepsia*, 10:363–395.

Freides, R. 1966. The histochemical architecture of Ammon's Horn as related to its selective vulnerability. *Acta Neuropathologica*, 6:1–13.

Goddard, G. V. 1964a. Functions of the amygdala. *Psychological Bulletin*, 62:89–109.

—— 1964b. Amygdaloid stimulation and learning in the rat. *Journal of Comparative and Physiological Psychology*, 58:23–30.

Graham, F. K. and R. K. Clifton. 1966. Heart rate change as a component of the orienting response. *Psychological Bulletin*, 65:305–320.

Groves, P. M. and R. F. Thompson. 1970. Habituation: A dual process theory. *Psychological Review*, 77:419–450.

Gruzelier, J. H. 1973a. Bilateral asymmetry of skin conductance orienting activity and levels in schizophrenics. *Biological Psychology*, 1:21–41.

—— 1973b. The investigation of possible limbic dysfunction in schizophrenia by psychophysiological methods. Unpublished Ph.D. thesis, University of London.

Gruzelier, J. H. and P. H. Venables. 1972. Skin conductance orienting activity in a heterogeneous sample of schizophrenics: Possible evidence of limbic dysfunction. *Journal of Nervous and Mental Diseases*, 155:277–287.

—— 1973. Skin conductance to tones with and without attentional significance in schizophrenic and non-schizophrenic psychiatric patients. *Neuropsychologia*, 11:221–230.

—— 1974a. Bimodality and lateral asymmetry of skin conductance orienting activity in schizophrenics: replication and evidence of lateral asymmetry in patients with depression and disorders of personality. *Biological Psychiatry*, 8:55–73.

—— 1974b. Two-flash threshold, sensitivity and β in normal subjects and schizophrenics. *Quarterly Journal of Experimental Psychology*, 26:594–604.

Heath, R. G. 1964. Developments toward new physiologic treatments in psychiatry. *Journal of Neuropsychiatry*, 5:318–332.

Jasper, H. H. 1958. Recent advances in our understanding of the ascending activities of the reticular system. In H. H. Jasper et al. (eds.), *Reticular Formation of the Brain.* London: Churchill.

Kimble, D. P. 1968. Hippocampus and internal inhibition. *Psychological Bulletin*, 70:285–295.

Kimble, D. P., M. H. Bagshaw, and K. H. Pribram. 1965. The GSR of monkeys during orienting and habituation after selective partial ablations of the cingulate and frontal cortex. *Neuropsychologia*, 3:121–128.

Koepke, J. E. and K. H. Pribram. 1966. Habituation of GSR as a function of stimulus duration and spontaneous activity. *Journal of Comparative and Physiological Psychology*, 61:442–448.

Kornetsky, C. 1972. The use of a simple test of attention as a measure of drug effects in schizophrenic patients. *Psychopharmacologia* (Berlin), 24:99–106.

Lacey, J. I. 1967. Somatic response patterning and stress: Some revisions of activation theory. In M. H. Appley and R. Trumbull (eds.), *Psychological Stress*. New York: Appleton-Century-Crofts.

Lane, E. and G. W. Albee. 1966. Comparative birth weights of schizophrenics and their siblings. *Journal of Psychology*, 64:227–231.

Lang, H., T. Tuovinen, and P. Valleala. 1964. Amygdaloid after discharge and galvanic skin response. *Electroencephalography and Clinical Neurophysiology*, 19:366–374.

Langfeldt, G. 1953. Some points regarding the symptomatology and diagnosis of schizophrenia. *Acta Psychiatrica et Neurologia Scandinavica*, Suppl., 80:7–43.

Luria, A. R. and E. D. Homskaya. 1963. Disturbance of the regulating activity with lesions of the frontal lobes of the brain. In *The Human Brain and Psychic Processes*. Moscow: Izd APN, RFSFR.

—— 1970. Frontal lobes and the regulation of arousal processes. In D. A. Mostovsky (ed.), *Attention: Contemporary Theory and Analysis*. New York: Appleton-Century-Crofts.

Lykken, D. T. and P. H. Venables. 1971. Direct measurement of skin conductance: A proposal for standardization. *Psychophysiology*, 8:656–672.

Lynn, R. 1963. Russian theory and research in schizophrenia. *Psychological Bulletin*, 60:486–498.

McGhie, A. 1969. *Pathology of Attention*, Harmondsworth: Penguin.

McGhie, A. and J. S. Chapman. 1961. Disorders of attention and perception in early schizophrenia. *British Journal of Medical Psychology*, 34:103–116.

MacLean, P. D. 1968. Ammon's Horn: A continuing dilemma. Foreword to S. Ramón y Cajal, *The Structure of Ammon's Horn*. Springfield: Thomas.

—— 1970. The limbic brain in relation to the psychoses. In P. Black (ed.), *Physiological Correlates of Emotion*. New York: Academic Press.

Malamud, M. 1967. Psychiatric disorders with intracranial tumours of the limbic system. *Archives of Neurology*, 17:113–123.

Mednick, S. A. 1970. Breakdown in individuals at high risk for schizophrenia: Possible pre-dispositional perinatal factors. *Mental Hygiene*, 54:50–63.

Mednick, S. A. and F. Schulsinger. 1968. Some pre-morbid characteristics related to breakdown in children with schizophrenic mothers. In D. Rosenthal and S. S. Kety (eds.), *The Transmission of Schizophrenia*. New York: Pergamon Press.

Obrist, P. A., R. A. Webb, J. R. Sutterer, and J. L. Howard. 1970. Cardiac deceleration and reaction time: An evaluation of two hypotheses. *Psychophysiology*, 6:695–756.

Orzack, M. H. and C. Kornetsky. 1966. Attention dysfunction in chronic schizophrenia. *Archives of General Psychiatry*, 14:323–326.

Pavlov, I. P. 1927. *Conditioned Reflexes: An Investigation of the Physiological Activity of the Cerebral Cortex* (trans. G. V. Anrep). Oxford: Oxford University Press.

Peck, C. K. and D. B. Lindsley. 1972. Average evoked potential correlates of two flash perceptual discrimination in cats. *Vision Research*, 12:641–652.

Pollack, M. and M. G. Woerner. 1966. Pre- and peri-natal complications and "childhood schizophrenia": A comparison of 5 controlled studies. *Journal of Child Psychology and Psychiatry*, 7:235–242.

Pollack, M., M. G. Woerner, and D. F. Klein. 1972. Pregnancy and birth complications in schizophrenics, personality disorders and their siblings. (Unpublished communication.)

Pribram, K. H. and F. T. Melges. 1969. Psychophysiological basis of emotion. In P. J. Yinken and G. W. Bru (eds.), *Handbook of Clinical Neurology*, Vol. 3. Amsterdam: North Holland.

Rothblat, L. and K. H. Pribram. 1972. Selective attention: Input filter or response selection? An electrophysiological analysis. *Brain Research*, 39:427–436.

Russell, I. S. 1966. Animal learning and memory. In D. Richter (ed.), *Aspects of Learning and Memory*. London: Heinemann.

Silverman, J. 1964. The problem of attention in research and theory in schizophrenia. *Psychological Review*, 71:352–379.

—— 1967. Variations in cognitive control and psychophysiological defense in the schizophrenias. *Psychosomatic Medicine*, 29:225–251.

Slater, E. and A. W. Beard. 1963. The schizophrenia-like psychoses of epilepsy. i. Psychiatric aspects. *British Journal of Psychiatry*, 109:95–150.

Smythies, J. R. 1969. The behavioural physiology of the temporal lobe. In R. N. Herrington (ed.), *Current Problems in Neuropsychiatry*. London: R.M.P.A.

Sokolov, E. N. 1960. Neuronal models and the orienting reflex. In M. A. B. Brazier (ed.), *The Central Nervous System and Behavior*. New York: Josiah Macy Foundation.

Sourek, K. 1965. The nervous control of skin potentials in man. Nakladatelstvi Ceskoslovenska Akademie Ved Praha.

Spector, R. G. 1965. Enzyme chemistry of anoxic brain injury. In C. W. M. Adams (ed.), *Neurohistochemistry*. New York: Elsevier.

Spinelli, D. N. and K. H. Pribram. 1966. Changes in visual recovery functions produced by temporal lobe stimulation in monkeys. *EEG and Clinical Neurophysiology*, 20:44–49.

Stabenau, J. R. and W. Pollin. 1967. Early characteristics of monozygotic twins discordant for schizophrenia. *Archives of General Psychiatry*, 17:723–731.

Stern, J. A. and D. G. McDonald. 1965. Physiological correlates of mental disease. *Annual Review of Psychology*, 16:225–264.

Tizard, J. and P. H. Venables. 1957. The influence of extraneous stimulation on the reaction time of schizophrenics. *British Journal of Psychology*, 48:299–305.

Treisman, A. and G. Geffen. 1967. Selective attention: Perception and response? *Quarterly Journal of Experimental Psychology*, 19:361–367.

Vaughan, H. G. and L. D. Costa. 1964. Applications of evoked potential techniques to behavioral investigation. *Annals of the New York Academy of Sciences*, 118:71–75.

Venables, P. H. 1960. The effect of auditory and visual stimulation on the skin potential response of schizophrenics. *Brain*, 83:77–92.

Venables, P. H. 1964. Input dysfunction in schizophrenia. In B. Maher (ed.), *Advances in Experimental Personality Research I* New York: Academic Press.
—— 1971. Schizophrenia as a disorder of input processing. *Proceedings of the Academy of Medical Sciences, USSR,* 5:10–12.
—— 1973. Input regulation and psychopathology. In M. Hammer, K. Salzinger, and S. Sutton (eds.), *Psychopathology: Contributions from the Social, Behavioral, and Biological Sciences.* New York: Wiley.
Venables, P. H. and M. J. Christie. 1973. Mechanisms, instrumentation, recording techniques, and quantification of responses. In W. F. Prokasy and D. C. Raskin (eds.), *Electrodermal Activity in Psychological Research.* New York: Academic Press.
Yokota, T., A. Sato, and B. Fujimori. 1963. Inhibition of sympathetic activity by stimulation of limbic system. *Japanese Journal of Physiology,* 13:137–143.
Zahn, T. P., D. Rosenthal, and W. G. Lawlor. 1968. Electrodermal and heart rate orienting reactions in chronic schizophrenia. *Journal of Psychiatric Research,* 6:117–134.

5

Psychometric Applications of the EEG

DAVID T. LYKKEN

MORE THAN forty years ago, Berger (1929) first reported that
faint electrical activity, apparently originating in the brain,
could be recorded from the human scalp. Since that time, although the inevitable iconoclasts have tried to attribute this activity to noncerebral sources, a mass of evidence has ac-
cumulated in support of Berger's original conclusion—the
electroencephalographer can indeed eavesdrop on at least some
of the spontaneous activity of the body's most complex and mysterious organ. Such a "window on the brain" is a source of fascination not only for the neurophysiologist but for the psychologist as well, since the brain is the great mediator of virtually all
behavior of any psychological interest. Spinal reflexes excluded,
if a stimulus is to affect behavior it must first affect the brain
and some aspect of that effect may be visible through the window of the EEG (as in the cortical evoked response, for example.) Individual differences in behavior dispositions, including important constitutional differences in aptitude,
temperament, and psychiatric diathesis, must have their origin
in differences in brain function, which again might be seen
through the window if one only knew where and how and when
to look.

To cite a specific example, Berger's first discovery—the so-
called "alpha rhythms" of the EEG—have received consider-

able recent attention. These are defined as roughly sinusoidal waves of from 8 to 13 Hz which appear in the waking EEG, especially when the subject is relaxed and has his eyes closed. These alpha waves have such high amplitude, on the order of 100 microvolts, that Berger was able to record them clearly on his primitive equipment. In recent years, biofeedback experiments have shown that it is possible to train subjects to increase their level of alpha activity, and people find the feeling state associated with this increased alpha to be relaxing and enjoyable (e.g., Kamiya, 1969). It is even possible to train some subjects to increase alpha selectively on one side of the brain (O'Malley and Conners, 1972).

One of the most interesting speculations about the alpha rhythm is the notion that it represents the ticking of one of the biological clocks, that alpha is associated with a kind of scanning or gating process involved in stimulus-input regulation and in cognitive processing. Lansing showed in 1957 that reaction times were quickest to visual signals which reach the visual cortex at a critical portion of the alpha cycle (the negative zero-crossing) and Surwillo (1963, 1964) has reported correlations of more than .7 between alpha period and reaction times although Boddy (1971) has since called Surwillo's findings into question.

Beginning with Craik in 1948, data have accumlated in support of the notion that the brain operates in a discontinuous or temporally segmented fashion, at least in respect to cognitive processing. Two related hypotheses, concerned with excitability cycles and the idea of cortical scanning, have been ably reviewed in a paper by Harter (1967). An interesting example of this approach is the theory of central intermittancy proposed by Kristofferson (1967) in which alpha figures as the central clock which determines the "moments"—from about 8 to 12 per second—during which attention can be switched from one input channel to another or when one stage of central processing can transmit its product to the succeeding stage.

If alpha frequency does in some way measure the speed of cognitive processing, then one naturally wonders whether this EEG parameter might not be related directly to the usual measures of intelligence. Munday-Castle (1958) reported a correlation of .51 between alpha frequency and Wechsler-Bellvue IQ and, in a later study (Munday-Castle and Nelson, 1960), a smaller but still significant correlation of .34. Knott, Friedman, and Bardsley (1942) obtained a similar value ($r = .50$) in a group of eight-year-old children but no appreciable correlation in a group of twelve-year-olds. Both Shagass (1946) and Gastaut (1960), working with large samples of young adults, found no relationship at all between alpha frequency and scores on group intelligence tests. It seems fair to say, however, that none of the studies reported thus far have provided the best possible opportunity for the alpha-intelligence relationship—if one exists—to show itself. Modern methods of spectral analysis (to be explained later in this chapter) should increase the reliability of measures of alpha frequency and thus enhance the possibility of finding meaningful correlations with other variables. Since there is some variation in alpha frequency within an individual subject, depending on the circumstances under which the recording is made, it may be that measurements should be obtained while the subject is engaged in systematic cognitive processing, e.g., while actually taking the intelligence test. Moreover, it is clear that processing speed cannot be the essence of intelligence although it may be an important facet or component. Therefore it may be that an intelligence measure like the Nufferno Tests (Furneaux, 1956) which assess separately speed, accuracy, and difficulty level, would provide the most promising correlate.

A scattering of studies have looked for relationships between EEG parameters and various personality and psychopathological characteristics (see Shagass, 1973, for a recent review). One of the few rather promising findings thus far uncovered has to do with the relative amount of alpha activity (alpha abundance) in relation to individual differences in the subject's inclination toward visual, rather than auditory or kinesthetic, imagery. Golla, Hutton, and Walter (1943) classified their S s into three groups on the basis of the amount and persistence of alpha activity. *M*-type (*M* for *minus*) S s had little alpha, even with their eyes closed, and were found to use predominantly visual imagery. *P*-type (*persistent*) *S*s seemed to think mainly in auditory or kinesthetic terms. *S*s whose alpha decreased substantially when they opened their eyes (*R* or *responsive* types), were less consistent than either *M*- or *P*-types in their use of imagery. A related study by Slatter (1960) found evidence for classifying *S*s along a continuum ranging from predominant visualizers, at one extreme, to persons whose thinking is predominantly verbal (auditory/kinesthetic?) at the other. Slatter reports a strong relationship between position on this continuum and both alpha abundance and persistence; habitually verbal thinkers were strong alpha generators. Walter and Yeager (1956) found that *S*s with high alpha abundance (mainly *R*-types, the *P*-type being rare) were less successful than low-alpha producers (*M*-types) in a task requiring reproduction of a figure drawn from memory. In a study of young-adult twins in our laboratory, Thorkelson (1973) found that extreme *M*-types and *P*-types both showed substantially higher scores on measures of hypnotic susceptibility than did the bulk of her sample.

These few illustrations may be enough to suggest that alpha abundance and alpha frequency may be variables of considerable psychological and even clinical interest. But this, in turn, requires that we look at these and other EEG variables with the scrutineering eye of the psychometrist, just as we would some alleged personality or aptitude measure. For example, Figure 5.1 shows some unpublished data from a study done with Peter Venables and John Gruzelier at a psychiatric hospital in London in which 1-minute resting, eyes-closed EEG samples were obtained from 27 chronic schizophrenic patients. The figure indicates that the mean alpha frequency was about 1.5 Hz lower for the schizophrenics than for a control group of nonpatients. This difference is highly significant and one might be tempted to relate it at once to the slowing of cognitive processing of schizophrenia and, with a little ingenuity, even to schizophrenic disorders of attention. But a first question to ask is whether this result is replicable; too often in psychology great effort has been spent on explaining findings which turn out later to be unrepeatable. This in turn raises questions like the following: Asked to find the alpha frequencies of a group of patients, would any two competent investigators produce essentially equivalent EEG samples? And would their independent analyses of the same EEG samples yield nearly identical estimates of alpha frequency? And would repeated testing of the same group of subjects produce similar results each time? More

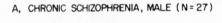

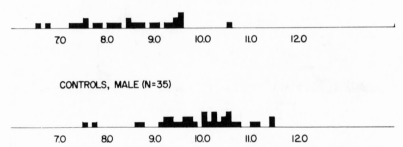

Figure 5.1 *Differences in EEG Alpha frequencies* between schizophrenics and control group. Mean alpha frequency in HZ (Schizophrenic mean = 8.4 HZ; Control mean = 9.9 HZ, t = 6.37).

generally, by what logic do we set the limits of alpha activity at 8 and 13 Hz in the first instance? By usual psychometric standards, this would imply that EEG activity at, say, 8.1 Hz has more in common with activity at 12.9 than at 7.9 Hz; what evidence supports that improbable contention? The truth seems to be that adequate techniques for studying these problems have only recently become available and that most of the necessary work has yet to be done. Meanwhile, there has accumlated a great wealth of clinical lore and data based on inadequate or at least idiosyncratic techniques; no doubt much of this body of doctrine is true but surely some of it is false and the problem is to tell the difference.

Spectral Analysis of EEG

One convenient way of studying the frequency characteristics of an EEG sample is by means of spectral analysis. The

EEG signal, either on-line or by means of tape recording, is fed into a computer which produces histograms of the types shown in Figure 5.2. These four magnitude spectra represent analyses of 3-minute eyes-closed EEG samples from both members of two fraternal twin pairs. The X-axes here are calibrated in cycles-per-second (Hertz) and the ordinates can be interpreted in

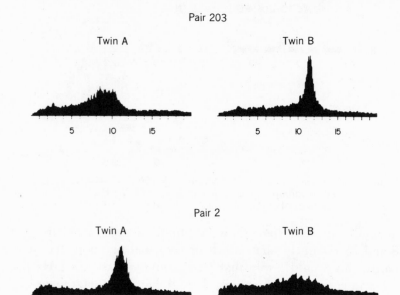

Figure 5.2 *Magnitude spectra for DZ twins* (pairs 203 and 2).

terms of microvolts input at the given frequency. A rough idea of how one can interpret such spectra can be deduced from the statement that Twin A of Pair 2 had more alpha activity in his sample than did his later born co-twin and that the alpha for both of these twins varied more in frequency during the three minutes than did that of Twin B in Pair 203.

We can get a clearer understanding by having a look at what spectral analysis does with input that is simpler than the EEG. The whole method is based on Fourier's Theorem, which (mathematicians please forbear) I shall now state in clear and simple language which the human mind can comprehend. Fourier tells us that just about any squiggly line, like those we record on a polygraph chart, can be synthesized by adding together a number of pure sine waves of different frequencies, amplitudes, and phase relationships. For example, to make the curve shown at the top in Figure 5.3, I set three sine wave generators going at 4, 5, and 8 Hz, respectively, and at about equal amplitudes, and then merely added their outputs together and fed them to the polygraph. The second curve is the sum of pure

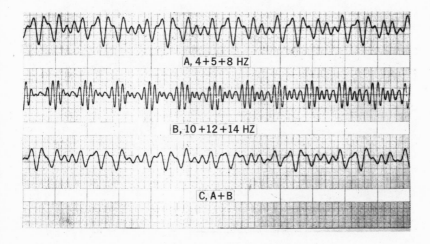

Figure 5.3 *Sine wave mixtures* (chart speed 50mm/sec.).

sine waves of 10, 12, and 14 Hz, and the bottom curve was formed by adding the first two and, hence, is the sum of six sine waves.

When we feed these three synthesized signals into the computer for spectral analysis, we get the result shown in Figure 5.4. Spectrum A shows spikes of about equal height at frequencies 4, 5, and 8 Hz; that is, the computer is telling us that our signal *could have been* composed of equal parts of these three pure sine waves. Now, of course, our signal need not have been actually synthesized from sine waves but might have been produced naturally by some device or even by the brain; the spectrum tells us only that an identical signal could have been so synthesized and that this recipe, equal parts of these three sine waves, is an adequate characterization of that signal. The second spectrum shows spikes at 10, 12, and 14 Hz, as it should, and also reveals that my 12 Hz generator was accidentally set to a slightly higher amplitude than the other two. Happily the third spectrum shows six spikes, all in their proper positions.

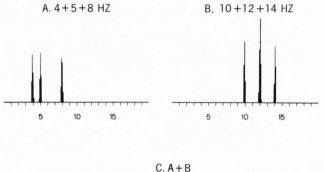

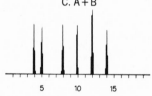

Figure 5.4 *Spectra of mixed sine waves.*

It is worth mentioning that we could have produced, say, the first spectrum with a single sine-wave generator by setting it at 4 Hz for one-third of the sample time, quickly switching it to 5 Hz for the next third and then to 8 Hz for the last. That is, the height of each spectrum ordinate is proportional to the product of the amplitude of the given frequency component times the time during which that frequency component is present in the input sample. Thus, a given "alpha bump" on an EEG spectrum could be produced either by intermittent alpha activity at high amplitude or by more continuous activity at lower amplitude. The computer actually produces two other histograms, called the sine and the cosine spectra, from which it is possible

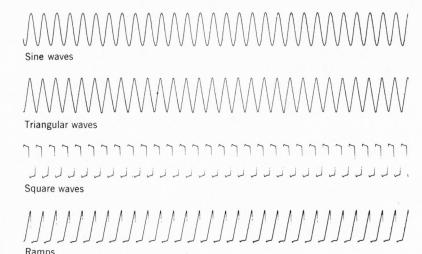

Sine waves

Triangular waves

Square waves

Ramps

Figure 5.5 *Four 5 HZ wave forms* (chart speed 50mm/sec.).

to uniquely characterize the input sample and, hence, to distinguish between intermittent high alpha and continuous low alpha, for example.

Figure 5.5 shows a polygraph write-out of four different wave forms, all at a fundamental frequency of 5 Hz. From top to

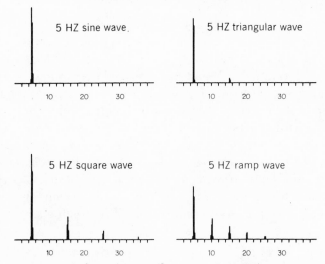

Figure 5.6 *Four wave forms* (magnitude spectra: 0–40 HZ).

bottom, these are known as sine waves, triangular waves, square waves, and ramps. Spectral analyses of these four wave forms are shown in Figure 5.6. The sine wave shows just the single spike at 5 Hz. The triangular wave, very much like a sine wave except less curved and more pointed, turns out to be analyzable into a large sine wave at the fundamental frequency and a very small sine wave at 15 Hz, the third harmonic. The square

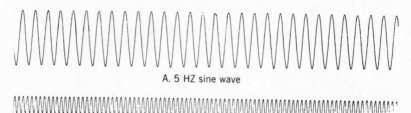

A. 5 HZ sine wave

B. 15 HZ sine wave

C. 25 HZ sine wave

D. sum of A + B + C

Figure 5.7 *Test of spectrum recipe*, with three odd harmonics of 5 HZ added.

wave appears to be a blend of all the odd harmonics, 1st, 3d, 5th, and so on, in decreasing amplitudes. The recipe for a ramp is to mix all the harmonics in the proportions shown. Finally, Figure 5.7 illustrates a test of one of these spectrum recipes. I set my three generators to frequencies corresponding to the first three odd harmonics of 5 Hz, and with amplitudes as shown and then added them to produce the curve at the bottom. The result is as close to a square wave as one could reasonably expect when only the three main ingredients of the recipe are used.

EEGs of MZ and DZ Twins

Having satisfied ourselves that the magnitude spectrum provides a convenient, quantitative, and reasonably fine-grained analysis of the frequency characteristics of an EEG sample, we can turn now to a comparison of EEGs obtained from monozygotic and dizygotic twins. When electroencephalography was still in its infancy, it had already been noticed that polygraphic records of EEGs produced by identical twins are often very similar and the literature abounds with references to that effect. The most recent and best quantified study is that of Young, Lader, and Fenton (1972) who recorded eyes-closed EEG from a sample of 32 adult male twins. The abundance and the mean amplitude of alpha activity were measured from the EEG tracings and gave intra-class correlations from the 17 MZ pairs of .51 and .42, respectively, as compared with .16 and .31 for the 15 DZ pairs. The amount of activity in four frequency bands was also quantified by passing the tape-recorded EEG through band-pass filters; the mean correlations for these four variables were .61 and .39 for the MZ and DZ pairs, respectively. The data I am about to show you suggest that the heritability of EEG frequency characteristics may be even greater than would be indicated by this British study, provided that one starts with the standardized spectrum as the basic datum.

Subjects in this experiment (Thorkelson, 1973) were 66 pairs of same-sex twins, all students at the University of Minnesota, who had been carefully diagnosed for zygosity by blood typing (14 systems) and by analysis of fingerprint ridge counts after the method of Slater (1963). In combination, these data allow us a confidence of at least .99 that the 39 MZ and 27 DZ pairs were each correctly classified. The twins sat side by side in the dimly lighted experimental chamber with a screen between them and an observer behind them. One channel of EEG was recorded from each twin, between electrodes on the vertex and the right ear lobe, with the left ear lobe serving as ground.

The EEG together with the electrocardiogram was recorded via a Beckman Dynograph onto FM tape continuously for the one-hour experimental session. During this hour, the subjects listened through earphones to a prerecorded standard hypnotic induction procedure, featuring the voice of my colleague, Auke Tellegen, whose Dutch accent and gentle, psychotherapist's manner combine to make him an effective Svengali. At the start

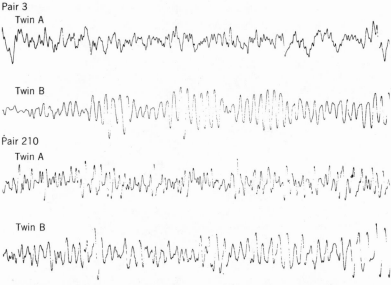

Figure 5.8 *Segment of raw EEG from two pairs of DZ twins* (pairs 3 and 210) (6 seconds of EEG at 50mm/sec.).

of the session, the subjects are asked to sit quietly with eyes closed for 3 minutes of physiological recording and this three-minute sampling was repeated again at the end of the hour, at which time the susceptible subjects were in fact in the hypnotic state. These two 3-minute EEG samples were subsequently analyzed from the tape by a PDP-12 computer which yielded the spectra that I am about to present.

Figure 5.8 shows a segment of raw EEG from 2 pairs of DZ twins. It is apparent that the tracings from the bottom pair are more similar than for the pair on the top, that Twin B of Pair 3 on top produced a lot of alpha activity while his earlier-born co-twin produced very little, and one can also see, though less dramatically, that Twin B of the lower pair also was a somewhat better alpha generator than his co-twin. These frequency relationships are considerably clearer when we look at the magnitude spectra for these same twins in Figure 5.9. By way of con-

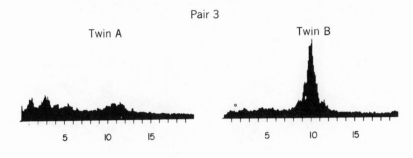

Pair 3

Twin A   Twin B

5   10   15   5   10   15

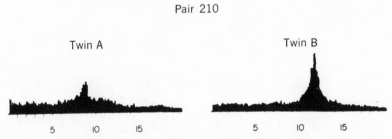

Pair 210

Twin A   Twin B

5   10   15   5   10   15

Figure 5.9 *Magnitude spectra for DZ twins* (pairs 3 and 210).

trast, Figure 5.10 shows four spectra from an MZ pair; samples 1 and 2 were the 3-minute rest periods at the start and end of the session. One might agree that these could be four samples from the same head.

All the spectra have been modified by the computer so that the total spectrum area—the dark area in the figures—is set equal to a constant; this is the process we call "standardization." The same four spectra we have just seen to be so similar are shown *un*standardized in Figure 5.11. As this illustrates,

David T. Lykken

standardization enhances the similarity of spectra obtained at different times from the same subject or of spectra from genetically identical subjects. What standardization does, in fact, is to partial-out differences in average apparent EEG amplitude, the amplified and recorded signal being played back into the computer. There are, of course, real and presumably meaning-

Sample 1

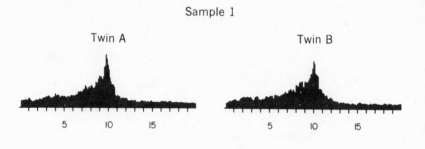

Sample 2

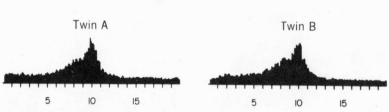

Figure 5.10 *Magnitude spectra for MZ twins* (pair 319).

ful differences in the mean size of the tiny voltages produced by the brain and these differences are lost in standardization. But recorded amplitudes are more strongly affected by factors which represent essentially errors of measurement. Small differences in the gain of any of the several stages of amplification which augment the orginal signal 10,000 times, differences in electrode resistance, in the location of the electrode on the scalp, in the thickness of the skull, and so on, all constitute a kind of noise which standardization removes.

This small example illustrates a useful general principle of psychological measurement: *viz.*, where alternative methods are available, that one is to be preferred which yields the more orderly data. Usually, stability is an aspect of orderliness, and for this reason we prefer methods which give higher retest reliability. In this case, spectra obtained from the same place on

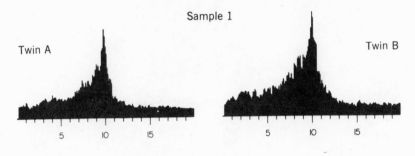

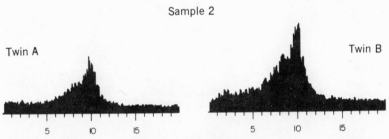

Figure 5.11 *Unstandardized magnitude spectra for MZ twins* (pair 319).

the same head under similar conditions but at different times are more similar or constant after standardization. The example also illustrates one of the advantages of using twins as subjects in psychological research. For many purposes, MZ twins can be thought of as "parallel forms" of the same subject; it is frequently reasonable to assume that a method which increases within-pair similarity probably does so by reducing errors of measurement. We have prior reason for assuming that MZ twins should have similar spectra and therefore since standardization of the spectra reduces the ratio of within- to between-pair variance, we can conclude that there is more bath water than baby in what is being thrown away in standardization and that the method is a useful one.

Figure 5.12 shows spectra from two more MZ pairs, also

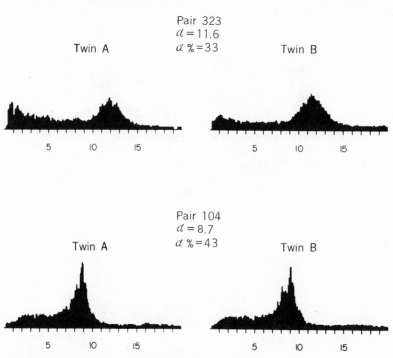

Figure 5.12 *Magnitude spectra from MZ twins* (pairs 323 and 104).

very similar. The computer has calculated alpha frequency for us by locating the peak of the "alpha bump" and then computing the mean frequency within a 3-Hz band centered on that peak. "Alpha percent" is the proportion of the total spectrum within a 3-Hz band centered on that calculated mean frequency. Both members of Pair 323 have an identical high alpha frequency of 11.6 Hz and an alpha abundance of 33 percent. Pair 104 have a low alpha frequency, 8.7 Hz, and a somewhat greater abundance. It should be noted that alpha abundance, defined from the spectrum, is the product of what other authors have called "alpha index" and "alpha amplitude." Figure 5.13 shows two more MZ pairs, very similar as usual, with the pair at the bottom being typical of that 6 or 7 percent of subjects who are said to show no alpha activity, a trait which Vogel

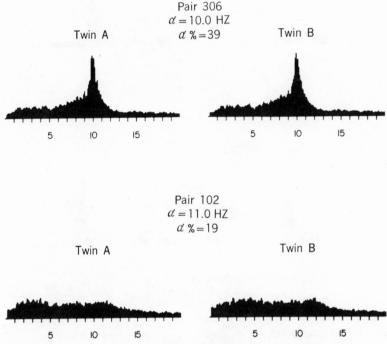

Figure 5.13 *Magnitude spectra for MZ twins* (pairs 306 and 102).

(1970) has shown to behave like a simple autosomal dominant. The spectrum reveals that, while there is virtually no "alpha bump," there is in fact activity from zero to 20 Hz and about 20 percent of the total activity is in the alpha range. But the spectrum is essentially flat and the raw record would reveal a virtual absence of the usual bursts or intervals of clear, sinusoidal alpha. Finally, Figure 5.14 shows a couple of MZ pairs who are real alpha generators. The pair on top, especially, produce tracings that look like nearly pure sinusoids; with a little amplifica-

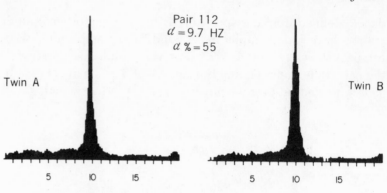

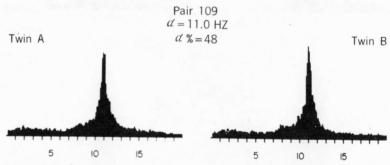

Figure 5.14 *Magnitude spectra for MZ twins* (pairs 112 and 109).

tion one could operate an electric clock from their EEGs and, geared up about 6 to 1, it would keep pretty good time.

Quantifying EEG Spectrum Similarity

The next task is to devise some quantitative index of spectrum similarity and a number of possibilities present themselves. Psychologists tend to think first of the correlation coefficient whenever an index of anything is wanted and one can, of course, compute a correlation between the envelopes of two spectra. The trouble is that spectra in general have a similar shape so that the correlation between any two spectra taken at random tends to average .5 or .6 rather than zero. Another, related, possibility is to compute the geometric mean (the root-mean-square) of the differences between corresponding ordinates. Since we had two spectra for each individual we could use this method to compare each twin with his co-twin twice and also each twin with himself. The ratio of the mean within-pair difference to the mean within-individual difference gives an index which is equal to unity when the twins' spectra are as much like each other as they are like themselves over time. For 35 of our 39 MZ pairs, this index proved to be less than 1.5 while it was greater than 1.6 for 21 of 27 DZ pairs, a hit-rate of 85 percent.

The trouble with the foregoing measure is that it compares between-twin differences of spectra taken at the same time with within-individual differences of spectra taken at different times, thus perhaps weighting the dice in favor of within-twin similarity. Therefore, we tried another approach which insures that variation over time will appear in both numerator and denominator of the ratio and, thus, cancel out. We computed the mean-squared-difference (MSD) between twin A's spectrum during Rest 1 and twin B's spectrum during Rest 2 or $MSD_{A_1B_2}$. This value, averaged with $MSD_{A_2B_1}$, gives a measure of between-twin similarity over time. Similarly, $1/2 (MSD_{A_1A_2} + MSD_{B_1B_2})$ measures within-individual similarity over time. The ratio of the former to the latter, therefore, provides an index of relative between-twin similarity with the effects of time variation eliminated. This "purified" index correctly classified 85 percent of the MZ pairs and 74 percent of the DZ pairs.

A judge who merely sorts the pairs of spectra for similarity to the eye and then classifies the 39 most similar pairs as "MZ" will get at least 90 percent "hits." Still another method is to divide each spectrum into ten adjacent 2-Hz bands and compute the proportion of the total spectrum in each band. These ten numbers can then be entered into a discriminant function analysis—actually, the absolute values of the ten within-pair differences serve as the variables of the function—with the result that 4 of 27 DZ pairs and only 1 of 39 MZ pairs are misclassified, a hit rate of 92 percent.

In this connection, it is worth remembering that no variable, no matter how completely determined by the genes, can be expected to produce perfect segregation of MZ from DZ twins. Figure 5.15 shows the idealized distributions one might

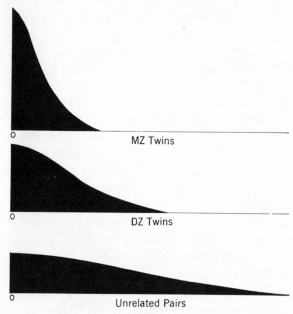

Figure 5.15 *Idealized distributions of (absolute) intra-pair differences* on any heritable traits.

expect from plotting the absolute values of within-pair differences on even a completely heritable trait. Clearly, even two unrelated persons off the street might happen to have identical heights or IQs or EEG spectra and one must expect that a few DZ or even unrelated pairs will sometimes prove to be so similar as to be misclassified "identical." Moreover, one should keep in mind that DZ twins "have 50 percent of their genes in common" *only on the average;* some fraternal pairs may chance to be no more similar genetically than people paired at random while others may have nearly all their genes in common.

Returning now to the problem of quantifying "similarity of spectra," a basic question we could ask is, "How many independent dimensions are required to adequately characterize a spectrum?" In the discriminant function referred to earlier, we used the ten 2-Hz bands as variables but that choice was entirely arbitrary. These spectra really consist of an ordered set of 200 numbers, the 200 ordinates at 0.1-Hz intervals from zero to 19.9 Hz. A psychometrist might think of a spectrum as a set of scores on a battery of 200 correlated tests. He might also think of factor analyzing those scores in order to determine nonarbitrarily how many independent dimensions are required to characterize a spectrum. We have invested a large amount of computer time in analyses of this kind and I have no intention of burdening you with the details of this effort. As I have commented elsewhere (Lykken, 1971), factor analysis is best regarded as an exploratory technique, better suited to suggesting ideas than to answering questions in any final way. Quite consistently we find that about 80 percent of the variance (and more than 90 percent of the common variance) in these spectra can be accounted for with only four to six orthogonal factors. Also quite consistently, it appears natural to identify one of these factors with activity above 13 Hz, i.e., what is classically referred to as Beta activity. Another recurrent theme is the covariation of activity from 2.0 to 7.9 Hz, i.e., roughly corresponding to the classic Theta band. We could probably claim a Delta factor as well, especially if we were to include a higher proportion of sleepy spectra. The remaining factors represent very narrow segments of the classic Alpha band or, when we analyze the standardized spectra, bipolar factors which contrast, e.g., 8 Hz with 10 Hz or 9 Hz with 11 Hz. One model which might produce such results would be a variable Alpha generator having three parameters—amplitude, center frequency, and variability. That is, we postulate a process, situated perhaps in the thalamus (cf. Andersen and Andersson, 1968), which generates activity of amount Alpha, varying about a central, peak frequency, which we call Phi. The third parameter, Kappa, measures the kurtosis of this distribution of frequencies, that is, whether the given quantity of alpha activity is concentrated near the central frequency or is rather spread out over a range of several Hz, giving a broad, flat distribution. Specifically, we define Kappa as the ratio $\mu_4/\mu_2{}^2$, where μ_4 and μ_2 are the fourth and second moments, respectively, of the 3-Hz segment of the spectrum centered on Phi. All three parameters vary from one brain to another with the center frequency, Phi, ranging from a low of about 7 Hz to a high of perhaps 13 Hz in our data. Alpha quantity varies from about 18 percent in a flat spectrum to a high of over 60 percent.

In other words, we find that we can account for at least 80 percent of the variance in our spectra with just five slightly correlated parameters (classic Beta and Theta, Alpha quantity, mean alpha frequency or Phi, and the variability of alpha frequency or Kappa), with classic Delta probably also being strong enough to be useful. Our kind of analysis cannot prove that these particular six factors are the best solution to the rotation problem—that these six parameters correspond to six discrete processes in the brain—but they do seem to comprise an adequate and convenient minimum statement of the information that is in a magnitude spectrum. Moreover, these six parameters allow us to compute heritabilities in the usual way, as well as correlations with other variables.

Table 5.1 shows some of these data. Body height and weight, as would be expected, show intraclass correlations greater than .9 for the MZ twins with values about half that size for the DZs. The total fingerprint-ridge count behaves similarly. The F ratio of within-pair variances for DZs over MZs is fairly large and highly significant for these three variables. Mean heart rate, taken during the same rest period when EEG was being analyzed, shows a barely significant F value and it can be seen that the intraclass correlation for the DZ sample is too low. Apart from ordinary sampling error, the only way I can think of to account for the DZ correlation being less than half as large as the MZ value would be to assume that common environmental experience works to increase trait similarity for MZs, as is usually postulated, but that common experience acts to *decrease*

Table 5.1 Intraclass Correlations and Heritabilities

Variable	R_{mz}	R_{dz}	H[a]	$F_{(w)}$[b]	P
Height	.91	.54	.76	3.22	.001
Weight	.93	.48	.90	5.22	.0001
Finger-ridge count	.98	.47	(.98)	6.14	.0001
Heart rate	.67	.20	(.67)	1.97	.05
High-school rank	.86	.67	.37	1.99	.05
ACT score	.85	.19	(.85)	3.10	.001
Delta	.76	−.01	(.76)	5.62	.0001
Theta	.86	−.03	(.86)	6.40	.0001
Beta	.82	.15	(.82)	4.09	.001
Alpha [c]	.82	−.20	(.82)	5.65	.0001
Phi [d]	.84	.21	(.84)	6.09	.0001
Kappa [e]	.83	.23	(.83)	7.22	.0001
ER (neuroticism)	.53	.39	.29	1.41	(ns)
EC (extraversion)	.57	.17	(.57)	2.23	.05
APQ	.72	.28	(.72)	3.52	.001
Rod and frame	.68	.18	(.68)	2.91	.01
Hypnotic susceptibility	.48	.23	(.48)	2.14	.05

[a] Heritability estimated by $H = 2 (R_{mz} - R_{dz})$, see Falconer (1960). Where R_{dz} is so low that $H > 1.0$, (R_{mz}) has been substituted as an upper-bound estimate of H.

[b] The F ratio of within-pair (Var. DZ)/(Var. MZ).

[c] Proportion of magnitude spectrum within 3-Hz band centered on Phi.

[d] Median frequency within 3-Hz band centered on peak frequency between 7 and 14 Hz.

[e] A measure of the kurtosis of the spectrum alpha peak.

similarity for DZ twins. Such a speculation might not be unreasonable in the case of, say, extraversion, where our results are similar as can be seen in Table 5.1. That is, one can imagine that same-sex fraternal twins might tend to form a sort of complementary relationship: "He's the extravert so I must be the introvert," whereas an identical twin might reason, "He's extraverted so I must be extraverted too." Admittedly, this line of thinking is a bit strained when applied to physiological variables, although it is conceivable, for example, when DZ pairs are confronted together by some stress situation, that one member of the pair commonly feels more responsibility for coping while the other feels more relaxed than he would if his twin wasn't with him. It may be, of course, that our DZ sample is simply peculiar for some reason but Monte Buchsbaum, who is doing a rather similar twin study at NIMH, tells me that they also have been getting very low DZ correlations on some variables. In any case, these low DZ values yield heritability estimates which are spuriously high. Therefore, wherever H^2 proved to be actually larger than the MZ correlation itself, I have listed the latter in parentheses in Table 5.1 as a sort of upper-bound estimate of the proportion of variance attributable to the genes.

Continuing down the table, an achievement measurement like high-school rank gives fairly high correlations in the DZ group and therefore very modest heritability. ACT scores, on the other hand, have a much higher loading on general intelligence and, for these students none of whom come from really deprived backgrounds, most of the variance in IQ seems to be genetic in origin. Again, however, the DZ correlation is inexplicably low.

The six spectrum variables all show MZ intraclass correlations of around .80 and negligible DZ correlations. The F ratios are all highly significant and it is clear that all six components of the spectrum are strongly genetically determined although again the DZ correlations remain unaccounted for. Finally, just out of curiosity, I have listed some values for certain personality test variables which may be of interest. Neuroticism, as measured by Block's Ego Resiliency Scale, shows modest correlations in both twin groups and therefore a low heritability. Extraversion, based on Block's Ego Control Scale, seems to owe about half its variance to genetic factors; similar findings have been reported by others. On the portable Rod and Frame Test, we find that MZs are quite similar in respect to field dependency while, again, the DZs are discrepant. Both the Rod and Frame and my anxiety reactivity scale, called the APQ, have heritabilities well over .50, if these results can be believed, a considerably stronger degree of genetic influence than I have seen previously reported for personality trait measures. Finally, our study indicated a very modest heritability for that mysterious trait, hypnotic susceptibility, with which no other trait has yet been found to correlate as much as .50; our findings here comport very well with the results from a large twin study done recently at Hilgard's laboratory by Morgan (1970) who reports MZ and DZ correlations of .56 and .18, respectively.

Psychological Correlates of Spectrum Parameters

Summarizing thus far, we have tried to show how the frequency characteristics of an EEG sample can be conveniently represented in a magnitude spectrum, and that the salient features of most spectra can be quantified in terms of just six parameters. We have demonstrated the strong heritability of these spectrum parameters and these same data also indicate that spectra are relatively stable over at least one hour's time. It's interesting, incidentally, to ask oneself the following question: Suppose we were to retest our twins under similar conditions a week or a month later, only to find that these parameters had low retest reliability over such longer periods? That is, what can we infer about a trait which gives high heritabilities when the twins are measured concurrently but which also shows considerable within-subject variation over time? One can imagine that a measure of "state anxiety" might behave in such a fashion. We assume that a subject's current anxiety level is a kind of product of his "trait anxiety" on the one hand—his constitutional level of anxiety reactivity, which may be a stable parameter of temperament—multiplied by the immediate environmental press. To the extent that our twins tend to share the same experiences, to move through the same period of stress concurrently, then their "state anxiety" at any time will be similar to the extent that their "trait anxiety" or "anxiety IQ" is similar. Therefore, if "trait anxiety" is determined by the genes, MZ twins—at least student-age twins like ours who are still living and doing things together—will tend to be "state anxious" at the same time, although their level of anxiety may be unpredictably different at some other time of testing. This illustrates another possible virtue of using twins in psychological research; normally we tend to be unenthusiastic about measures which have poor retest reliability but clearly we should pay more respect to such a measure if it does at least show high within-twin correlations.

Pair 203

Twin A   Twin B

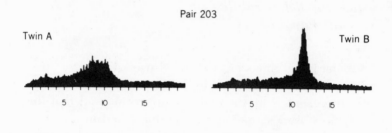

Pair 202

Twin A   Twin B

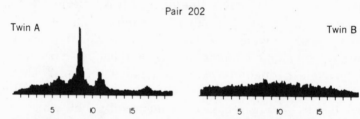

Figure 5.16 *Magnitude spectra of DZ twins* (pairs 203 and 202).

Two small studies we have done with singletons, however, indicate that most EEG spectrum variables are in fact quite stable over periods of weeks, giving retest correlations of .60 to about .85. Having reached this point, it would be delightful if I could proceed to demonstrate to you what these quantitative, stable, heritable variables *mean* psychologically, these brain processes that we can observe through the window provided by the EEG. Figure 5.16, for example, shows the spectra of 2 more pairs of DZ twins, selected for their interesting dissimilarity. Those four shapes represent stable, genetically determined differences in the functioning of these four brains; surely there are important and interesting psychological differences correlated with them? Alas, we have not found them yet (nor has anyone else, to my knowledge) but on the other hand we have only started to look. Twins scoring high on a global intelligence test like the ACT do not differ consistently in spectrum properties from those who have low scores. Our measures of neuroticism, extraversion, anxiety reactivity, and field dependence do not show any striking correlations with spectrum variables. Maybe nothing does that is of psychological interest and the whole exercise has been a waste of time. I do not believe it but we shall see.

References

Andersen, P. and S. A. Andersson. 1968. *Physiological Basis of the Alpha Rhythm*. New York: Appleton-Century-Crofts.

Berger, H. 1929. Über das Elektrenkephalogramm des Menschen. *Archiv für Psychiatrie und Nervenkrankheiten*, 87:527–570.

Boddy, J. 1971. The relationship of reaction time to brain-wave period: A re-evaluation. *Electroencephalography and Clinical Neurology*, 30:229–235.

Craik, K. W. J. 1948. Theory of the human operator in control systems. II: Man as an element in a control system. *British Journal of Psychology*, 38:142–148.

Falconer, D. S. 1960. *An Introduction to Quantitative Genetics*. New York: Ronald Press.

Furneaux, W. D. 1956. *The Nufferno Manual of Speed Tests*. London: National Foundation for Education and Research.

Gastaut, H. 1960. Correlations between the electroencephalographic and the psychometric variables (MMPI, Rosenzweig, intelligence tests). *Electroencephalography and Clinical Neurophysiology*, 12:226–227.

Golla, F., E. L. Hutton, and W. G. Walter. 1943. Objective study of mental imagery; physiological concomitants: Appendix on a new method of electroencephalographic analysis. *Journal of Mental Science*, 89:216–223.

Gruzelier, J. H., D. T. Lykken, and P. H. Venables. 1972. Schizophrenia and arousal revisited: Two-flash thresholds and electrodermal activity in activated and nonactivated conditions. *Archives of General Psychiatry*, 26:427–432.

Harter, M. R. 1967. Excitability cycles and cortical scanning: A review of two hypotheses of central intermittency in perception. *Psychological Bulletin*, 68:47–58.

Kamiya, J. 1969. Operant control of the EEG alpha rhythm and some of its reported effects on consciousness. In Charles Tart (ed.), *Altered States of Consciousness*. New York: Wiley.

Knott, J. R., H. Friedman, and R. Bardsley. 1942. Some electroencephalographic correlates of intelligence in eight-year- and twelve-year-old children. *Journal of Experimental Psychology*, 30:380–391.

Kristofferson, A. B. 1967. Successiveness discrimination as a two-state, quantal process. *Science*, 158:1337–1339.

Lansing, R. W. 1957. Relation of brain and tremor rhythms to visual reaction time. *Electroencephalography and Clinical Neurology*, 9:497–504.

Lykken, D. T. 1971. Multiple factor analysis and personality research. *Journal of Experimental Research in Personality*, 5:161–170.

Morgan, A. H., E. R. Hilgard, and E. C. Davert. 1970. The heritability of hypnotic susceptibility of twins: A preliminary report. *Behavior Genetics*, 1:213–224.

Munday-Castle, A. C. 1958. Electrophysiological correlates of intelligence. *Journal of Intelligence*, 26:184–199.

Munday-Castle, A. C. and G. K. Nelson. 1960. Intelligence, personality and brain rhythms in a socially isolated community. *Nature*, 185:484–485.

O'Malley, J. E. and C. K. Conners. 1972. The effect of unilateral alpha training on visual evoked response in a dyslexic adolescent. *Psychophysiology*, 9:467–470.

Shagass, C. 1946. An attempt to correlate the occipital alpha frequency of the electroencephalogram with performance on a mental ability test. *Journal of Experimental Psychology*, 36:88–92.

—— 1972. Electrical activity of the brain. In N. S. Greenfield and R. A. Sternbach (eds.), *Handbook of Psychophysiology*. New York: Holt, Rinehart and Winston.

Slater, E. 1963. Diagnosis of zygosity by fingerprints. *Acta Psychologica Scandinavica*, 39:78–84.

Slatter, K. H. 1960. Alpha rhythms and mental imagery. *Electroencephalography and Clinical Neurophysiology*, 12:851–859.

Surwillo, W. W. 1963. The relation of simple reaction time to brain wave frequency and the effects of age. *Electroencephalography and Clinical Neurology*, 15:105–114.

—— 1964. The relation of decision time to brain wave frequency and to age. *Electroencephalography and Clinical Neurology*, 16:510–514.

Thorkelson, K. E. 1973. The relationship between hypnotic susceptibility and certain personality, physiological, and EEG variables in monozygotic and dizygotic twin pairs. Unpublished doctoral dissertation, University of Minnesota.

Vogel, F. 1970. The genetic basis of the normal human electroencephalogram (EEG). *Humangenetik*, 10:91–114.

Walter, R. D. and C. L. Yeager. 1956. Visual imagery and electroencephalographic changes. *Electroencephalography and Clinical Neurophysiology*, 8:193–199.

Young, J. P. R., M. H. Lader, and G. W. Fenton. 1972. A twin study of the genetic influences on the electroencephalogram. *Journal of Medical Genetics*, 9:13–16.

6

Acquisition of Heart-Rate Control:
Method, Theory, and Clinical Implications

PETER J. LANG

THIS CHAPTER is concerned with the study of methods by which man can gain voluntary control over the action of his visceral organs. The research to be described here is focused on modification of the cardiovascular system, and more specifically on the learned control of cardiac rhythm. In defining the topic to be "voluntary control" I mean to undertake no review of subjective concepts such as "will" or conscious intention. For the purposes of these investigations, volition is defined as the achievement of instructional control over a behavioral event. That is to say, we are trying to train human subjects to respond to specific commands (e.g., increase your heart rate) with the appropriate cardiovascular response (a more rapid heart rhythm), much as individuals accomplish complex motor acts when simply told to so perform. While experimental study calls for experimenter-manipulated instructions, it is presumed that with training the same behaviors could be controlled by our subjects' spontaneous self-instructions.

This research was supported in part by grants from the National Institute of Mental Health (MH-10993, MH-35,324) and the Wisconsin Alumni Research Foundation. The on-line programs used in this project were written by Michael Falconer.

Broadly considered, this research is relevant to the issue of the language control of behavior, which is both a fundamental and a unique characteristic of human psychology. More specifically, three clinically related concerns have prompted our experimental program. First of all, we hope this research will bear on the understanding of emotional behavior and its expression in human beings. Most investigators would probably agree that the phenomenon of emotion involves a complex of responses which include verbal behavior, gross motor acts, and physiological events. Thus, behavior we consensually label as "fearful" includes reports of a fear "experience," motor avoidance, and some performance deficit, as well as evidence of increased heart rate, skin conductance, peripheral vasoconstriction, and decreased intestinal motility.

Efforts to explain such emotional behavior have often emphasized the latter, visceral component, giving it a special determining function in the instigation or maintenance of the total affective response. Thus, William James (1884) defined emotional experience as the percept of visceral arousal—a position recently revived and modified by Schachter (1964)—and Lange (1885) contended that emotion literally was a cardiovascular event. Learning theorists such as Mowrer (1947) hold that the fundamental aspect of the fear response is autonomic and, in conformity with this view, Wolpe (1958) designed desensitization therapy with the specific purpose of modifying sympathetic activity level.

From this perspective, avoidance behavior and verbal report of fear are secondary manifestations of a conditioned visceral response. While it is certainly true that sympathetic arousal is a common accompaniment of affective behavior, there is an increasing body of evidence which shows that visceral, verbal, and motor acts in emotion are poorly correlated (Ericksen, 1958; Lang, 1968). Assertions of intense anxiety can occur in the absence of strong autonomic arousal, as can performance or cognitive deficits which we are inclined to attribute to emotional factors. In attempting to bring cardiovascular events under instructional control, we mean to forge a tool for directly testing the interactions between physiological and behavioral responses in emotion. We intend to explore these relationships both in the context of specific instigating stimuli (e.g., anticipated pain or social disapproval) and as represented in chronic, aversive emotions.

The above considerations prompt a second, long-range goal of this research: to examine the feasibility of learned visceral control as a treatment for anxiety and phobia. In recent years, a variety of therapies have appeared which are designed to alter the physiological substrata of aversive emotional states. These include progressive relaxation therapy (Jacobson, 1938), autogenic training (Schultze and Luthe, 1959), transcendental meditation (Benson and Wallace, 1972), as well as various treatments utilizing biofeedback (Barber et al., 1971). However, laboratory research has not yet provided support for the basic hypothesis on which they are predicated. Utilizing the heart-control techniques under development here, we hope to examine the following questions: If instructional control over a viscus can be achieved, can such control be maintained in the context of an emotional stressor? If control is in the direction of lowered sympathetic activity, what are the consequences for the performance deficits, psychomotor and cognitive, often seen with fear and anxiety? Finally, can learned visceral control become a basis for practical therapy, i.e., will effects transfer beyond the laboratory setting and will this approach be effective with pathological emotional states?

A third aim of this research is to provide information relevant to the etiology and treatment of cardiac disease. Lown and Wolf (1971) point out that deaths from coronary heart disease have "now reached the staggering figure of 625,000 annually." Many of these deaths result from sudden, acute myocardial infarction, attributable to an "electrical derangement in heart rhythm manifesting as ventricular fibrillation." Fibrillation appears to be preceded by a pattern of premature ventricular beats, and among patients in coronary-care units, an erratic rhythm involving premature beats (systoles) identifies patients susceptible to sudden death. Furthermore, epidemiological studies suggest that the presence of such extra systoles in outpatients or older normal subjects is correlated with a higher than average risk of cardiac death.

Lown, Verrier, and Corbalan (1973) recently showed that erratic heart rhythm and fibrillation could be stimulated in physiologically prepared animals through psychological stress. This suggests that the extent and nature of psychological determination of heart rate may be a significant factor in cardiac disease. It is also clear that the inhibition of arrhythmias (without the debilitating side-effects of anti-arrhythmic drugs) is an important therapeutic goal in cardiovascular illness. Recently Weiss and Engel (1971) achieved some success in training patients to reduce the incidence of heart-rate anomalies using feedback techniques. During the course of this project we hope to assess the ability of cardiac patients to develop instructional control over heart rhythm. We are interested both in relationships between psychological determination of heart rate and the presence of heart disease, and in the possible development of instructional control as a treatment for disorders of heart rhythm.

While the potential of this line of investigation seems vast, it is also true that our methodological understanding of learned heart-rate control is still primitive. Only a beginning has been made at analyzing the relevant parameters, which facilitate the acquisition and transfer of this skill. One approach has adapted the methods developed in the instrumental conditioning of animals. From this perspective, a visceral event is presumed to be analogous to an operant response, such as a bar press. It is held that the response can be brought under control simply by following each occurrence of the event with some reinforcer. The studies of animal subjects by Miller and his associates (1969) are models of this procedure. In training rats to alter heart rate, subjects were first implanted with stimulating electrodes in the medial forebrain bundle of the hypothalamus. They were then curarized and artificially respirated. Logic circuitry was so arranged that when the animal's heart rate exceeded a preset criterion, positive brain stimulation was administered. In a series of dramatic experiments, Miller's group demonstrated the instrumental conditioning of a whole host of visceral responses, including heart-rate acceleration and deceleration, stomach motility, and localized vasoconstriction. It was hoped that the basic methodology might be adapted to the study of human subjects. Investigators anticipated a rapid increase in our knowledge of visceral control and a clear path to the previously described practical benefits. Unfortunately, these procedures have proved difficult to replicate by other investigators (Brener, 1974) and are not now reproducible within Miller's own laboratory (1974). A review of the data suggests that some modification of the animal's viscera through instrumental conditioning is possible; however, the effects are much smaller than previously suggested, less persistent, and apparently more narrowly dependent on unique details of procedure than was previously supposed.

Work on visceral control with human subjects has also relied heavily on the instrumental conditioning model. For example, Shapiro, Tursky, and Schwartz (1970) have reported a series of experiments in which operant methods have been used to modify heart rate and blood pressure. In these experiments a criterion level of performance is defined prior to training (usually the median of a resting distribution), subjects are rewarded when their response (e.g., heart rate) exceeds this criterion—with the illumination of a light, attractive slides, or money, depending on the experiment. Significant acquisition of heart-rate control has been obtained with this method, and comparable results were found in several laboratories (Blanchard and Young, 1973). It is also true that the size of the effects have been modest and the evidence for transfer minimal.

An alternative approach is illustrated by the work of the Russian investigator Lisina (1958). Her procedure emphasized the importance of continuous exteroceptive feedback in teaching voluntary control of vasomotor responses. While conditioning methods were employed, the training technique more closely resembles those used to teach motor skills.

In her initial study, subjects were administered electric

shock while the arm plethysmograph was recorded. This shock stimulus prompted marked vasoconstriction; however, over time some relative dilation occurred. Lisina attempted to increment overall dilation by stopping the shock coincident with these minimal responses. Nevertheless, "despite numerous reinforcements (up to 80)" no learning was observed. After analyzing her data, Lisina suggested that learned vasodilation did not develop "because the interoceptive stimuli are very weak and do not produce an orientation (behavioral) in the subject towards these stimuli and cannot be isolated in the overall experimental situation as a significant component" (p. 453).

For a subsequent experimental series, she developed a procedure designed to mobilize the "orienting-exploratory activity" of subjects in the direction of discriminating vasomotor changes. Subjects were provided with "additional afferentation," which consisted of a light beam, controlled by the plethysmograph, which changed coincident with variations in the volume of the blood vessels. This second experimental series was successful. Over trials subjects learned to increase dilation and escape the electrical stimulation. Some subjects reported an early awareness of the relationship between light-beam variations and shock, and many described various maneuvers (muscle relaxation, respiration changes, efforts to reduce emotion) that they used to control the response. It is interesting to note that the intentional use of such mediators diminished over trials, as actual control increased.

In a third experimental series the escape-conditioning paradigm was not employed. Subjects were simply trained to perceive the skin-tactile sensations associated with the vascular response. A variety of psychological stimuli were administered and the subject was instructed to sense their effect on the skin (of a finger enclosed within a glass container). Subjects soon learned to report when vasoconstriction or dilation occurred. After this initial training, subjects were required to evoke vascular changes "according to verbal instruction of the experimenter and self-instruction. It turned out that all of the subjects could immediately perform this task." While the first reactions were small, with practice their "voluntary" vascular responses became larger and were sustained over long periods.

Influenced by Lisina's work and the results of pilot exploration, the first studies in our laboratory used a system for training heart-rate control which similarly emphasized augmented afferentation and instruction. Instead of receiving only specific rewards for correct performance, subjects in these experiments were presented with a continuous display of the visceral function to be trained. For heart rate this was done with a meter display, driven by a cardiotachometer, so that lateral movements of the dial provided a continuous, analogue indication of beat-by-beat changes in heart rate. We were successful in these experiments in training subjects to restrict their heart rate to a narrow target area, marked on the meter face, varying within ± 3 beats per minute of their resting heart rate (Hnatiow and Lang, 1965; Lang, Sroufe, and Hastings, 1967). Other investigators have since used this same method to teach heart-rate slowing and speeding (Blanchard and Young, 1973).

An overview of the above experiments raised an important methodological question: Is the instrumental learning paradigm the best way to train subjects to control heart rate, or is it more efficient to use techniques similar to those of Lisina, which depend on orienting subjects to the discrimination of visceral changes, providing "additional afferentation," and the development of instructional sets or strategies which the subject can use to mediate the correct autonomic responses? The latter approach assumes that the acquisition of voluntary control over a viscus is a skill. It assumes that cardiovascular control involves more than a single conditioned reflex, but that it requires an organized sequence of activities, movements, and symbolic information, such as those required to play darts or hit a tennis ball accurately. Thus, the body of literature most relevant to this study is perhaps not the instrumental conditioning of animals but research on the acquisition of motor skills and the performance theories of Fitts and Posner (1968) and Bilodeau and Bilodeau (1969).

From the perspective of information analysis, the distinction between these two approaches is one of type of feedback. That is to say, in the instrumental paradigm information about cardiac rate is provided in binary form. The subject is cued when his performance exceeds a preset criterion heart rate, and this signal is absent or replaced with a different cue, when the subject fails to achieve criterion. In some early studies (Engel and Hansen, 1966) using the operant method, subjects were not told that this performance cue referred to the relative rate of their hearts, nor even that heart rate was involved. Thus, subjects only knew if they were correct or incorrect, with almost no "additional afferentation." When information is provided in analogue form, subjects attend to a signal which is in continuous covariation with beat by beat changes in heart rate. If the target or criterion level is a part of the display, the subject may also be provided with a proportional representation of their own relative performance. In this case, analogue feedback of both performance and organ activity is provided.

In a recent experiment (Lang and Twentyman, 1974), we studied the difference in effectiveness of two procedures, one emphasizing analogue and the other binary feedback. Subjects were seen for seven separate sessions, which included initial practice with the display and two sessions each of speeding and slowing training. The timing of the experiment, presentation of instructions, feedback, data acquisition, and primary data reduction were all accomplished in real-time by a Digital Equipment Corp. PDP-12 computer. The use of a computer to control the experimental environment permits an unusual degree of precision in the execution of an experiment, and considerable flexibility in developing appropriate feedback displays.

The analogue display used in the present experiment had the following characteristics:

The subject is seated in a reclining chair before a large oscilloscope screen. Each heart cycle initiates a moving line, starting at the left, which extends itself across the screen at a constant rate. In the standard program, this line is turned off by the next EKG cycle, a vertical marker is briefly illuminated at the terminus, and within microseconds a new line starts across the screen. Thus, the length of successive horizontal lines is exactly proportional to the length of each successive R-R interval.

The screen also contains a fixed, vertical line, running from the top to the bottom of the screen. This is the subject's target. If the subject is asked to speed his heart rate, his job is to terminate the horizontal line before it crosses the target. If his task is slowing, the horizontal line must extend past the target for a success to be recorded. Each success is underscored for the subject by the appearance of the word "good" on the screen, at the completion of the cycle. The display is illustrated in Figure 6.1.

The target line is initially set at the subject's median R-R interval. This is done during a one-minute period, at which time the subject is asked to perform the desired task (speed or slow) without feedback. The target may be altered subsequently, depending on subject performance. The schedule is as follows: If during a feedback trial, a slowing

Figure 6.1 *The display oscilloscope* used in training subjects to control heart rate. A moving horizontal line is initiated by each electrical systole of the heart, and its length is proportional to the subsequent interpulse interval. The vertical line provides a target. In this case the subject has been successful in slowing his heart rate (i.e., lengthening the interpulse interval), and the word "good" appears on the screen.

subject's median heart interval should exceed that of the previous trial, a new target is set for the next feedback period, which is midway between his previous median and his current median. A similar adjustment to a less difficult target is made for subjects who show "poorer" performance on a trial. We call this schedule the "rule of halves." It is designed to prompt improved performance without making discouraging demands.

The format of the experimental session is the same for all subjects. Following the attachment of a respiration sensor and heart-rate electrodes, the adjustments of heart-cycle and respiration-input levels, and a brief rest period, control of the experiment is assumed by the computer. Three minutes of baseline data are acquired. The subject is then instructed to attempt heart-rate control (speed or slow depending on the task, for a 1 minute period). He is subsequently instructed to use the feedback display for the same purpose, and the display is then presented for 3 minutes. After termination of the display, subjects are asked to continue control (speeding or slowing for 1 minute). Subjects are then given a 1 minute rest. This sequence of feedback trial, transfer trial, and rest is repeated five times during an experimental session. (Lang, 1974, pp. 394–95)

The procedure for the binary feedback group was exactly the same, with the following modification of the subject's display. During feedback trials the screen remained blank when interpulse intervals failed to achieve criterion. When an interval fell within the target range, the word GOOD briefly appeared on the screen. Thus, subjects received only binary (right/wrong) information about performance in the manner of an instrumental conditioning session. As they were instructed in which direction to change their heart rate, speed or slow, the condition of the screen also provided binary feedback (fast/slow) of organ activity.

Twenty-two subjects participated in the experiment, equally divided between the analogue and binary feedback groups. They did not differ significantly in either heart rate or respiration rate. Furthermore, prior to training all subjects were instructed to try to increase or decrease their heart rate without feedback. No significant changes in heart interval were found in these brief, initial try periods.

Results for the feedback trials are presented in Figure 6.2.

Average heart interval is represented for successive trials as a deviation from initial base performance. It will be noted that the analogue group shows a palpable increase in both speeding and slowing performance. While the binary group performed similarly to analogue subjects when slowing, it does not match the marked acceleration of the analogue group during instructed speeding. The conclusions prompted by the figure

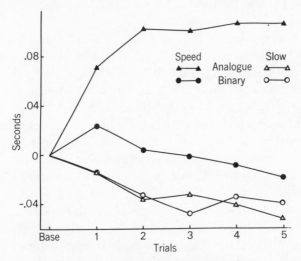

Figure 6.2 *Change in average heart interval from rest* for two groups of subjects—one trained to speed and slow heart rate using binary feedback and the other trained with an analogue procedure. The data represent average performance over two training sessions.

were confirmed statistically. A comparison of the analogue and binary subjects yielded a significant effect for display type and heart-rate task and an interaction between display group and task.

In order to assess the changes in heart rate which might be attributable to the stimulus properties of the display or subjects' task involvement, binary and analogue subjects were compared with a group that performed a simple tracking task (Gatchel, 1974). This latter group observed exactly the same display of moving lines as the analogue feedback subjects. However, the display was a random distribution of intervals controlled by the computer, rather than the subject's heart. Subjects were told to track the display and press a hand-held microswitch whenever the line terminated to the right or left of the target line depending on group assignment. Both analogue and binary groups showed significantly greater heart-rate slowing than tracking subjects. However, while the analogue subjects showed significantly better speeding performance than tracking controls, the same comparison for the binary group did not approach significance.

The properties of the analogue display were further explored in a second experiment, in which the frequency of information feedback was systematically manipulated. Through a minor alteration in the PDP-12 program which ran the experiment, the display could be modified such that the sweep line initiated by an electrical cycle of the heart was not terminated by the next cycle to occur. Rather, it could be set so that the sweep line was terminated after a number of successive cycles (five, ten, or whatever was programmed). In this latter case, subjects would observe a summary of their performance, i.e., a sweep line whose length was proportional to the sum of a group of beats. The information would be provided to the subject at a rate controlled by the number of cycle intervals the sweep line was programmed to represent. Using this modified program, Gatchel (1974) studied the acquisition of heart-rate increases and decreases at three different feedback frequencies. One group received feedback every beat, as in the previously discussed analogue sample. A second group was administered feedback every five heart intervals, and a third subject group worked with a ten-beat display. All groups were compared to the tracking control group previously described.

All feedback groups yielded significant speeding and slowing, relative to the performance of tracking subjects. Furthermore, the degree of heart-rate speeding achieved co-varied significantly with feedback frequency. As may be seen in Figure 6.3, the one-beat subjects showed significantly better speeding performance than the ten-beat group. The five-beat group fell

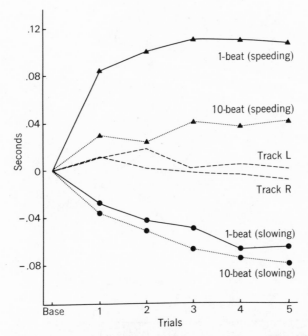

Figure 6.3 *The speeding and slowing performance of subjects trained to mod-ify heart rates presented as heart interval deviations from rest. The results are an average of two sessions of training. The figure shows the performance of subjects who received feedback every heart interval (1-beat), a subject group that received a summary of their per-formance every 10 heart intervals, and a control group that was ad-ministered a motor tracking task that utilized a similar display.*

midway between, but has not been included on the graph for the sake of clarity. A trend analysis over all groups yielded a significant linear component for feedback frequency. Similar patterns of performance were found for transfer trials. Further-more, all groups showed an improvement in speeding perfor-mance from the first to the second session.

Very different findings were obtained for the slowing task. While feedback subjects showed greater deceleration during feedback trials than tracking controls, there was no systematic relationship between frequency and performance (see Figure 6.3). Furthermore, no significant difference was found between

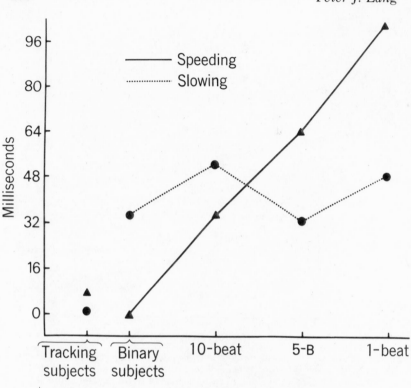

Figure 6.4 *Subject performance in the heart-rate task presented as average heart interval deviation from pretraining resting rate.* Improvement is indicated by an upward movement on the ordinate for both speeding and slowing. Triangles indicate performance in speeding sessions or during the tracking task which was used as a control for the speeding display. The circles indicate slowing performance or the tracking control sessions for slowing. Tracking subjects received no heart-rate feedback. The remaining groups defined along the abscissa received increasingly more information about their heart rate. The figure includes data from Lang and Twentyman (1974) and Gatchel (1974).

feedback groups and tracking subjects for the transfer periods, nor was there any improvement in heart-rate slowing for feedback subjects over sessions.

The differential effects of information feedback on instructed heart rate speeding and slowing are clearly illustrated in Figure 6.4. Data from the two previous experiments are combined. The groups presented along the x-axis differ in the extent to which they provide a continuous analogue display of information. Maximum information is provided by the one-beat group; least information ("additional afferentation" and performance data) is provided by the binary display. For heart-rate speeding an increasing monotonic function of performance exists from low information to high information. However, for heart-rate slowing there is no performance gradient. Binary or low information frequency subjects do as well as the analogue group.

Considered together, these experiments suggest that instructed heart-rate speeding and slowing depend on different mechanisms. The effects of information on speeding performance is similar to that which would be expected from a psychomotor task. In point of fact, the results of manipulating frequency of heart-rate feedback exactly parallel the findings obtained by Bilodeau and Bilodeau (1958) in a study of lever control. These latter investigators required subjects to adjust a lever within one-hundredth of a degree of an arc. Performance varied systematically with frequency of feedback, with the best results achieved by subjects who were informed of their performance after every response, and the poorest results obtained from subjects receiving information every tenth trial. It is tempting to speculate that heart-rate speeding is dependent on some central coupling between somatic and autonomic innervation systems (Obrist et al., 1970).[1] As previously suggested by Lang and Twentyman (1974, p. 628):

Perhaps, subjects need only activate somatic behaviors already in their repertoire to increment heart rate. In this case we presume no new learning of specific visceral responses, but only a use of feedback to confirm the appropriateness of recruiting a somatic-autonomic response unit which includes heart rate acceleration. The very rapid

[1] Respiration was the only parallel system involving somatic muscle that was recorded in these experiments. While modest correlations have been obtained between respiration rate and speeding performance ($r = .41$, $p < .05$; $r = .59$, $p < .05$), respiration rate did not differentiate between analogue and binary feedback or among groups receiving different feedback frequencies.

acquisition observed in speeding sessions (near maximum performance on the first two trials) is consistent with this view.

On the other hand, heart-rate slowing developed gradually over a session. Invariably we observed a significant trials effect which was not characteristic of speeding training. Furthermore, the absolute change in beats per minute was palpably less for slowing, and there was little evidence of transfer to no-feedback trials. Finally, slowing was accompanied by marked rebound during Time-out periods, which indicates that it is, more than speeding, in competition with short term homeostatic controls. These facts suggest a different innervation pattern. One is tempted to speculate that slowing is closer to true visceral learning, perhaps involving a modification of vagal firing and vascular changes which are relatively independent of centers which control somatic activity.

Differences between speeding and slowing performance were pursued in a third experiment, conducted in collaboration with Dr. William Troyer. Twenty patients diagnosed as having had a myocardial infarction or unequivocal angina pectoris formed one of the subject groups (mean age = 58.05 years). A second group of 20 subjects, age matched to the patients but

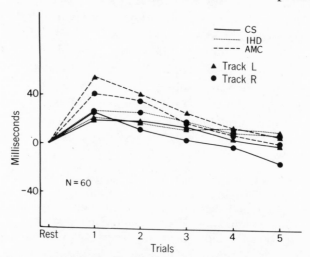

Figure 6.5 *A comparison of the heart-rate change* prompted by the motor tracking task. Subjects were college students (CS), patients with histories of ischemic heart disease (IHD), and nonpatient age-matched controls (AMC). Scores are presented as average heart interval deviations from pretraining resting heart rate.

free from any known cardiac disease, were also studied (mean age = 60.60 years). Twenty college students, similar to the sample used in the previous studies formed a third, control, group. Subjects were seen for six experimental sessions. Three sequential sessions were devoted to training in heart-rate control (one speeding session between two slowing), using the five-beat display program. The previously described tracking

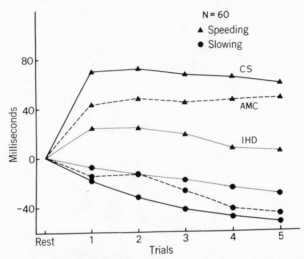

Figure 6.6 *A comparison of college students (CS), heart patients (IHD), and their age-matched controls (AMC) on the heart-rate slowing and speeding tasks. Scores are presented as average heart interval deviations from pretraining resting heart rate.*

task was administered during the remaining three sessions. Order of presentation was balanced, such that half the subjects in each group began with tracking and the other half started with the heart-rate control task.

The results for the tracking task are presented in Figure 6.5. Analysis of variance confirmed the impression of no difference between groups in tracking performance.

Results for the heart-rate task may be found in Figure 6.6. A significant groups effect was obtained for instructed heart-rate change. That is to say, ignoring the direction of change, perfor-

Peter J. Lang

mance was best for the college students, next best for the age-matched controls, and least adequate for the patients with heart disease. However, when heart-rate task performance relative to tracking was considered, an interesting difference between speeding and slowing sessions was apparent.

In Figure 6.7, each group's slowing heart rate is compared

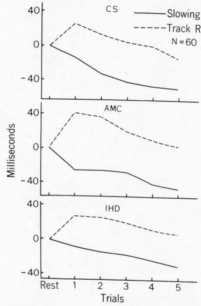

Figure 6.7 *Average heart-rate slowing task performance* compared to tracking heart interval changes for college students (CS), heart patients (IHD), and their age-matched controls (AMC).

to their tracking heart rate. Patients as well as normals display the same pattern, with significantly greater slowing during the heart-rate feedback task than when tracking the computer generated display.

In Figure 6.8, speeding task heart rate is compared with tracking. Only the college students show a significantly faster heart rate than that obtained during the psychomotor task; neither of the older subject groups were able to increase heart rate significantly more than during tracking.

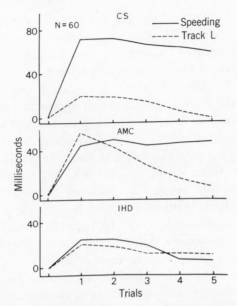

Figure 6.8 *Average heart-rate speeding task performance* compared to tracking heart interval changes for college students (CS), heart patients (IHD), and their age-matched controls (AMC).

We were at first surprised by these data, having gained the impression in the earlier research that speeding was the easier, more natural task, and had conjectured that slowing might present more of a problem for heart-disease patients. However, on reflection these results are not inconsistent with the previous interpretation of speeding-slowing differences. If the acquisition of instructional control over heart-rate speeding is analogous to the learning of a psychomotor task, and possibly based on a related neurophysiology, it is reasonable to expect that it would be similarly influenced by age and disease. That is to say, performance would be deleteriously affected by both of these variables.[2] In point of fact, our previous studies of college

[2] We are, of course, sensitive to the possibility that these results represent a differential response to instructions by the college students and patients. It might even be hypothesized that the patients simply refused to increase heart rate because they suspected it might aggravate their condition. A number of factors argue against this interpretation: (1) the older subjects without heart disease (and presumably no more reason than the college students to be uncooperative)

students suggested that the degree of instructed speeding is related to the variability and responsivity of the individual's cardiovascular system. Significant correlations were obtained between speeding performance and resting variability ($r = .48$, $p < .01$; $.40$, $p < .05$), and heart rate during the tracking task ($r = .32$, $p < .10$; $.36$ $p < .05$). Research in gerontological physiology (Thompson and Nowlin, 1973) indicates that a diminution of reactance and variability of the cardiovascular system is a reliable consequence of the aging process. It would appear that instructed heart-rate speeding follows a similar course.

In an absolute sense, the patients showed the least instructed speeding. While this could be a consequence of the disease process, it could as well be speculated that an inability to bring heart rate under instructional control is a characteristic of individuals predisposed to cardiac disease. Psychosomatic theories of cardiovascular disorder usually hypothesize a special susceptibility in this population to system arousal through psychological events. However, it is perhaps more logical to consider the system which is insusceptible to psychological control to be more vulnerable to stress. That is to say, an individual who readily learns to tune cardiac events to changes in his experience may be much better able to cope with stress than the individual whose visceral response cannot be brought under language control.

In any event, the ability to speed heart rate on command appears to be a talent which is not distributed equally in the human population. College-age males are superior "autonomic athletes" relative to the elderly or those with a cardiac disorder. These facts raise the possibility that the acquisition of cardiac control as a treatment manuever may not generally be practical. It may be that the very population for which treatment is intended is the group least able to profit from such instruction.

------

also showed attenuated speeding, (2) all subjects were interrogated after the experiment and none reported this concern, (3) in intensive care, bradycardia rather than tachycardia is often the precursor of fibrillation and sudden death. Many of our subjects were aware of this, and yet there was no apparent attenuation of slowing performance.

It remains unclear why instructed heart-rate slowing fails to co-vary with variables that traditionally modify performance. A recent pilot investigation in which monetary incentives were provided for improved performance yielded similar differential effects on heart-rate speeding and slowing. Thus, the addition of incentives prompted subjects to increase rate an average of over 20 b/m, with individual subjects achieving feedback rates approaching maximum treadmill rates. However, little palpable effect was noted for slowing. Subjects showed significant rate reductions, but little more than under nonincentive conditions.

It is, of course, possible that this is an initial values effect. Subjects in these experiments are well habituated to the experimental environment, having average resting heart rates of approximately 70 b/m. It is clear that while the normal variance of an individual's heart rate extends well above this value, the range below this level is much narrower. It could be argued that the amount of change that can be achieved from slowing is simply too small to distribute significantly the effects of the independent variables studied. Arguing against this position are these facts: waking heart rate in young males does descend to around 40 b/m. Considering the small effects achieved here (5 to 10 b/m) a 30-beat range should be large enough to differentiate stimuli. Furthermore, the correlation between resting rate and slowing is not very impressive (r = .36, $p < .10$), arguing that initial value is controlling little of the slowing variance.

Perhaps the problem lies in the nature of the task itself as it affects a dually innervated organ like the heart. Low heart rates are achieved in states of low arousal, e.g., just after waking in the morning. Watching a visual display and processing feedback require an organismic state which makes palpable cardiovascular demands. In effect, the unconditioned sympathetic effects of the task may block rate reduction, with the degree of their reciprocal inhibition proportional to the potency of the variable. This is easily understood in the case of incentives, where an increase in the value of an incentive would be expected to increment sympathetic arousal. However, a more rapid processing of information, as in the high frequency information condition, might produce a similar effect. Thus, the sympathetic activation of the heart prompted by the task would exactly counter efforts to train in greater vagal (parasympathetic) inhibition of cardiac rate.

The previous argument suggests that refined control of heart-rate slowing is not likely to be achieved through a direct attack. Instructional control of slowing may require indirect training, which operates broadly on organismic activation. The thought-stopping techniques used in meditation may be one vehicle for achieving greater slowing. It may be that more specific attention must be given to control of respiration and general somatic muscle activity. In effect, refined control of heart slowing, as well as large effects, may depend on training multiple behaviors. If this program follows the pattern of other skills learning, it might be anticipated that these ancillary maneuvers would become less important over time, and that a more direct instructional control could then be achieved (Kimble and Perlmuter, 1970).

There are three aspects of our research to date which have implication for emotional disorders and their treatment. First of all, it is clear from the above that we do not yet have sufficient control over heart-rate slowing to consider it as a practical method for inhibiting emotional responding. It is important to remember that there is presently no adequate demonstration from any laboratory that biofeedback training can inhibit anxiety through inhibition of the sympathetic components of a stress response. If biofeedback methods are effective in individual cases, they may achieve this indirectly as placebos, through the confidence and sense of well-being provided by accomplishing a difficult task. This is not to say that such methods might not be direct inhibitors of the physiology of anxiety, only that such an effect has not yet been clearly shown.

Second, we have found little relationship between the development of instructional control over heart rate and personality trait factors such as impulsivity, manifest anxiety, or internal-external orientation. The few significant correlations that we have obtained, have been with slowing, and not when feedback was being presented. Thus, Gatchel (1974) found a correlation between slowing Transfer trials performance and the Autonomic Arousal scale of the Epstein-Fenz anxiety inventory ($r = .37, p < .05$). Slowing performance during a test period prior to feedback training was associated with an external locus of control on Rotter's (1966) I-E scale ($r = .54, p < .01$). A marginally significant relationship was found with a report of subjects' degree of sensitivity to visceral and somatic events ($r = .31, p < .10$). Thus, there is a tendency for subjects to show more instructed slowing (in the absence of training), if they are more concerned with and aware of their own physiology and if they are more dependent on external reinforcers than on their own preset goals and ambition. The fact that speeding does not relate to personality seems consistent with the hypothesis that its acquisition is a learned skill, based more on training and talent than subtleties of temperament. The fact that naive slowing is at least marginally related to personality factors may suggest that it is determined more by temperamental, unconditioned factors, and perhaps for this reason less responsive to training.

The ability to gain instructional control over heart-rate speeding seems, at first, irrelevant to the treatment of aversive emotions. However, studies of the physiology of desensitization therapy suggest that language control of heart-rate acceleration may be an important prognostic consideration in behavioral treatment. Lang, Melamed, and Hart (1970) recently found a high correlation between success in desensitization and the extent to which heart rate increased with aversive visual images. That is to say, when instructed to visualize the phobic object, those subjects who reported that the image was upsetting *and also showed large heart-rate increases,* tended to profit most from treatment. In this case the instruction was to produce aversive imagery and heart-rate change was a byproduct. However, the route from language behavior to cardiac activity is analogous. It may be that the ability to speed heart rate is related to good prognosis for behavioral disorders as well as cardiac disease.

In summary, our research program is well underway. While

our preliminary work is necessarily concerned with the formal parameters which accentuate or diminish instructed control of heart rate, our data have already raised a variety of provocative issues for clinical theory and research. As our understanding of the basic phenomenon becomes surer, we look forward to their intensive exploration.

References

Barber, T. X., L. V. DiCara, J. Kamiya, N. E. Miller, D. Shapiro, and J. Stoyva (eds.). 1971. *Biofeedback and Self-Control*. Chicago: Aldine-Atherton.

Benson, H. and R. K. Wallace. 1972. Decreased drug abuse with Transcendental Meditation—A study of 1,862 subjects. In C. J. D. Zarafonetis (ed.), *Drug Abuse–Proceedings of the International Conference*. Philadelphia: Lea and Febiger.

Bilodeau, E. A. and I. M. Bilodeau. 1958. Variable frequency of knowledge of results and the learning of a simple skill. *Journal of Experimental Psychology*, 55:379–383.

—— (eds.). 1969. *Principles of Skill Acquisition*. New York: Academic Press.

Blanchard, E. B., and L. B. Young. 1973. Self-control of cardiac functioning: A promise as yet unfulfilled. *Psychological Bulletin*, 3:145–163.

Brener, J. 1974. A general model of voluntary control applied to the phenomena of learned cardiovascular change. In P. Obrist, A. Black, J. Brener, and L. DiCara (eds.), *Contemporary Trends in Cardiovascular Psychophysiology*. Chicago: Aldine-Atherton.

Engel, B. T. and S. P. Hansen. 1966. Operant conditioning of heart rate slowing. *Psychophysiology*, 3:176–187.

Ericksen, C. W. 1958. Unconscious processes. In M. R. Jones (ed.), *Nebraska Symposium on Motivation*. Lincoln: University of Nebraska Press.

Fitts, P. M. and M. I. Posner. 1968. *Human Performance*. Belmont, Calif.: Brooks/Cole.

Gatchel,R.1974.Frequencyoffeedbackandlearnedheartratecontrol.*JournalofExperimental Psychology*, 103:274–283.

Hnatiow, M., and P. J. Lang. 1965. Learned stabilization of cardiac rate. *Psychophysiology*, 1:330–336.

Jacobson, E. 1938. *Progressive Relaxation*. Chicago: University of Chicago Press.

James, W. 1884. What is emotion. *Mind*, 19:188–205.

Kimble, G. A. and L. C. Perlmuter. 1970. The problem of volition. *Psychological Review*, 77:361–384.

Lang, P. J. 1968. Fear reduction and fear behavior: Problems in treating a construct. In J. M. Shlien (ed.), *Research in Psychotherapy*. Washington, D.C.: American Psychological Association, III, 90–103.

—— 1974. Learned control of human heart rate in a computer directed environment. In P. Obrist, A. Black, J. Brener, and L. DiCara (eds.), *Contemporary Trends in Cardiovascular Psychophysiology.* Chicago: Aldine-Atherton.

Lang, P. J., B. G. Melamed, and J. Hart. 1970. A psychophysiological analysis of fear modification using an automated desensitization procedure. *Journal of Abnormal Psychology,* 76:220–234.

Lang, P. J., L. A. Sroufe, and J. E. Hastings. 1967. Effects of feedback and instructional set on the control of cardiac rate variability. *Journal of Experimental Psychology,* 75:425–431.

Lang, P. J. and C. T. Twentyman. 1974. Learning to control heart rate: Binary vs. analogue feedback. *Psychophysiology,* 11:616–629.

Lange, C. G. 1885. *On Sindsbevaegelser et psyko. fysiolog. studie.* Copenhagen: Krønar.

Lisina, M. I. 1958. The role of orienting in the conversion of involuntary into voluntary reactions. In L. G. Voronin, A. N. Leontiv, A. R. Luria, E. N. Sokolov, and O. S. Vinogradova (eds.), *The Orienting Reflex and Exploratory Behavior.* Moscow: Acad. Pedag. Sci.

Lown, B., R. Verrier, and R. Corbalan. 1973. Psychological stress and threshold for repetitive ventricular response. *Science,* 182:834–836.

Lown, B. and M. Wolf. 1971. Approaches to sudden death from coronary heart disease. *Circulation,* 44:130–142.

Miller, N. E. 1969. Learning of visceral and glandular components. *Science,* 163:434–445.

—— 1974. In P. Obrist, A. Black, J. Brener, and L. DiCara (eds.), *Contemporary Trends in Cardiovascular Psychophysiology.* Chicago: Aldine-Atherton.

Mowrer, O. H. 1947. On the dual nature of learning—A re-interpretation of "conditioning" and "problem-solving." *Harvard Educational Review,* 17:102–148.

Obrist, P. A., R. A. Webb, J. R. Sutterer, and J. L. Howard. 1970. The cardiac-somatic relationship. Some reformulations. *Psychophysiology,* 6:569–587.

Schacter, S. 1964. The interaction of cognitive and physiological determinants of emotional state. In L. Berkowitz (ed.), *Advances in Experimental Social Psychology,* Vol. 1. New York: Academic Press.

Schultze, J. H., and W. Luthe. 1959. *Autogenic Training: A Psycho-Physiologic Approach in Psychotherapy.* New York: Grune and Stratton.

Shapiro, D., B. Tursky, and G. Schwartz. 1970. Differentiation of heart rate and systolic blood pressure in man by operant conditioning. *Psychosomatic Medicine,* 32:417–423.

Thompson, L. W. and J. B. Nowlin. 1973. Relation of increased attention to central and autonomic nervous system states. In L. F. Jarvik, C. Eisdorfer, and J. E. Blum (eds.), *Intellectual Functioning in Adults.* New York: Springer.

Weiss, J. M. and B. Engel. 1971. Operant conditioning of heart rate in patients with premature ventricular beats. *Psychosomatic Medicine,* 33:301–321.

Wolpe, J. 1958. *Psychotherapy by Reciprocal Inhibition.* California: Stanford University Press.

7

Theoretical Approaches and Methodological Problems in Clinical Research

DON C. FOWLES

THE PRECEDING six papers were chosen in order to present to nonpsychophysiologists a wide variety of approaches to clinical research utilizing psychophysiological techniques. I will now call attention to the theoretical approaches implicit or explicit in these chapters and review some of the methodological problems which have arisen. By cutting across the chapters in this fashion I hope that an appreciation of some of the basic issues in this type of research will be developed which might otherwise be missed in a reading of individual papers. The analysis of theoretical approaches will begin with a discussion of the view of the *general* nature of psychopathology which is assumed in much of this research. It will then turn to the more specific hypotheses used to guide individual research programs and to interpret experimental results. The consideration of methodological issues will be subdivided into sections on the selection of subjects, stimulus conditions, and physiological response systems.

The author wishes to thank T. C. Weerts for his critical comments.

Theoretical Issues

THE DIATHESIS-STRESS MODEL AND
BIOLOGICAL INDIVIDUAL DIFFERENCES

The common assumption in the clinical applications of psychophysiology is, of course, that biological variables play an important role in the development of psychopathology. The credibility of this assumption has been greatly increased by important developments during the past decade in the field of psychiatric genetics, especially in the area of schizophrenia. Moreover, the implications of these developments underscore the importance of the type of psychophysiological research described here. A description of these developments and their implications, therefore, will help to place this research in perspective.

As Gottesman and Shields (1972) note, it was still possible in 1960 for Jackson (1960) to dismiss Kallman's data on genetic influences in schizophrenia as methodologically too weak to be persuasive. The dominant attitudes in American psychiatry and psychology were favorably disposed toward theories proposing an environmental etiology for psychopathological disorders and hostile toward those proposing genetic influences (Meehl, 1962). The psychogenic versus organic dichotomy seemed reasonable enough and the disorders covered in this volume were seen as primarily psychogenic in origin.

The *Zeitgeist* changed dramatically in the decade which followed. In the case of schizophrenia this change was brought about by two major developments. First, the twin study by Gottesman and Shields (1966) corrected many of the methodological faults of Kallman's work and yet reported very similar results. Next, the *coup de grâce* was delivered by the adoption studies (Heston, 1966; Heston and Denny, 1968; Karlsson, 1966; Kety et al., 1968; Rosenthal et al., 1968; Wender, Rosenthal, and Kety, 1968) which demonstrated an increased risk of developing schizophrenia for the biological rather than the adoptive relatives of a schizophrenic proband. The combined weight of the evidence, carefully reviewed by Gottesman and Shields (1972) and by Rosenthal (1970), is so persuasive as to leave little doubt concerning the importance of genetic influences. Although research has not progressed quite as far as in schizophrenia, there is increasing evidence of the importance of genetic factors in anxiety neurosis (Miner, 1973) and the affective psychoses (Rosenthal, 1970). In a parallel fashion, it appears that genetic vulnerability is a major factor in the development of physical illnesses, even when the illness involves a known infectious organism as in tuberculosis (Wiggins et al., 1971).

In part, the earlier rejection of the genetic hypothesis was based on a misunderstanding of the nature of genetic influences. It was not clearly recognized that a genetic influence in no way precluded a substantial contribution of environmental factors. The essence of the genetic position is that genetic vulnerability is necessary but not sufficient, as emphasized by Meehl (1962) in his discussion of the meaning of "specific etiology" and more recently by Rosenthal (1970) and by Gottesman and Shields (1972).[1] What is inherited, then, is what Rosenthal (1970) calls psychiatric diathesis, a vulnerability to the development of a specific type of psychopathology, and not the disorder itself. In order for the diathesis to develop into a psychiatric disorder some type of (as yet unspecified) environmental stress is necessary. Hence the term "diathesis-stress" which is used to identify this theoretical position.

Although at first glance, this position may appear simply to be restating the axiom that both nature and nurture are important, it is in fact a very strong position which assumes that the harmful effects of pathogenic environments will be found *only* in genetically vulnerable individuals. For example, the notion of a schizophrenogenic environment without reference to gene-

[1] Gottesman and Shields (1972) do not preclude a simple additive, as opposed to an interactive, model of genetic influence. Strictly speaking, in an additive model the genetic contribution might not be absolutely necessary in order for schizophrenia to develop. However, even in an additive model it is unlikely that schizophrenia would develop without some genetic liability.

tic vulnerability would be untenable from this point of view, since an environment could be schizophrenogenic only for individuals who were genetically vulnerable to schizophrenia. Once this view is accepted, one reaches the somewhat ironical conclusion that the best (and perhaps the only) way to study environmental influences is to study genetically vulnerable individuals!

Another way in which the diathesis-stress model is more than simply a restatement of the nature plus nurture axiom is that it implies that the "choice of symptom" may be strongly determined by genetic factors. That is, the factor which determines who will develop schizophrenia or depression or an anxiety neurosis or an ulcer when placed under stress may well be more a matter of genetics than of the specific nature of the stress. It is improbable that this somewhat extreme genetic position will be completely true. Instead, it seems more likely that the nature of the stressor will also be important. If this is the case, then the choice of symptom will be determined by the *interaction* of genetic and environmental factors rather than by either one alone. Whichever position proves to be most valid, it is clear that both imply that the etiology of psychiatric disorders can only be understood by examining genetic contributions. This conclusion demonstrates the importance of the diathesis-stress model and the extent of the change which has occurred in just over a decade.

The diathesis-stress model and the data which support it call attention to the contribution of biological variables in the development of psychopathology. The exact nature of these biological individual differences is not altogether clear, but presumably they would involve an alteration in the structure and/or function of some aspect of the central nervous system which, in turn, would influence the effect of the environment on the individual. An example might be a more labile sympathetic nervous system which would make the individual generally more responsive to anxiety-provoking situations.

So far, however, there is an enormous gap between the genetic endowment at the moment of conception, on the one

hand, and a fully developed clinical disorder such as schizophrenia, on the other hand. The answer to the question, "What
is inherited?" is required to fill that gap. A related question of
the utmost theoretical and practical significance is whether or
not the psychiatric diathesis is detectable other than as the clinically defined disorder in question. If it is, a number of important consequences follow, as detailed below.

Meehl's (1962) speculations on the nature of the diathesis
in schizophrenia serve to illustrate the general structure of the
most plausible view of the manner in which genetic influences
are exerted. Adopting a single gene model for schizophrenia,[2]
Meehl suggested that *all* individuals with this genotype develop schizotaxia, defined as an integrative neural defect directly caused by a biochemical abnormality associated with the
gene producing vulnerability to schizophrenia. This neural abnormality is so slight that it cannot be detected by the standard
techniques for assessing neural damage. Thus schizotaxia is the
vulnerability to schizophrenia at a neural level and is not visible without special and possibly as yet undeveloped procedures. Schizotaxia, in turn, has a pervasive effect on the individual's reaction to his social environment with the result that all
or almost all schizotaxic individuals will develop a personality
which consists of the symptoms of schizophrenia in mild degree. This personality, which reflects the interaction of the genotype and the environment and thus is not directly inherited, is
called "schizotypy." Schizotypy is viewed as falling within the
range of normal personality types and consequently is not
pathological in itself. However, given a schizophrenogenic environment (the nature of which is uncertain, though Meehl
speculates that the mother-child relationship is of critical importance), the schizotype will develop clinically diagnosable
schizophrenia. Meehl speculates that only about one out of
every four schizotypes actually develops schizophrenia.

There are four levels of psychiatric diathesis in this simple
model: the genetic-biochemical defect, the neural defect (schizo-

---

[2] Polygenic variations on this theme are similar, though somewhat more complicated.

taxia), the possibly identifiable phenotype at the personality level (schizotypy), and the clinically diagnosable condition itself. Thus this model offers two answers to the question of what is inherited—the neural defect and the personality type. Of the two, the neural defect is a more direct manifestation of gene action and thus is a better reflection of the diathesis. In a similar discussion of the possibility of a detectable phenotype associated with psychiatric diathesis, Gottesman and Shields (1972) employed the term "endophenotype," defined as the phenotypic expression of a genetic characteristic which is "discernable only after aid to the naked eye" (p. 319). This aid to the naked eye was said to consist of either biological or behavioral assessment techniques. An example of an endophenotype in physical medicine is chemical or latent diabetes, which has none of the overt symptoms of diabetes but is detectable by means of chemical tests (Rosenthal, 1970). Although Gottesman and Shields did not make this comparison, it would seem that schizotaxia is closer to their view of an endophenotype than is schizotypy, since schizotypy presumably involves behavior which is easily observed without the aid of tests.

So far, no endophenotypes have been discovered for the functional disorders. The literature on psychological deficit in schizophrenia does involve the type of behavioral or physiological assessment techniques which may prove fruitful in this endeavor, and a number of them look promising. However, this approach has not yet demonstrated a reliable identification of individuals at genetic risk for schizophrenia. Along the same lines, there has been considerable discussion in the schizophrenia literature of the possibility of detecting a "schizoid personality" (a concept very similar to Meehl's schizotype) (Gottesman and Shields, 1972; Heston, 1970; Rosenthal, 1970), but it has not yet proved possible to diagnose the schizoid in such a way that it includes all schizoids without also including too many nonschizoids to be useful (Gottesman and Shields, 1972). It may well be the case that the schizoid personality can be adequately defined only by the inclusion of measures of the endophenotype. In both the literature on the schizoid personality and that on psychological deficit there have been partial successes. These successes and the widespread belief that in many cases the premorbid personality exhibits some aspects of later pathology encourage the hope that it will prove possible to detect endophenotypes. Nevertheless, this has not yet been accomplished in the case of schizophrenia where the interest has perhaps been greatest, and for other disorders the search for an endophenotype has hardly begun.

As noted above, the absence of information on the nature of the diathesis constitutes a serious theoretical gap in our understanding of the etiology of psychopathology. One can only cite evidence that inheritance is a critical factor without being able to fill in any of the crucial details concerning how genes influence the development of pathology. Furthermore, filling this gap would bring about practical as well as theoretical benefits. For example, the study of environmental contributors to etiology would be facilitated by the ability to identify individuals who are "at risk." It would then be possible to study the environmental influences on the transition from the diathesis alone to the psychiatric disorder itself. At present it is extremely costly to execute prospective studies of this transition. One example is the "high risk" study by Mednick and Schulsinger (1968), in which 200 children of schizophrenic mothers are being studied over a period of twenty years or more in order to obtain data *prior* to the development of approximately 30 cases of schizophrenia. It is assumed that at most only about 100 of these children are in fact at genetic risk for schizophrenia, and the number may be considerably smaller than that. Thus the identification of the endophenotypes would reduce the number of children being studied by at least a factor of two with the attendant reduction in costs. Moreover, once the etiological factors are better understood, the detection of endophenotypes might well make possible the introduction of prophylactic measures which could have a major therapeutic impact. In view of these considerations, the measurement of psychiatric diathesis is a problem of paramount importance to both etiology and prevention.

Before looking at the way in which the diathesis-stress model has influenced the research reported in the preceding chapters, it would be well to comment on the significance of the genetics literature for the field of personality, since the concept of psychiatric diathesis is concerned with the premorbid personality. The notion of diathesis-stress as used here bears some similarity to the view that personality is related to the probability of psychiatric disturbance, and that it also shapes the form of that disturbance. The two views have in common the assumption that an increased risk of psychiatric breakdown is associated with the premorbid personality and that this personality is visible to some degree. The major difference is the specification of a significant genetic contribution in the diathesis-stress model. There is also a much stronger tendency for a genetically oriented approach to turn to biological variables (e.g., an autonomic nervous system lability, a sensory input disturbance such as a deficient inhibition of irrelevant stimuli, or a biochemical abnormality) than has been the case for the field of personality as a whole.

The most important aspect of this comparison is the theoretical support for the field of personality provided by the genetic evidence. The field of personality has had few triumphs in recent years. The personality-trait approach, which by virtue of its emphasis on the measurement of personality should be most suitable for applications to clinical research, has been strongly criticized by Mischel (1968, 1969, 1971) for its weak empirical support. In contrast, the diathesis-stress model is riding the crest of a wave of positive findings in the clinical area. Moreover, there has been an increasing recognition of the influence of genes on behavior generally, not just on pathological behavior (e.g., Fuller and Thompson, 1960; Lockard, 1971; Manosevitz, Lindzey, and Thiessen, 1969; McClearn and DeFries, 1973). These hereditary influences are understood in the context of the evolution of adaptive behavior. Since a fundamental aspect of evolution is within-species genetic diversity (necessary for the operation of natural selection), this tradition offers a firm scientific basis for a view of personality involving biological individual differences. The clinical research, which deals with within-species genetic variation, directly supports this conclusion.

The implications of behavior genetics for the field of personality have not gone unnoticed. A recent personality text (Wiggins et al., 1971) proposes a genetic-biological view of personality along the lines being discussed here. Similarly, Mischel's criticisms of personality theory have been countered by Bowers (1973), who articulates a view of personality in which biological individual differences interact with situational variables to produce overt behavior.[3] In these approaches the "trait" is an underlying biological variable rather than an overt behavior, a conceptualization similar to that of the endophenotype discussed above. It can be seen from this brief discussion that these developments in personality theory mesh nicely with the diathesis-stress model, both of them stressing the importance of biological individual differences.

It has been argued that the diathesis-stress model and the associated view that biological individual differences constitute an important aspect of personality provide the theoretical foundation for many clinical applications of psychophysiology. This influence, therefore, should be visible in varying degrees in the research described in the preceding chapters, and that is the case.

The strongest and most explicit instance of this influence is found in Lykken's paper, since the diathesis-stress model was the focus of his research. The data he presented showed that all aspects of the electroencephalogram which he was able to assess (with a sophisticated computer analysis of the EEG) showed high heritability as estimated from the twin studies. This demonstration provides an important first step—the measurement of an endophenotype. The second and equally important step, the demonstration that this particular endophenotype does in fact reflect a psychiatric diathesis, remains to be taken.

---

[3] Bowers' emphasis is on "biocognitive" individual differences and hence tends to focus on cognitive factors more than in the examples presented here. Nevertheless, the basic argument is similar.

Given the thoroughness of Lykken's analysis of the EEG and the likelihood that the EEG does include important information concerning psychological functions, there would seem to be a better than even chance that the second step will be successful.

The influence of the diathesis-stress model can also be seen in Lykken's reference to trait anxiety, described as the individual's "constitutional level of anxiety reactivity, which may be a stable parameter of temperament" (p. 163). Lader uses the same concept when he refers to emotional traits. A person high on an emotional trait is said to be more likely to experience that emotional state than are others. However, Lader's comment that "someone with a high trait for an emotion may avoid experiencing it by minimizing situations which might provoke that emotion" (p. 15) makes it clear that the definition here is one of vulnerability to anxiety rather than of the frequency of anxiety. Thus Lykken and Lader both view emotional traits as being defined in terms of an underlying vulnerability to environmental stresses, and Lykken explicitly implicates genetic influences in the development of such traits.[4]

A suggestion similar in form to the Lader-Lykken conceptualization can be seen in Lang's proposal that people who develop psychosomatic disorders probably did so at least in part because they were poor "autonomic athletes" (p. 186). This can be seen as a form of psychiatric diathesis in which the person's inability to control (the physiological component of) his emotional reactions predisposes him to excessive responding during stress.

Although the exact nature of the individual difference parameter contributing to psychopathy is not clear—e.g., reduced ability to learn a conditioned fear response or a superior ability to "modulate aversive cues and cope with an impending

---

[4] This underlying vulnerability may be detected by placing the individual in the right type of situation. For example, it is likely that a subject with trait anxiety will be made anxious by situations which are not stressful enough to produce anxiety in most individuals. It is probably for this reason that, as Lader reports, differences are found between anxiety neurotics and controls only under conditions of minimal stimulation—conditions which produce anxiety in the patients but not the controls.

stressor" (p. 93)—one clearly is postulated in the research reported by Hare. Thus the general approach taken is that an important contributor to the etiology of psychopathy is an underlying biological process. While no evidence is presented to indicate that this process is genetically based, the clinical histories of psychopaths suggest a lifelong pattern of such behavior.

As might be expected because of the extensive genetic research in schizophrenia, Venables' theory is explicitly concerned with genetic influences. In this case there appear to be two levels of vulnerability. In the first, the amygdala-hippocampal portion of the limbic system is more than usually vulnerable to damage—e.g., because of anoxia during pregnancy. Once this damage has occurred, the individual has a considerably elevated probability of developing the clinical symptoms of schizophrenia. Venables does not propose a way of detecting the initial vulnerability, but the second stage is reported to be at least partly detectable through measures of electrodermal activity (Mednick, 1970) prior to the development of schizophrenia. In Venables' work, therefore, there is an explicit hypothesis of psychiatric diathesis and some indication that at least the second stage may be measurable.

The research which is least involved with the diathesis-stress model is Mendels' work on disturbed sleep in depression. The comparisons of the sleep of depressed patients with nonpatient controls and with themselves when not depressed requires little by way of assumptions as to the nature of pathology. The major emphasis is on monitoring abnormalities in sleep which begin at or near the onset of clinically visible depression and improve as the patient recovers clinically. Thus the primary interest is in changes from the premorbid to morbid state rather than in traits characteristic of the premorbid period. While this approach is not at all incompatible with the diathesis-stress model, it is less closely tied to that model than are many of the other investigations reported here. On the other hand, Mendels and Chernik found some evidence in their data that the sleep of depressed patients does not return completely to normal during an apparently complete clinical recovery, and he speculates that there may be some chronic abnormalities of the sleep of patients who become depressed—a statement more consistent with the trait approach found in the other papers.

In summary, the last decade has witnessed a dramatic increase in the evidence supporting a diathesis-stress model in the etiology of psychiatric disorders. The diathesis-stress model, in turn, leads to a view of personality-as-related-to-psychopathology in terms of biological individual differences which convey a vulnerability to the development of psychopathology. These biological individual differences or endophenotypes cannot be seen with the naked eye, but it is hoped that they may be detected with biological or behavioral methods (perhaps under very highly controlled circumstances). Much of the psychophysiological research reported in this volume is being conducted within this context.

It should be stressed, on the other hand, that simply because the diathesis is fundamentally biological in nature it does not follow that psychophysiological techniques are the only (or even the best) way it can be assessed. The diathesis is likely to be manifest in any one of the three systems—verbal-cognitive, overt-motor, or physiological—which Lang (1971) identified as interacting components of behavior. The primary concern is that the response being observed be fairly closely coupled to the basic deficit, and for that reason it must be relatively uninfluenced by social learning. Although verbal and motor behavior are perhaps more likely to be influenced by social learning, since they are more directly subject to reinforcement contingencies, it is easy to find exceptions. In the verbal-cognitive realm, for example, the effect of distraction on memory for letters or digits has been used to assess psychological deficit in schizophrenia (McGhie, 1970). In the overt-motor realm, simple reaction time has been used for the same purpose (Salzinger, 1973). Thus, physiological responses are not the only basis for assessing psychiatric diathesis, but they are too important to be ignored.

SPECIFIC EXPLANATORY CONCEPTS

The ink tracings on a sheet of polygraph paper in and of themselves are of little use. It is only when they are interpreted in terms of psychological or physiological concepts that they become interesting. These concepts are more specific than those just discussed and serve to define certain aspects of the disorder in question. A second matter of concern is how these concepts are related to the behavior which brought the patient to the clinic. If the connection is not obvious, then a theory is required which relates the descriptive concept (e.g., habituation of the orienting response) to the symptoms of interest to the clinician. Finally, insofar as it is assumed that the peripheral responses being measured are indices of events occurring within the central nervous system, it must be counted as a theoretical advance if these central events can be specified in more detail—e.g., the anatomical sites or the functional systems of most importance. In this section the specific explanatory concepts used in the preceding papers will be examined with these points in mind.

One of the simplest and most direct applications of psychophysiological techniques is to anxiety neurosis. Because physiological responses are commonly accepted as an essential component of anxiety, there is little difficulty in relating the responses being measured to the clinical symptoms. On the basis of what is known about anxiety, one would expect that anxiety neurotics would show a relatively generalized overarousal, and Lader's review (paper 1) confirms this expectation. The precise nature of this overarousal, on the other hand remains unclear. Some of the possibilities include (1) simple overreactivity as if all responses were amplified; (2) failure to habituate to repeated occurrences of a stimulus, as in a series of tones or shocks; (3) failure to adapt to a continued stressor; (4) failure to recover rapidly once the stress has ended. Any one or a combination of these could produce overarousal. Some hypotheses have been put forth emphasizing poor habituation (Lader and Wing, 1966; Lader, 1972) or a slow recovery following the termination of stress (Malmo, 1957; 1966), but a final verdict is not yet in. Nor has the physiological substrate in the central nervous system been identified.

At the other end of the arousal continuum much of the data reviewed by Hare is consistent with an *under*arousal hypothesis for psychopaths in experiments involving aversive stimulation. This underarousal can be related to the psychopath's antisocial behavior by borrowing concepts from Mowrer's (1947) two-factor learning theory. Thus avoidance conditioning is said to require a conditioned emotional response (CER) in order to be successful, and psychopaths, it is suggested, do not develop CERs as readily as do other individuals. Avoidance conditioning, in turn, is assumed to be an essential component in the learning of socialized behavior. With respect to the cause of the underarousal, Hare tentatively proposes that psychopaths are able to modulate their sensory input in such a way that they tune out cues related to impending aversive stimulation. A point of interest in this explanation is that Hare has placed the cause of the reduced responsiveness in the sensory input rather than in the response output apparatus. Disentangling these two influences on psychophysiological responses will not be an easy matter, but it will represent an important theoretical advance if it is achieved.

So far the concepts of overarousal and underarousal have been used as if various physiological responses are interchangeable. It may be the case that in anxiety neurosis the overarousal is very general, but some degree of response specificity seems to be involved in psychopathy and depression. The studies of psychopathy have found underarousal with electrodermal activity but not with heart rate. In fact, it was the pattern of diminished electrodermal activity combined with adequate or greater than normal cardiovascular responding which led Hare to think in terms of differences in the processing of sensory input as the critical variable in psychopathy.

The numerous physiological responses on which patients were found to differ from controls in Lader's review of depression cannot be incorporated into a simple over- or underarousal model—e.g., the results for salivation and muscle activity are more easily interpreted as overarousal whereas sweat-gland activity and catecholamine secretion suggest the opposite conclusion. It is not clear whether these findings represent a theoretically significant degree of response specificity or simply a failure in the general literature to separate subtypes, such as agitated versus retarded depressives. An attractive possibility suggested by some of Lader's work is that anxiety, retardation, and severity of depressive mood are distinct dimensions, each of which may be related to some physiological measures but not others. Nevertheless, at present the findings in depression must be viewed as descriptive only, having neither a postulated cause nor any clear theoretical relationship to clinical depression.

Venables' theory of schizophrenia is unusually comprehensive. The basic schizophrenic process is seen as a disturbance in the functioning of the limbic system (especially the amygdala and hippocampus). This disturbance is manifested, on the one hand, in deviant orienting responses and, on the other hand, in a disturbance of selective attention. The problems with selective attention, in turn, are related to the various perceptual symptoms associated with schizophrenia. In addition, the interpretation of the orienting response as the simplest form of learning provides a basis for understanding the cognitive symptoms of schizophrenia. Thus with respect to the psychophysiological measures (skin conductance orienting responses), there is both an explanation for their deviance and a relatively straightforward relationship to schizophrenic symptoms.

Unlike most of the experiments in the preceding chapters, Mendels and Chernick's review of sleep disturbance in depression involves direct examination of a clinical symptom. This being the case, the measures are of obvious relevance to depression and they represent the more complex analysis of this symptom which is possible only with psychophysiological techniques. The major concepts applied to this analysis are the interpretation of the recordings in terms of stages of sleep and the associated concept of REM pressure. Little is offered, however, by way of speculation as to the causes and/or consequences of the sleep disturbance. The authors do suggest at one point that a biochemical abnormality may underlie changes in depression, but the nature of this abnormality is not spelled out.

Lang's research on the control of heart rate differs from the other papers in that it is most concerned with how best to manipulate a variable (heart rate) rather than with the assessment of biological individual differences. The initial question was whether control of heart rate can be achieved and, if so, whether its acquisition should be viewed as instrumental conditioning or as the learning of a motor skill. However, this research has already led to the speculation that psychosomatic cardiovascular disorders arise in part from the individual's inability to achieve control over his autonomic responses. Thus the psychiatric diathesis in this case is that of being a poor "autonomic athlete." At this point it is not clear how general this deficiency would be—whether it is specific to a given response system or applies to the entire autonomic nervous system. Perhaps even more important from a theoretical point of view are the long-range possibilities of manipulating the activity of a specific physiological system, which would greatly facilitate our understanding of the relationship between these variables and other aspects of behavior. In view of the minimal knowledge on this score at present, the importance of such a development could hardly be overstated.

This brief summary of the specific theoretical concepts appearing in the preceding chapters and the way in which they are related to clinical problems reveals the wide range of approaches being taken. Theoretical concepts have been borrowed from other areas of psychology—learning theory, perception, and physiological psychology—to supplement those which have been developed within psychophysiology itself. At the same time, it is equally clear that this research is in a very early stage. Much of it is still basically descriptive in nature. The theories which are proposed are almost always to be taken as tentative, the fit between the theory and data not being so close as to warrant strong conclusions.

Two general but related problems contribute largely to this state of affairs. First, the currently available theories can account for only a relatively small portion of the variance in any one response system, the rest of the variance being accounted for by factors which are either unrecognized or beyond control. Second, there is a considerable discrepancy between technology and theory. It is possible for psychophysiologists to score far more responses than the currently available theories can explain. That is, as the number of responses being recorded increases, so does the probability of finding patterns of responses which are not interpretable with our present theories. These are basic problems in the field of psychophysiology, not problems unique to clinical research. Consequently, the future progress of clinical applications will depend upon the continued development of both theory and methodology in the field of psychophysiology as a whole. In the meantime, many new frontiers have been opened by the application of these techniques to clinical research.

Methodological Issues

Methodological problems are common in research on psychopathology. In addition, as mentioned in the introduction, the field of psychophysiology has been heavily involved from the outset in methodological concerns of its own. This strong emphasis on methodology is clearly evident in the papers which appear in this volume. For the sake of convenience, the discussion of this topic will be organized around the selection of the subjects to be studied, the stimulus conditions under which they are studied, and the physiological responses which are to be recorded.

SELECTION OF PATIENTS AND CONTROLS

Among the general problems in clinical research is the method by which patients to be studied are selected. The two most frequent approaches are clinical judgment and psychological tests (e.g., the MMPI), and in the research described here physiological measurements offer a third basis for classification. In practice, clinical diagnosis was by far the most frequent method used to define patient groups in these papers. There was also a unanimous concern to minimize the heterogeneity within the groups of patients selected in this manner. This took the form of adopting a conservative diagnosis in the initial screening of subjects as in Venables' mention of the more conservative British view of schizophrenia, Hare's restriction of his Group P to those subjects who clearly met Cleckley's criteria for psychopathy, and Lader's emphasis on restricting studies of anxiety to patients with few symptoms other than anxiety. These more conservative diagnoses were also based on clinical judgment. Only in one instance was another method used to define clinical groups, and in that instance Hare used the MMPI *after* the groups were defined by the usual clinical method. Thus clinical diagnosis served as the starting point in all cases.

The physiological measures frequently provided a basis for evaluating the wisdom of the initial groupings of patients or for suggesting alternative groupings. Venables strongly emphasized the manner in which his distinction between responder and nonresponder was forced on him by his data. In equally dramatic fashion Lader used electrodermal measures to compare various patient groups: these measures produced a dichotomy between monosymptomatic, specific phobics, on the one hand, and social phobias, agoraphobias, anxiety states, and anxiety with depression, on the other hand. Physiological measures also provided more consistent results when depressed patients were subdivided into agitated versus retarded depression than when the endogenous-reactive subdivision was used, thereby providing support for the former classification. In another application to diagnosis, Mendels confirmed the importance of the neurotic versus psychotic distinction in terms of sleep characteristics and also found that age was an important variable which interacted with depression. Perhaps the most radical use of physiological measures for the purposes of assessment is Lykken's development of six factors which can be used to assess individual differences in EEG activity.

From these examples it is clear that physiological recordings were most often used to complement or evaluate traditional diagnosis. However, Venables' responder-nonresponder distinction and Lykken's EEG factors represent dimensions which are defined solely in terms of physiological measures. If these approaches are successful in defining categories of patients or personality dimensions which are clinically significant, then physiological assessment could well become a part of diagnosis in the clinic.

The selection of an appropriate control group for clinical research is more difficult than diagnosing the patients of interest. One of the first and most difficult problems derives from the medications which most patients receive. Although medication is a confounding variable for most clinical research, it is particularly serious in psychophysiological research because the effects on physiological responses are known to be quite significant. For example, chlorpromazine produces a lowering of blood pressure with a compensatory increase in heart rate (Goodman and Gilman, 1965) and a dampening effect on electrodermal activity (Tecce and Cole, 1972). In this volume Lader reported that hypnotics had an effect on the EEG twelve hours after administration, and Mendels found that the drugs used to treat depression or the associated sleep difficulty have a residual effect on the sleep EEG which may persist for several weeks after the drugs are discontinued. Thus the effects are widespread and have been of practical concern to many investigators. The difficulty of obtaining unmedicated patients is apparent from Lader's comment that during a one-year period he was able to find only 10 acutely ill schizophrenics who had not received medication for four weeks *prior* to hospitalization, and this was in spite of canvassing an area containing a population of one million.

In addition to medication, a number of other confounding variables are difficult to eliminate when patients are compared with controls. These have been enumerated by Mednick (1967; Mednick and McNeil, 1968) and include such factors as a history of social failure, various forms of treatment (e.g., electroconvulsive therapy, psychotherapy, etc., in addition to medication), the effects of institutionalization, and the meaning of the experimental situation to the subject. In part, these problems can be handled by comparing one patient group with another and matching the groups in terms of duration of institutionalization and time since onset of the disorder. It is difficult, nevertheless, to match patients on all variables, especially when comparing different diagnostic categories, since different treatments and a different course of the disorder are likely to be encountered.

These problems have been approached in a number of ways in the previous chapters. The obvious way to handle the medication problem is to arrange to test patients who are off drugs for a long period of time. Practical and often ethical considerations preclude this ideal solution in most instances, leaving the investigator to find other ways to cope with medication. One way is to demonstrate that differences in physiological activity are not accompanied by differences in medication. Thus Venables reported that the amount and type of medication administered did not differ between patients who were responders and those who failed to give responses. Carrying this approach one step further, Venables' demonstration of laterality differences in electrodermal activity would be very difficult to attribute to drugs.

Comparison of a patient with himself at another time offers a method of eliminating some of the problems of between-subject comparisons. The longitudinal studies of depressed patients described by Mendels and Chernik allowed the investigators to look at changes within a given patient and study their relationship to clinical improvement. Unfortunately, insofar as treatments being administered concurrently have a direct effect on the physiological responses being monitored, these effects will be indistinguishable from those attributable to clinical improvement. In some cases it was even possible to monitor the sleep of patients who had recovered and to note changes in their sleep prior to relapse. This is a particularly attractive procedure, especially if treatment has been discontinued and if measurements can be obtained often enough to detect the early stages of relapse prior to the reintroduction of treatment. Due to its cyclical course, depression seems well suited to this approach.

More indirect ways of coping with these methodological problems are presented by Lykken and Hare, both of whom suggest studying personality dimensions presumed to be important in the etiology of psychopathology. At the end of his paper Hare comments that because of the difficulties of selecting appropriate samples of psychopaths and controls, he plans to extend his work to noncriminal populations. He would prefer to study psychopaths who are functioning reasonably well in society, but both detection and lack of cooperation are likely to be insurmountable problems. As an alternative, he plans to look at personality dimensions such as "impulsivity, lack of anxiety and empathy, etc.," which seem closely related to the concept of psychopathy. This approach will avoid many of the problems associated with studying institutionalized patients or prisoners, and it may result in valuable information concerning the way in which these dimensions combine to produce psychopathy, or which ones are more primary in the etiology of psychopathy.

Lykken's study used "normal" subjects and hence faced none of the problems associated with studying patients. On the other hand, ultimately he must demonstrate the validity of his hope that his EEG factors are assessing psychiatric diathesis. Assuming that he can accomplish that, this approach avoids the many methodological difficulties associated with studying patients and will be a valuable addition to the study of psychopathology.

A final approach to this problem and one which is closely tied to the notion that there are measurable premorbid characteristics which predict pathology is the "high risk group" study (Mednick and Schulsinger, 1968) mentioned above. The major advantages of this type of study are that (1) the data are obtained prior to the development of pathology and thus are not contaminated by "halo" effects, (2) the effects of chronicity are minimized, and (3) matched control groups can be selected from "low risk" children and from high risk children who do not develop pathology. As noted above, the disadvantages are the high cost and the great amount of time required for completion of the study.

The basic similarity of several of these approaches should be recognized. Hare's interest in the dimensions of psychopathy in normal populations, Lykken's EEG dimensions which may reflect psychiatric diathesis, and Mednick's high risk studies all assess the functioning of individuals who are not defined as patients at the time they are being studied, permitting the selection of adequate control groups.[5] These studies also have in common the problem of demonstrating the relevance to clinical disorders. Studies with patients, on the other hand, have difficulty in matching patients and controls on all of the variables associated with patienthood, even when it is possible to obtain unmedicated patients. Thus neither of these approaches is fully adequate when taken alone. It is only when a combination of approaches reaches the same conclusion that one can view that conclusion with a high degree of confidence.

SELECTION OF STIMULUS CONDITIONS

There are a number of considerations in the selection of stimulus conditions which are specifically associated with psychophysiological approaches. The first of these centers around the fact that most physiological activity monitored in these studies is sensitive to many aspects of the experiment. Simply appearing for an experiment has been found stressful enough to produce a measurable activation of adrenocortical activity (Oken, 1967). Similarly, differences in the experimenter's appearance and behavior (Hicks, 1969) or sex (Fisher and Kotses, 1974)

---

[5] Even in this case it may be difficult to distinguish between the onset of symptoms and the individual's reaction to those symptoms (e.g., anxiety in response to feelings of loss of control). This still represents, nevertheless, a much better matching of experimental and control subjects than is possible when studying patients with a disorder of many years' duration.

have been found to influence physiological measures, and even the method of recruiting subjects for an experiment can affect physiological activity (Kotses, Glaus, and Fisher, 1973).

The task of demonstrating often subtle physiological differences between various subject groupings when so many factors other than subject differences also affect these measures requires that considerable care be taken in the choice of the tasks to be employed and the general experimental conditions. Numerous examples of this concern are evident in the papers in this volume. Lang reports that since he has been using a computer to interact with his subjects, thereby eliminating the experimenter interaction, he has been much more successful at replicating his results. Lader expressed concern over the complexity of the laboratory situation and the possibility that it may have different effects in different subjects. It is difficult to know whether a patient might be threatened by the experiment, seeing it as a test which will reveal his pathology further, or whether he would view it as a potentially helpful test. Similarly, nonpatient controls sometime express a fear that they might produce responses similar to those of the patients, while others appear to be unthreatened by the experiment. The most frequently adopted solution to this problem appears to be that of making the subjects familiar with the experimenter and the laboratory before obtaining the measurements of interest: Lader, Lang, and Mendels all stressed the importance of using habituated subjects and Mendels found that more than one night of adaptation to the laboratory was necessary to overcome this problem. Unless the nature of the investigation requires the use of nonhabituated subjects, this practice seems to have much in its favor in spite of the extra time required.

A parallel problem arises in the choice of tasks or stimulus conditions within the experiment itself. The possibilities are, of course, infinite, but in practice they are rather circumscribed. Generally speaking, it is desirable (perhaps even absolutely essential) to use stimuli and tasks which require only a minimal amount of motor activity from the subject. This is because the physiological systems being monitored are called into play by the energy requirements of general physical activity, and the changes produced by physical activity are powerful enough to override those of psychological interest. Lang (1971) described this state of affairs metaphorically:

> R. C. Davis and his associates (1955) described the multitudinous responses of the body as a vast somatic sea, with waves, tides and deep currents all commingling. If we are to follow the course of a specific event, it is wise to let this sea settle as much as possible before we begin observation. . . . with the subject moving about, the psychological cockleshell is swamped in the general turbulence of gross energy demands. (p. 89)

It is probably for this reason that there has not been more extensive use of telemetry in spite of the fact that telemetry was heralded a few years ago as permitting observation of subjects during their normal daily activities. The constraints of having wires connected to the subject have been consistent with the need to keep the subject relatively immobilized anyway, and thus there has not been strong pressure to expand into telemetry.[6]

The requirement that the subject show little movement does not preclude the use of psychophysiologically meaningful stimuli and/or tasks. However, the examples in the previous chapters tend, on the whole, to involve relatively simple stimuli, often even simple physical stimuli with a minimum of psychological meaning. Probably the most frequently used paradigms are the orienting response and the reaction-time paradigms, which are about as simple as it is possible to make a stimulus and a task. Hare's slides of female nudes are not simple stimuli, but they are not as complex as would be a taped conversation or story or a movie or a clinical interview focused on the patient's psychological problems. Undoubtedly, the need to exert maximum control over the stimulus conditions so as to

[6] The requirements that subjects be immobilized does severely restrict the range of phenomena which can be investigated, and eventually telemetry may be used to study more active subjects. In contrast to the early interest in monitoring daily activities, it is likely that any such studies will involve *controlled* motor activity so that the physical demands can be equated for all experimental groups.

make the results of an experiment replicable is the reason for the absence of unstandardized stimuli such as clinical interviews. However, many easily standardized stimuli are seldom used compared with those already mentioned. Thus it appears that simple stimuli are used in the majority of cases and that this reflects a theoretical preference rather than the constraints of psychophysiological measures. The reason for this probably is so that, as Venables suggests, the psychological part of the experiment will be most easily interpretable. This is especially important in view of the theoretical problems facing this type of research as discussed below.

SELECTION OF PHYSIOLOGICAL RESPONSE SYSTEMS

The general point of view that it is important to study physiological responses does not offer much guidance as to which of the many possible responses should be recorded. For many years the notion that there was a dimension of generalized, nonspecific arousal (e.g., Hebb, 1955; Lindsley, 1951; Malmo, 1958; Duffy, 1962) suggested that response systems were relatively interchangeable. This hope was contradicted, however, by the repeated finding that the intercorrelations among different response systems are relatively low (Lang, 1971; Sternbach, 1966), thus demonstrating a considerable degree of response specificity.

Two principles which are traditionally applied to the problem of response specificity are individual response (I-R) and stimulus response (S-R) specificity (Sternbach, 1966). I-R specificity refers to the observation that when several measures are obtained simultaneously some individuals show their maximal responsiveness in one system (e.g., heart rate), while other individuals are most responsive in another system (e.g., skin conductance). Thus an individual's position relative to other subjects in terms of reactivity is likely to be determined to some extent by which response is being measured. S-R specificity refers to the equally reliable observations that the patterning of responses for a given subject will vary according to the stimulus conditions—e.g., the pattern of responses in a fear situation may differ from those in an anger situation.

The importance of I-R specificity varies with the interests of the investigator. If one is interested only in demonstrating that a given category of patient is more or less aroused than control subjects, I-R specificity is only a source of noise or error variance. Assuming that response specificity is distributed randomly among the patients and controls, it should be possible to demonstrate differences in arousal across a number of response systems, thereby establishing the generality of the difference in arousal. In this case, the major interest is in minimizing the effects of response specificity.

Aside from simply increasing the sample size, two major methods of reducing the effects of I-R specificity have been used. One is to record many physiological responses simultaneously, convert each to standard scores, and use the most responsive system for each individual as the best index of his arousal (e.g., Mandler et al., 1961; Zahn, 1964). It is interesting to note that not one of the contributors to this volume employed this solution, nor has it achieved a great popularity in the clinical literature generally. This is probably due to a combination of practical, theoretical, and empirical factors. On the practical side, such a technique requires a large investment in equipment and the development of recording techniques, and the massive amounts of data generated per subject require an automated system for data analysis. From a theoretical perspective, the number of systems for which the measurement techniques have been developed is too small compared to the vast number of possible physiological responses to insure that an adequate sampling has been achieved. Finally, there have been no dramatic demonstrations that this approach yields results which warrant the cost involved.

The second and more widely used solution is to find some method of adjusting the scores on a single measure for I-R specificity. Usually this takes the form of what are called "ipsative" (Opton and Lazarus, 1967) or "range-corrected" (Lykken, 1968) measures, which involve quantifying the response in such a way that it is scored relative to other aspects of the same physiological system for that individual. This can be seen when, for example, *changes* in SCR amplitude across trials is used rather than the absolute amplitude or when the subject is required to increase or decrease his heart rate *relative* to his own heart rate under resting conditions. Lykken's correction of his power spectrum data for the overall energy content for that subject is an application of this technique. Thus, the use of ipsative measures reduces the seriousness of the problems caused by I-R specificity and appears to be a helpful partial solution.

One aspect of S-R specificity is the expectation that each emotion might have a characteristic pattern of physiological activity. Some success has been achieved in demonstrating differences between fear and anger in this respect (Martin, 1961; Martin and Sroufe, 1970). The hope that specific emotions could be inferred from the pattern of responses has not been fulfilled, however, because the patterns associated with these emotions are not consistent enough from subject to subject (Lang, 1971). Consequently, this aspect of S-R specificity has not had a significant impact on clinical research.

Taken in its broadest sense, S-R specificity underscores the importance of the stimulus conditions in determining the responses obtained. This leads to a general concern with the selection of the most appropriate stimulus conditions and with the theoretical significance of the responses measured under those conditions. Examples of this approach are found in the papers by Hare and Venables. Hare's use of the concepts of orienting and defensive responses in connection with heart-rate acceleration and deceleration reflects a theory which relates fairly specific stimulus conditions to particular types of responses. Similarly, Venables' use of the orienting response paradigm and electrodermal responses was based on a quite specific theory as to how the responses are to be interpreted—i.e., when recorded under these particular stimulus conditions they reflect one aspect of the functioning of the limbic system. One of the best-known attempts at this type of theory is Lacey's (1967) intake-rejection hypothesis in which heart rate acceleration is seen as facilitating rejection and heart rate deceleration as facilitating intake of sensory input. Obrist and his colleagues (Obrist et al., 1970) have proposed an alternative formulation in which heart rate is viewed as being closely coupled to somatic activity in order to serve the increased energy demands associated with somatic activity. Along the same lines, Edelberg (1973) has recently discussed a number of specific functions (fine motor, locomotor, and defensive activity) in which electrodermal activity is involved. Theories of this type are few in number at present, but they are crucially important inasmuch as they provide guidance as to which response should be recorded for a given purpose.

Finally, the importance of technology in the determination of what can be measured must be mentioned. In a field as dependent on technology as is psychophysiology, this influence can be enormous. Three examples will serve to illustrate this point. The widespread scoring of heart-rate responses to discrete stimuli was greatly facilitated by the development of the cardiotachometer, which displays the amount of time between heartbeats (or the reciprocal in beats per minute) in a much more readable form than in the raw electrocardiogram. Similarly, the increased availability of computers has revolutionized the analysis of EEG, the analysis of which otherwise is limited and extremely tedious. On the other hand, the measurement of blood pressure—a variable of great importance in part because of its direct relevance to essential hypertension—is infrequent because satisfactory techniques have not been developed.

Although the problems of limited technology and I-R specificity are a matter of concern, they are not so serious as is the need for theories on which to base the choice of response. These are critical to the interpretation of the results of clinical studies. Thus a consideration of the problem of selecting response systems reinforces the earlier emphasis on the importance of theory and the dependence of clinical applications on basic research in psychophysiology.

Summary

Recent developments in psychiatric genetics have strongly supported the inference that genetic factors are important in the etiology of schizophrenia and probably other disorders as well. This conclusion, in turn, leads to the hypothesis that there should be genetically based biological individual differences which contribute substantially to the etiology of psychiatric disorders. Psychophysiological techniques offer an important means of assessing and helping to define the nature of these individual differences. Much of the research reported in this volume can be seen as the beginnings of an attempt to achieve that goal.

In order for the application of physiological measures to reach its full potential, it will be necessary to understand the relation of the response being monitored to the central neural structures which control it and to the behavior which brought the patient to the clinic. Several theories have been proposed which attempt to do this, but on the whole research in this area has not reached a point at which these proposals can be regarded as anything more than working hypotheses. A strengthening of these hypotheses is dependent in part on further research with clinical populations and in part on basic theoretical developments in the field of psychophysiology.

Several methodological problems are common to most studies in this area and require the investigator's attention if experimental results are to be meaningful. Some of these, such as finding adequate control groups when studying patients, are difficult to handle with complete satisfaction in a single experiment, but are not so serious when it can be demonstrated that the results obtained with different methodologies are in agreement. Others can be avoided by exerting maximum control over the stimulus conditions and the subject's activity so as to minimize physiological activity for reasons other than those of primary interest. Finally, the choice of the response(s) to be measured must be resolved primarily on a theoretical basis. That is, the choice must be determined by knowing how the activity of a particular physiological system is to be interpreted when measured under specific stimulus conditions. At present, there are some theories available which offer assistance in making this choice, but our understanding of the many factors affecting physiological responses has not kept pace with our ability to measure them.

The rapidly developing technology of psychophysiology has made possible the observation of hitherto invisible responses and has opened a vast new frontier of clinical research. The initial exploration of this frontier has already begun to pay dividends and further advances can be anticipated in the future. It is hoped that someday this research will lead to a much more complete understanding of the nature and causes of psychopathology and to more adequate means of prevention or treatment.

References

Bowers, K. S. 1973. Situationism in psychology: An analysis and a critique. *Psychological Review*, 80:307–336.

Davis, R. C., A. M. Buchwald, and R. W. Frankmann. 1955. Autonomic and muscular responses, and their relation to simple stimuli. *Psychological Monographs*, 69:(20, Whole No. 405).

Duffy, E. *Activation and Behavior.* 1962. New York: Wiley.

Edelberg, R. 1973. Mechanisms of electrodermal adaptations for locomotion, manipulation, or defense. *Progress in Physiological Psychology*, 5:155–209.

Fisher, L. E. and H. Kotses. 1974. Experimenter and subject sex effects in the skin conductance response. *Psychophysiology*, 11:191–196.

Fuller, J. L. and W. R. Thompson. 1960. *Behavior Genetics.* New York: Wiley.

Goodman, L. S. and A. Gilman. (eds.). 1965. *The Pharmacological Basis of Therapeutics.* 3d ed. New York: Macmillan.

Gottesman, I. I. and J. Shields. 1966. Schizophrenia in twins: 16 years' consecutive admissions to a psychiatric clinic. *British Journal of Psychiatry*, 112:809–818.

—— 1972. *Schizophrenia and Genetics: A Twin Study Vantage Point.* New York: Academic Press.

Hebb, D. O. 1955. Drive and the CNS (conceptual nervous system). *Psychological Review*, 62:243–254.

Heston, L. L. 1966. Psychiatric disorders in foster home reared children of schizophrenic mothers. *British Journal of Psychiatry*, 112:819–825.
—— 1970. The genetics of schizophrenic and schizoid disease. *Science*, 167:249–256.
Heston, L. L. and D. Denney. 1968. Interactions between early life experience and biological factors in schizophrenia. In D. Rosenthal and S. S. Kety (eds.), *The Transmission of Schizophrenia*. Oxford: Pergamon.
Hicks, R. G. 1969. Experimenter effects on the physiological experiment. Paper presented at the meeting of the Society for Psychophysiological Research, Monterey, California (October 1969).
Jackson, D. D. 1960. A critique of the literature on the genetics of schizophrenia. In D. D. Jackson (ed.), *The Etiology of Schizophrenia*. New York: Basic Books.
Karlsson, J. L. 1966. *The Biologic Basis of Schizophrenia*. Springfield, Ill.: Thomas.
Kety, S. S., D. Rosenthal, P. H. Wender, and F. Schulsinger. 1968. The types and prevalence of mental illness in the biological and adoptive families of adopted schizophrenics. In D. Rosenthal and S. S. Kety (eds.), *The Transmission of Schizophrenia*. Oxford: Pergamon.
Kotses, H., K. D. Glaus, and L. E. Fisher. 1973. Effects of subject recruitment procedure on heart rate and skin conductance measures. Paper presented at the meeting of the Society for Psychophysiological Research, Galveston, Texas (October 1973).
Lacey, J. I. 1967. Somatic response patterning and stress: Some revisions of activation theory. In M. H. Appley and R. Trumbull (eds.), *Psychological Stress: Issues in Research*. New York: Appleton-Century-Crofts.
Lader, M. 1972. The nature of anxiety. *British Journal of Psychiatry*, 121:481–491.
Lader, M. H. and L. Wing. 1966. *Physiological Measures, Sedative Drugs, and Morbid Anxiety*. London: Oxford University Press.
Lang, P. J. 1971. The application of psychophysiological methods to the study of psychotherapy and behavior modification. In A. E. Bergin and S. L. Garfield (eds.), *Handbook of Psychotherapy and Behavior Change*. New York: Wiley.
Lindsley, D. B. 1951. Emotion. In S. S. Stevens (ed.), *Handbook of Experimental Psychology*. New York: Wiley.
Lockard, R. B. 1971. Reflections on the fall of comparative psychology: Is there a message for us all? *American Psychologist*, 26:168–179.
Lykken, D. T. 1968. Neuropsychology and psychophysiology in personality research. In E. F. Borgatta and W. W. Lambert (eds.), *Handbook of Personality Theory and Research*. New York: Rand McNally.
McClearn, G. E. and J. C. DeFries. 1973. *Introduction to Behavioral Genetics*. San Francisco: Freeman.
McGhie, A. 1970. Attention and perception in schizophrenia. In B. A. Maher (ed.), *Progress in Experimental Personality Research*, Vol. 5. New York: Academic Press.
Malmo, R. B. Anxiety and behavioral arousal. *Psychological Review*, 64:276–287.

—— 1958. Measurement of drive. In M. R. Jones (ed.), *Nebraska Symposium on Motivation*. Lincoln: University of Nebraska Press.

—— 1966. Studies of anxiety: Some clinical origins of the activation concept. In C. D. Spielberger (ed.), *Anxiety and Behavior*. New York: Academic Press.

Mandler, G., J. M. Mandler, I. Kremen, and R. D. Sholitan. 1961. The response to threat: Relations among verbal and physiological indices. *Psychological Monographs*, 75:(9, Whole No. 513).

Manosevitz, M., G. Lindzey, and D. D. Thiessen. (eds.) 1969. *Behavioral Genetics: Method and Research*. New York: Appleton-Century-Crofts.

Martin, B. 1961. The assessment of anxiety by physiological-behavioral measures. *Psychological Bulletin*, 58:234–255.

Martin, B. and L. A. Sroufe. 1970. Anxiety. In C. G. Costello (ed.), *Symptoms of Psychopathology: A Handbook*. New York: Wiley.

Mednick, S. A. 1967. The children of schizophrenics: Serious difficulties in current research methodologies which suggest the use of the "high-risk group" method. In J. Romano (ed.), *The Origins of Schizophrenia*. New York: Excerpta Medica Foundation.

Mednick, S. A. and T. F. McNeil. 1968. Current methodology in research on the etiology of schizophrenia. *Psychological Bulletin*, 70:681–693.

Mednick, S. A. and F. Schulsinger. 1968. Some premorbid characteristics related to breakdown in children with schizophrenic mothers. In D. Rosenthal and S. S. Kety (eds.), *The Transmission of Schizophrenia*. Oxford: Pergamon.

Meehl, P. E. 1962. Schizotaxia, schizotypy, schizophrenia. *American Psychologist*, 17:827–838.

Miner, G. D. 1973. The evidence for genetic components in the neuroses. *Archives of General Psychiatry*, 29:111–118.

Mischel, W. 1968. *Personality and Assessment*. New York: Wiley.

—— 1969. Continuity and change in personality. *American Psychologist*, 24, 1012–1018.

—— 1971. *Introduction to Personality*. New York: Holt, Rinehart and Winston.

Mowrer, O. H. 1947. On the dual nature of learning—a reinterpretation of "conditioning" and "problem-solving." *Harvard Educational Review*, 17:102–148.

Obrist, P. A., R. A. Webb, J. R. Sutterer, and J. L. Howard. 1970. The cardiac-somatic relationship: Some reformulations. *Psychophysiology*, 6:569–587.

Oken, D. 1967. The psychophysiology and psychoendocrinology of stress and emotion. In M. H. Appley and R. Trumbull (eds.), *Psychological Stress: Issues in Research*. New York: Appleton-Century-Crofts.

Opton, E. M., Jr. and R. S. Lazarus. 1967. Personality determinants of psychophysiological response to stress: A theoretical analysis and an experiment. *Journal of Personality and Social Psychology*, 6:291–303.

Rosenthal, D. *Genetic Theory and Abnormal Behavior*. New York: McGraw-Hill.

Rosenthal, D., P. H. Wender, S. S. Kety, F. Schulsinger, J. Welner, and L. Ostergaard. 1968. Schizophrenics' offspring reared in adoptive homes. In D. Rosenthal and S. S. Kety (eds.), *The Transmission of Schizophrenia*. Oxford: Pergamon.

Salzinger, K. 1973. *Schizophrenia: Behavioral Aspects*. New York: Wiley.

Sternbach, R. A. 1966. *Principles of Psychophysiology.* New York: Academic Press.

Tecce, J. J. and J. O. Cole. 1972. Psychophysiologic responses of schizophrenics to drugs. *Psychopharmacologia* (Berl.), 24:159–200.

Wender, P. H., D. Rosenthal, and S. S. Kety. 1968. A psychiatric assessment of the adoptive parents of schizophrenics. In D. Rosenthal and S. S. Kety (eds.), *The Transmission of Schizophrenia.* Oxford: Pergamon.

Wiggins, J. S., K. E. Renner, G. L. Clore, and R. J. Rose. 1971. *The Psychology of Personality.* Reading, Mass.: Addison-Wesley.

Zahn, T. P. 1964. Autonomic reactivity and behavior in schizophrenia. *Psychiatric Research Reports,* 19:156–173.

Author Index

Ackerman, P. T., 135
Ackner, B., 21, 23, 37
Agnew, H. W., 32, 38, 47, 48, 54, 73
Albee, G. W., 108, 136
Alexander, A. A., 38
Altschule, M. D., 23, 37
American Psychiatric Association, 78, 103
Andersen, P., 159, 165
Andersson, S. A., 159, 165
Arieti, S., 81, 82, 103
Aserinsky, E., 43, 73

Bagg, C. E., 31, 37
Bagshaw, M. H., 114, 134
Barber, T. X., 169, 190
Bardsley, R., 141, 166
Basowitz, H., 40
Beard, A. W., 108, 137
Beck, A. T., 54, 60, 73
Ben-Horin, P., 75
Bensch, G., 74
Benson, H., 169, 190
Benzies, S., 114, 134
Berger, H., 42, 139, 165
Berger, R. J., 5, 10, 40, 47, 54, 55, 73, 75
Berger, S. M., 89, 103
Bergsman, A., 33, 37
Bernstein, A. S., 115, 117, 134
Bever, J., 93, 99, 105
Bilodeau, E. A., 173, 181, 190
Bilodeau, I. M., 173, 181, 190
Blackburn, R., 96, 103
Blackwell, B., 30, 31, 40

Blackwood, W., 108, 134
Blanchard, E. B., 171, 173, 190
Board, F. A., 32, 37, 40
Boddy, J., 140, 165
Bond, A. J., 27, 37
Bostock, H., 28, 37
Bowers, K. S., 200, 221
Brazier, Mary A. B., 23, 38
Brener, J., 171, 190
Broadbent, D. E., 109, 134
Broen, W. E. Jr., 101, 103
Brooksbank, B. W. L., 38
Brotsky, S., 86, 99, 103
Brown, C. C., 1, 10
Buchwald, A. M., 221
Bunney, W. E., 32, 38, 64, 73
Busfield, B. L., 31, 38
Buss, A. H., 5, 10

Cargill, W. H., 39
Carlson, V. R., 46, 73
Carroll, B. J., 33, 38, 72, 73
Chapman, J. S., 109, 110, 125, 136
Chernik, D. A., 7, 48, 59, 60, 68, 71, 73, 74, 75, 202, 206, 211
Christie, M. J., 116, 138
Cleckley, H., 78, 80, 103
Cleghorn, J. M., 74
Clifton, R. K., 92, 93, 99, 103, 113, 135
Clore, G. L., 224
Cobb, S., 23, 38
Cochrane, C., 55, 60, 74, 75
Cohen, H., 14, 38
Cohen, H. B., 54, 73

Cohen, M. J., 99, 103
Cohen, S. I., 41
Cohn, A. E., 23, 40
Cole, J. O., 210, 224
Conners, C. K., 140, 166
Cooper, J. E., 12, 38, 116, 134
Copeland, J. R. M., 38
Coppen, A., 33, 38, 72, 73
Corbalan, R., 170, 191
Costa, L. D., 123, 137
Craigen, D., 82, 87, 89, 90, 92, 102, 104
Craik, K. W. J., 140, 165
Cromwell, R. L., 107, 110, 134
Crookes, T. G., 31, 37

Dahlstrom, W. G., 82, 103
Davert, E. C., 166
Davies, B., 33, 38
Davies, B. M., 30, 31, 38, 40, 73
Davis, J. F., 22, 39
Davis, R. C., 215, 221
Deane, G. E., 21, 38
DeFries, J. C., 222
Dement, W. C., 44, 51, 54, 59, 73
Denney, D., 193, 222
Depue, R. A., 5, 10
Deutsch, D., 109, 134
Deutsch, J. A., 109, 134
Diaz-Guerrero, R., 48, 73
DiCara, L. V., 190
Dim, B., 32, 41
Dodson, W. E., 32, 41, 48, 55
Douglas, R. J., 109, 110, 114, 134, 135
Dronsejko, K., 93, 103
Duffy, E., 216, 221
Duker, J., 96, 103
Dykman, R. A., 115, 135

Edelberg, R., 97, 103, 104, 219, 221
Ellis, R. M., 31, 41, 72, 76
Engel, B. T., 170, 174, 190, 191
Epstein, S., 113, 133, 135
Erbaugh, J. K., 73
Ericksen, C. W., 168, 190

Falconer, D. S., 161, 165
Farkas, T., 134
Feinberg, I., 46, 73

Fenton, G. W., 149, 166
Fenz, W., 82, 103
Finesinger, J. E., 23, 38
Finkelstein, J., 72, 75
Fisher, L. E., 214, 221, 222
Fitts, P. M., 173, 190
Fitzgerald, R. G., 74
Flor-Henry, P., 108, 135
Floris, V., 32, 41
Fowles, D. C., 5, 10
Frankmann, R. W., 221
Frazer, A., 74
Freides, R., 108, 135
Friedman, H., 141, 166
Fujimori, B., 114, 138
Fuller, J. L., 199, 221
Furneaux, W. D., 141, 165

Galbrecht, C. R., 135
Gale, E., 86, 103
Gantt, W. Horsley, 103
Gastaut, H., 141, 165
Gatchel, R., 177, 178, 180, 189, 190
Geffen, G., 109, 137
Gibbons, J. L., 32, 38
Gilberstadt, H., 96, 103
Gildea, E. F., 23, 41
Gilman, A., 210, 221
Glaus, K. D., 214, 222
Goddard, G. V., 114, 115, 122, 135
Golden, A., 21, 39
Goldstein, I. B., 22, 31, 38
Golla, F., 141, 165
Goodman, L. S., 210, 221
Goodwin, F. K., 73
Gorsuch, R. L., 15, 41
Gottesman, I. I., 193, 194, 197, 221
Gottlieb, G., 31, 38
Gottlieb, J. S., 73
Graham, F., 92, 93, 99, 103, 113, 135
Granda, A. M., 45, 73
Green, W. J., 48, 54, 73, 75
Greenfield, N. S., 1, 10, 31, 38
Gresham, S. C., 32, 38, 48, 54, 62, 73
Grinker, R. R., 40
Groves, P. M., 117, 135
Gruzelier, J. H., 116, 123, 124, 126, 131, 135, 142, 165

Gullickson, G. R., 1, 10
Gurland, B. J., 38, 134
Gurland, J. B., 30, 38

Hamburg, D. A., 32, 37, 38, 40
Hammack, J. T., 45, 73
Hansen, S. P., 174, 190
Hare, R. D., 8, 77, 80–82, 84–93, 96, 99, 101–4, 202, 205, 209, 212, 215, 218
Harrington, A., 79, 104
Hart, J., 189, 191
Harter, M. R., 140, 165
Hartmann, E., 47, 71, 74
Harvey, E. N., 42, 74
Haruei, P., 64, 74
Hastings, J. E., 173, 191
Hawkins, D. R., 31, 32, 39, 40, 48, 51–56, 58, 64, 68, 71, 74, 75
Heath, H. A., 40
Heath, R. G., 109, 135
Hebb, D. O., 216, 221
Hellman, L., 72, 75
Hemsi, I. K., 31, 39
Hertz, M., 40
Herz, M. J., 1, 11
Heston, L. L., 193, 197, 222
Hickam, J. B., 21, 39
Hicks, R. G., 213, 222
Hilgard, E. R., 163, 166
Hinsie, L. E., 30, 41
Hinton, J. M., 31, 39
Hnatiow, M., 173, 190
Hobart, G. A., 42, 74
Homskaya, E. D., 130, 136
Howard, J. L., 136, 191, 223
Huhmar, E., 31, 40
Hunt, W. A., 21, 39
Hutton, E. L., 141, 165

Jackson, D. D., 193, 222
Jacobson, A., 45, 74
Jacobson, E., 169, 190
James, W., 168, 190
Jaramillo, R. A., 40, 75
Jarvis, M. J., 28, 37
Jasper, H. H., 113, 135
Johnson, H. J., 99, 103
Jouvet, M., 47, 74

Kales, A., 5, 10, 44, 50, 59, 75
Kamiya, J., 140, 165, 190
Karlsson, J. L., 193, 222
Karpman, B., 81, 82, 96, 104
Katz, D., 38
Katzenmeyer, G., 82, 104
Keddie, K. M. G., 40, 75
Kelly, D. H. W., 23, 39
Kendell, R. E., 38, 134
Kety, S. S., 193, 222, 223, 224
Kimble, D. P., 109, 114, 115, 122, 134, 135
Kimble, G. A., 188, 190
Kirschner, N., 41
Klein, D. F., 108, 137
Kleitman, N., 43, 44, 51, 59, 73
Knott, J. R., 73, 141, 166
Koepke, J. E., 114, 135
Korchin, S. J., 40
Kornetsky, C., 109, 133, 136
Kotses, H., 93, 99, 105, 214, 221, 222
Kremen, I., 223
Kristofferson, A. B., 140, 166

Lacey, J. I., 92, 93, 104, 113, 125, 136, 218, 222
Lader, M. H., 4–7, 10, 20–23, 25, 27, 30, 33–37, 39, 40, 201, 204–6, 209, 210, 214, 222
Landis, C., 21, 39
Lane, E., 108, 136
Lang, H., 114, 136
Lang, P. J., 5, 9, 10, 168, 173, 174, 176, 178, 180, 181, 189, 190, 191, 201, 203, 207, 214, 215, 222
Lange, C. G., 168, 191
Langfeldt, G., 107, 136
Lansing, R. W., 140, 166
Latane, B., 84, 105
Lawlor, W. G., 115, 138
Lazarus, R. S., 217, 223
Levander, S., 89, 105
Levitt, E. E., 15, 39
Lewis, S. A., 49, 62, 74
Lhamon, W. T., 23, 40
Lindsley, D. B., 23, 39, 123, 137, 216, 222
Lindzey, G., 199, 223

Lippert, W. W., 89, 104
Lisina, M. I., 171, 172, 173, 191
Lockard, R. B., 199, 222
Loomis, A. L., 43, 74
Lown, B., 169, 170, 191
Lowy, F. H., 48, 55, 74
Luria, A. R., 130, 136
Lushene, R. E., 15, 41
Luthe, W., 169, 191
Lykken, D. T., 3, 4, 9, 11, 80, 82, 84, 85, 88, 89, 93, 96, 104, 116, 136, 159, 165, 166, 200, 201, 209, 210, 212, 218, 222
Lynn, R., 115, 136

McCallum, W. C., 24, 39
McClearn, G. E., 199, 222
McClure, D. J., 74
McDonald, D. G., 133, 137
McGhie, A., 109, 110, 125, 136, 203, 222
MacLean, P. D., 108, 111, 136
McMenemey, W. H., 134
McNeil, T. F., 210, 223
Mailer, N., 79, 104
Malamud, M., 109, 136
Malmo, R. B., 5, 11, 22, 30, 39, 205, 216, 222
Malmstrom, E. J., 10
Mandell, A. J., 45, 74
Mandell, M. P., 45, 74
Mandler, G., 217, 223
Mandler, J. M., 223
Manosevitz, M., 199, 223
Marks, I., 21, 39
Martin, B., 21, 40, 218, 223
Martin, F. I. R., 33, 38, 73
Martin, I., 1, 11, 31, 40
Mason, J. W., 32, 38
Mathews, A., 27, 39
Mechanic, D., 13, 40
Medawar, P. B., 17, 40
Mednick, S. A., 108, 115, 136, 198, 202, 210, 212, 223
Meehl, P. E., 193, 194, 196, 197, 223
Melamed, B. G., 189, 191
Melges, F. T., 110, 137
Mendels, J., 7, 31, 32, 39, 40, 48, 51–55, 58, 60, 68, 71, 72, 73, 74, 75, 202, 206, 209, 210, 211, 214

Mendelson, M., 73
Mercer, M., 32, 41
Metz, J. T., 59, 75
Meyer, A., 134
Michel, F., 59, 75
Miller, N. E., 170, 171, 190, 191
Miner, G. D., 194, 223
Mischel, W., 199, 200, 223
Mock, J., 73
Molinari, S., 75
Mordkoff, A. M., 97, 104
Morgan, A. H., 163, 166
Morocutti, C., 32, 41
Mowrer, O. H., 84, 104, 168, 191, 205, 223
Munday-Castle, A. C., 141, 166
Murphy, D. L., 64, 73
Myers, G. M., 75

Nelson, G. K., 141, 166
Neumann, C., 23, 40
Noble, P. J., 34, 35, 40
Noguera, R., 38, 73
Norman, R. M., 134
Nowlin, J. B., 186, 191

Obrist, P. A., 86, 93, 104, 125, 136, 181, 191, 219, 223
Oken, D., 213, 223
Olley, P. C., 40, 75
O'Malley, J. E., 140, 166
Opton, E. M., Jr., 217, 223
Orzack, M. H., 109, 133, 136
Ostergaard, L., 223
Oswald, I., 5, 11, 31, 40, 48, 49, 54, 55, 62, 73, 74, 75

Palmai, G., 30, 31, 38, 40
Parkes, C. M., 15, 40
Parsons, L. B., 82, 105
Patterson, M. M., 1, 11
Paulson, G., 31, 38
Pavlov, I. P., 112, 136
Peck, C. K., 123, 137
Peck, R. E., 30, 31, 40
Peeke, H. V. S., 1, 11
Perez-Reyes, M., 93, 104
Perlmuter, L. C., 188, 190

Persky, H., 24, 32, 37, 40
Plunkett, H. G. B., 40, 75
Pollack, M., 108, 137
Pollin, W., 107, 137
Posner, M. I., 173, 190
Post, F., 31, 39
Prange, A. J., Jr., 73
Pribram, K. H., 109, 110, 114, 122, 123,
    134, 135, 137
Prokasy, W. F., 1, 11

Quay, H. C., 82, 105
Quinn, M., 80, 81, 84, 86–89, 90, 91,
    101, 104

Ramsey, T. A., 74
Raskin, D., 1, 11, 93, 99, 105
Rechtschaffen, A., 44, 50, 59, 75
Reese, W. G., 135
Renner, K. E., 224
Richter, C. P., 31, 40
Rimón, R., 31, 40
Roessler, R., 38
Rose, R. J., 222, 224
Rosen, A., 84, 105
Rosenthal, D., 115, 138, 193, 194, 197,
    223, 224
Rothblat, L., 109, 137
Rotter, J., 189
Rubin, R. T., 10
Russell, D. S., 134
Russell, I. S., 113, 137

Sabshin, S., 40
Sachar, E. J., 72, 75
Salzinger, K., 203, 223
Sartorius, G., 29, 39
Sartorius, N., 134
Sato, A., 114, 138
Scadding, J. G., 12, 41
Schachter, S., 84, 105
Schachter, S., 168, 191
Schalling, D., 84, 89, 105
Scharf, M. B., 10
Schlosberg, H., 1, 11
Schmauk, F. J., 84, 105
Schoenherr, J. C., 84, 105

Schulsinger, F., 108, 115, 136, 198, 212,
    222, 223
Schultze, J. H., 169, 191
Schwartz, G., 171, 191
Scott, J., 74
Senter, R. J., 89, 104
Shagass, C., 5, 11, 22, 32, 39, 41, 141,
    166
Shakow, D., 19, 20, 41
Shapiro, D., 171, 190, 191
Sharpe, L., 38
Shields, J., 193, 194, 197, 221
Shmavonian, B. M., 41
Sholitan, R. D., 223
Silverman, A. J., 24, 41
Silverman, J., 107, 109, 125, 133, 137
Simon, R., 38
Slater, E., 108, 137, 149, 166
Slatter, K. H., 142, 166
Smith, A. A., 5, 11
Smythies, J. R., 111, 137
Snyder, F., 45, 48, 55, 62, 64, 75
Sokolov, E. N., 93, 99, 105, 114, 115,
    137
Sourek, K., 130, 137
Speck, L. B., 32, 41
Spector, R. G., 108, 137
Spielberger, C. D., 15, 41
Spinelli, D. N., 123, 137
Sroufe, L. A., 21, 40, 173, 191, 218, 223
Stabenau, J. R., 107, 137
Stajduhar, P. P., 48, 54, 73
Stenbäck, A., 31, 40
Stern, J. A., 4, 11, 86, 103, 133, 137
Sternbach, R. A., 1, 3, 4, 6, 10, 11, 216,
    224
Stokes, J. W., 74
Stoyva, J., 169, 190
Strongin, E. I., 30, 41
Sunderman, R. S., 135
Surwillo, W. W., 140, 166
Sutterer, J. R., 136, 191, 223
Szasz, T. S., 12, 41

Taylor, F. K., 14, 41
Teachey, W., 74
Tecce, J. J., 210, 224
Tellegen, A., 82, 104

Thiessen, D. D., 199, 223
Thompson, L. W., 186, 191
Thompson, R. F., 1, 11, 117, 135
Thompson, W. R., 199, 221
Thorkelson, K. E., 142, 149, 166
Tizard, J., 106, 137
Traub, A. C., 75
Treisman, A., 109, 137
Tuovinen, T., 114, 136
Tursky, B., 171, 191
Twentyman, C. T., 174, 180, 181, 191

Ustick, M., 97, 104

Valleala, P., 114, 136
Van de Castle, R. L., 58, 75
Vasconetto, C., 32, 41
Vaughan, H. G., 123, 137
Vaughan, T., 48, 75
Veldman, D., 95, 105
Venables, P. H., 1, 8, 9, 11, 101, 105–7,
    109, 112, 116, 123, 124, 131, 135–38,
    142, 165, 202, 206, 209, 210, 211, 218
Verrier, R., 170, 191
Vogel, F., 155, 166
Vogel, G. W., 48, 62, 75

Wallace, R. K., 169, 190
Walter, C. J. S., 39
Walter, R. D., 142, 166
Walter, W. G., 23, 24, 39, 141, 165
Ward, C. H., 73
Watson, R., 59, 75
Webb, R. A., 136, 191, 223
Webb, W., 73
Wechsler, H., 31, 38

Weinstein, N., 55, 75
Weiss, J. M., 170, 191
Welner, J., 223
Welsh, G. S., 82, 103
Wender, P. H., 222, 223, 224
Wenger, M. A., 23, 41
Whatmore, G. B., 31, 41, 72, 76
White, B. V., 23, 41
Whitehead, A., 31, 39
Whybrow, P. C., 72, 73
Wiggins, J. S., 194, 200, 224
Wilkinson, R. T., 28, 41
Williams, R., 32, 38, 47, 48, 54, 62, 73
Wilson, D. A., 38
Wilson, W. P., 32, 41, 45, 48, 55
Wincor, M. Z., 75
Wing, L., 20, 22, 23, 25, 30, 33, 39, 204,
    222
Wishner, J., 23, 41
Woerner, M. G., 108, 137
Wolf, M., 169, 191
Wolpe, J., 168, 191
Wood, D. M., 93, 104
Woodworth, R. S., 1, 11
World Health Organization, 78, 105
Wright, D. J., 97, 103
Wyatt, R. J., 75

Yeager, C. L., 142, 166
Yokota, T., 114, 138
Young, J. P. R., 149, 166
Young, L. B., 171, 173, 190

Zahn, T. P., 115, 117, 122, 138, 217, 224
Zung, W. W. K., 32, 41, 45, 48, 55

Subject Index

Activation, *see* Arousal
Activity Preference Questionnaire (APQ), 82, 83, 162
Adaptation, *see* Laboratory, adaptation to
Adoption studies, of schizophrenia, 193
Adrenal cortex, 32, 213
Adrenaline, 24
Adrenal medulla, 24, 33
Affective psychoses, genetic factors, 194; *see also* Depression
Afferentation, additional, 172–74, 181
Aggression, in responders and nonresponders, 122, 123
Amygdala, 8, 110, 111, 114, 115, 122, 123, 202, 206
Anger, 4, 22, 24, 217, 218
Angina pectoris, 182
Anoxia, 108, 111
Antisocial behavior: neurotic, 83; psychopathic, 83; subcultural, 83
Anxiety, 3, 6–9, 15–17, 20–30, 32–35, 37, 84, 123, 168, 169, 188, 195, 201, 204, 206, 209, 212; anxiety-proneness, 16; anxiety-provoking environment, 195; genetic factors, 194; neurosis, *see* Neurosis, anxiety states; pathological trait, 15; phobia, *see* Phobia; reactivity, 82, 163, 165, 201; state, 163; trait, 163, 201
Anxiety Inventory, Epstein and Fenz, 189
Arousal (activation), 1, 5, 7, 8, 22, 26, 30, 43, 46, 92, 93, 113, 117, 168, 186–88, 204, 205, 213, 216, 217; cortical, 93; tonic level of, 117
Attention, 112, 113, 140, 142; *see also* Schizophrenia, disturbances of attention
Autogenic training, 169
Autonomic Arousal Scale, 189
Autonomic athletes, 186, 201, 207
Autonomic nervous system, 107, 113, 168, 181, 199, 207
Averaged evoked response, 27, 28, 36, 123, 139

Barbiturates, *see* Drugs, hypnotics
Behavior: adaptive, 199; divided into verbal-cognitive, overt-motor, and physiological components, 203; genetic influences on, 199, 200; language control of, 168
Behavior Problem Checklist, 82, 83
Biochemical abnormality, 8, 196, 199, 207
Biofeedback, 2, 3, 9, 140, 169, 170, 174, 188; analogue vs. binary, and heart-rate control, 174, 176–78, 180, 181
Biological clocks, 140
Blood flow: forearm, 6, 23, 34, 35; muscle, 23; skin, 23
Blood pressure, 21, 23, 123, 171, 219; effect of chlorpromazine on, 210

Cardiac activity, *see* Heart rate
Cardiac output, 21

Cardiac-somatic coupling, 125, 181, 219
Cardiovascular system, 5, 8, 22, 86, 91, 167, 170; *see also* Heart rate; Vasomotor activity
Card-sorting task, 36
Catecholamines, 24, 33, 206
Central intermittancy, theory of, 140
Central nervous system, 112, 195, 204, 205
Cerebellum, 108
Chlorpromazine, 210, 211
Choice of symptom, 195
Classical conditioning, *see* Conditioning and learning
Clinical improvement or recovery, changes associated with, 7, 31, 32, 34, 54, 56, 64, 72
Cognitive deficits, 168, 169
Cognitive processing, 140-42
Computer, used to control experiment, 174, 214
Conditioning and learning, 83-94; avoidance learning, 84, 94, 168, 205; conditioned anticipatory responses, 85, 89-94, 97; conditioned emotional response (CER), 8, 205; differential conditioning, 84-86; discrimination conditioning, 88-90; instrumental conditioning of visceral responses, 170, 171, 173, 174, 207; mediation of visceral conditioning, 172, 173; Mowrer's two-factor theory, 8, 84, 205; social learning, 8, 84, 196, 203, 205; temporal conditioning and signal value of stimulus, 122; vicarious conditioning, 91; visceral conditioning, 168, 170, 171
Contingent negative variation (CNV), 23, 24
Continuous performance test, 133
Control groups, 8, 17-20, 22, 60, 81, 101, 116, 177, 178, 183, 208, 210-13, 220; confounding variables, 210-13
Cooperation, subjects' lack of, 112
Correlation, intraclass, 149, 160
Cortex: cortical arousal, 93; cortical recovery cycle, 32; cortical scanning,
140; inferotemporal, 114; visual, 140
Corticosteriods, 32
Corticotrophin, 32, 33
Cortisol, 24, 32, 33
Cosine spectra, in analysis of EEG, 146
Curare, 170

Defenses, psychological, 32
Defensive response, 93, 99, 100, 114, 124, 218
Depersonalization, 111
Depression, 6, 7, 15, 16, 24, 25, 30-37, 47-72, 124, 129, 131, 132, 195, 202, 203, 205-7, 209-11; age and, 209; associated with strokes, 109; associated with temporal lobe epilepsy, 109, 126; electroconvulsive therapy (ECT), 34, 35, 54, 56-58, 210; Hamilton Depressive Scale, 35; heterogeneity of, 48, 71; pathological state, 14; severity of, 54, 55, 60, 72, 206; symptoms of, 47, 60
Depression, subtypes: agitated vs. retarded, 7, 25, 26, 33-37, 71, 206, 209; endogenous vs. reactive, 7, 16, 35, 60, 209; neurotic vs. psychotic, 54-56, 72, 209; primary, 33; unipolar vs. bipolar, 60, 63
Depression Inventory (Beck), 54, 55, 60
Desensitization, systematic, 168, 169
Dexamethasone, 72
Diabetes, 197
Diathesis, psychiatric, 139, 194, 196-98, 201-3, 207, 212, 213
Diathesis-stress, 9, 193-203
Digit symbol substitution test, 36
Disease, definition of, 12-16; *see also* Heart disease
Distractibility, 23, 24
Dreams, 2, 7, 44
Drugs: alcohol, 5; anti-arrhythmic, 170; chlorpromazine, 210, 211; effect on physiological measures, 18, 19, 49, 54, 62, 63; hypnotics, 5, 36, 37, 210; phenothiazines, 120; *see also* Medication; Patients, without medication

Ego control, 162
Ego resiliency, 162
Electric shock, *see* Stimulation, electric shock
Electroconvulsive therapy, 34, 35, 54, 56–58, 210
Electrodermal activity, 1, 6–9, 19–22, 24–29, 31, 33–35, 84–91, 94, 95, 97, 102, 113–33, 168, 202, 205, 206, 209–11, 216, 218, 219; chlorpromazine and, 210; contralateral vs. ipsilateral innervation, 129–31; laterality differences, 126–32, 211; methodology, 116, 117
Electrodes, implanted, 109, 112, 170
Electroencephalogram (EEG), 5, 6, 9, 23, 26–28, 31, 32, 36, 42–72, 139–65, 200, 201, 209, 210, 212, 213, 219; alpha and theta states, 3; genetic influences, 149–65; hypnotics and, 210; influence of the thalamus on, 159
Electroencephalogram (EEG) spectra, 141, 144, 149–65, 218; alpha frequency, 154; alpha percent, 154; factor analysis, 9, 159, 160; method of spectral analysis, 144–48; methods of quantifying similarity in twins, 156, 157, 159; reliability, 141, 163, 164; standardization, 151–54, 218
Electromyogram (EMG), 6, 21, 22, 31, 34, 35, 45, 50, 59, 206
Electro-oculogram, 6
Emotion, 3, 111, 168, 169, 172, 189, 218; emotional arousal, 92, 93; emotional behavior, 168; emotional disorders/disturbance, 4, 188; emotional expression, 168; emotional states, 201; emotional traits, 201; theories of, 168
Empathy, lack of, 212
Endophenotype, 197, 198, 200, 203
Environmental press, 163
Epidemiology, 169, 170
Epilepsy, temporal lobe, 108, 109, 126
Etiology, 8, 9, 198; contributions of personality to, 212; environmental contributions to, 193, 195, 198; genetic contributions to, 193–99, 220; psychogenic vs. organic dichotomy, 193
Evoked response, *see* Averaged evoked response
Evolution, 199
Excitability cycles, 140
Excitation, 111, 119, 122
Experimental environment: controlled by computer, 174, 214; habituation to, 187; as stimulus, 211, 213, 214
Experimental psychology, 126
Exteroceptive feedback, 171

Fear, 4, 8, 22, 84, 85, 168, 169, 217, 218; anticipatory, 84, 85, 91; conditioned, 84, 201; temporal gradient of, 84
Field dependence, 162, 165
Figure-ground, 110
Forearm blood flow, 6, 23, 34, 35
Fornix, 114
Fourier's Theorem, 144, 145
Frontal lobes, 131

Gastrointestinal symptoms, 35
Gating, 109–11, 125, 140
Genetics: genetic diversity, 199; genetic influences in schizophrenia, *see* Schizophrenia, genetic influences; genetic risk, 198; genetic variation, 200; genetic vulnerability in physical illness, 194; psychiatric, 193, 220
Gerontological physiology, 186
Growth hormone, 72
GSR (galvanic skin response), *see* Electrodermal activity

Halo effects, 212
Hamilton Depressive Scale, 35
Heart disease, 10, 169, 170, 182–84, 186
Heart rate, 6, 10, 21–23, 29, 34, 43, 85–88, 91–99, 102, 113, 123–25, 150, 160, 167–90, 205, 210, 216, 218, 219; chlorpromazine and, 210; information processing and, 187, 188; response to psychological stimuli in animals, 170, 171

Heart-rate control, 167–90, 207; age and, 184, 185; binary vs. analogue feedback and, 174, 176–78, 180, 181; frequency of feedback and, 178–81; heart rate variability and, 186; incentives and, 187; individual differences in, 186; instrumental conditioning in, 207; method of recording heart rate and providing feedback, 173–76; in patients with heart disease, 182–86; as skill, 181, 185, 188, 189, 207; speeding vs. slowing, 176–89; state of methodology, 170, 171; voluntary, 167, 173; *see also* Instructional control

Heritability, 9, 162, 200

High risk method, 198, 199, 212, 213

Hippocampus, 8, 108–11, 114, 122, 123, 202, 206

Homeostasis, 182

Hormonal function, 24

5-hydroxyindoleacetic acid, 72

Hyperponesis, 72

Hypertension, 10, 219

Hypnosis, 150

Hypnotics, *see* Drugs, hypnotics

Hypnotic susceptibility, 142, 163

Hypothalamus, 33, 170

Hysteria, 25–26

Illness: deviation model of, 14, 15, 30; medical or process model of, 14; *see also* Heart disease

Imagery: auditory, 141, 142; kinesthetic, 141, 142; visual, 141, 142

Impulsivity, 123, 188, 212

Individual differences, biological, 193, 195, 199, 200, 203, 207, 220

Inhibition, 111, 119, 122, 133, 187, 188, 199; reciprocal, 187

Insomnia, 2

Instructional control, 167–70, 172, 173, 181, 185, 186, 188–90

Instrumental conditioning, *see* Conditioning and learning

Intake-rejection, Lacey's theory of, 113, 114, 125, 218, 219

Intelligence (IQ), 141, 162, 165

Internal-external orientation, 188, 189

Interoceptive stimuli, 172

Intervention, preventive, 8, 68, 198

Intestinal motility, 168

Introversion/extraversion, 161, 162, 165

Ipsative measures, 217, 218

Kluver-Bucy syndrome, 114

Laboratory, adaptation to, 18, 48, 49, 52, 55, 63, 214

Law of initial value, 120, 187

Learning, *see* Conditioning and learning

Libido, 35

Lie detection, 3

Limbic system, 8, 107–12, 114, 115, 119, 202, 206, 218

Lithium carbonate, 64, 68, 69

Longitudinal studies, 6, 7, 50, 55–68, 211

Mania, 33, 60, 67, 68, 70, 71; symptoms of, 60

Manifest anxiety, 188

Medial forebrain bundle, 170

Medication, 2, 170, 210–12; *see also* Drugs; Patients, without medication

Meditation, 169, 188

Memory, 114

Menstrual cycle, 122

Methodology: electrodermal activity, 116, 117; heart-rate control, 173–76; importance of, 1, 112; problems and issues, 10, 192, 193, 208–20

MMPI, 31, 60, 82, 83, 94–96, 101, 102, 208, 209; hierarchical grouping analysis of, 95, 102

Mood, 111

Motor response/activity, 5, 113, 133, 167, 181, 184, 185, 214

Motor skills, 171, 173, 174, 207

Muscle relaxation, 172

Myocardial infarction, 169, 182

Neural abnormality, 196

Neurology, 126, 131

Neurophysiology, 5
Neurosis, 13, 14, 22, 23; anxiety states, 7, 22–30, 194, 195, 204, 205, 209
Neuroticism, 162, 165
Nitrazepam, *see* Drugs, hypnotics
Noradrenaline, 24
Nufferno Tests, 141

Occipital lobes, 131
Organic brain pathology, 8, 107, 108, 112, 116, 130, 131
Orienting response, 99, 100, 112–15, 117–34, 172, 204, 206, 215, 218; amplitude of initial response, 118; asymptotic value, 117, 118, 128; electrodermal, 85, 90, 97, 99, 113–28, 130–33; heart rate, 92, 97, 99; instructions and, 120, 131; interstimulus interval and, 122, 124; laterality differences, 127–32; menstrual cycle and, 122; neural model, 114, 115; nonresponders among normal subjects, 121, 122; signal value of stimulus and, 120–22, 131, 132; vasomotor, 99
Overarousal, 204, 205; caused by poor habituation, 204; caused by slow recovery following stress, 204, 205

Pain, 21, 89, 90, 169; *see also* Stimulation, painful; Stimulation, electric shock
Parasympathetic nervous system, 93, 188
Parietal lobes, 131
Patients: changes associated with clinical improvement or recovery, 31, 64–68, 72, 125, 202, 203, 211; grouped according to research data, 106, 107, 122, 209; heterogeneity of, 209; relapse, 8, 66–68, 72, 212; relapse, prediction of, 66–68; selected by clinical judgment, 208, 209; selected by MMPI, 208, 209; without medication, 19, 49, 58, 62–65, 70, 71
Perceptual distortions, 111
Performance deficit, 168, 169

Peripheral resistance, 21
Personality: criticisms of trait approach, 199; dimensions of, 212; implications of diathesis-stress model for, 199, 200, 203; state-trait distinction, 15, 18; traits, 188, 189, 199, 200, 202, 203
Personality disorders, 124, 131, 132
Phenothiazines, 120
Phenotype, 197
Phobia, 7, 25, 169, 189, 209
Physical activity, effect on physiological measures, 215
Physiological psychology, 3, 4, 126
Placebo, 188
Premature ventricular beats (systoles), 169, 170
Premorbid personality, 199
Premorbid state, compared with morbid state, 202
Progressive relaxation therapy, 169
Prophylaxis, 8, 68, 198
Psychiatry, 5
Psychomotor activity, *see* Motor response/activity
Psychopathy, 6, 8, 77–105, 201, 202, 205, 209, 212, 213; Cleckley's criteria used in selection of subjects, 79–81, 94, 95, 101, 209; disregard for future consequences of behavior, 84; heterogeneity of, 81, 95; importance of as a topic for research, 83; psychopaths who remain out of prison, 81, 102; selection of subjects, 94, 95, 101, 102; symptoms, 77–79, 102
Psychopathy, subtypes: aggressive, 82; complex, 82; neurotic, 96; neurotic delinquent, 96; passive, 82; pseudo, 81; secondary, 81, 96; simple, 82
Psychophysiology, compared with physiological psychology, 3, 4
Psychoses, endogenous, 111
Psychoses, toxic, 111
Psychosomatic disorders, 3, 5, 6, 9, 201, 207; theories of, 186
Psychotherapy, *see* Treatment
Pulse rate, *see* Heart rate

Punishment, 84
Pupillary response, 21, 29, 30

Range-corrected measures, 217
Reaction time, 27, 36, 106, 140, 215
Recovery or improvement, 31, 64–68, 72, 125, 202, 203, 211
Relapse, 8, 66–68, 72, 212
Relaxation, as condition maximizing differences between anxious patients and controls, 30
Reliability, 4, 141, 163, 164; inter-rater, 50, 80; test-retest, 153, 163, 164
Repeated testing (of same Ss), 143
Replication, need for, 142
Respiration, 6, 43, 44, 95, 170, 172, 176, 181, 188
Response patterns, 208, 218
Response specificity, 5, 6, 205–7, 216–9
Rod and frame test, 162

Salivation, 21, 30, 31, 34, 35, 206
Scanning: cortical, 140; sensory input, 140
Schizophrenia, 5, 6, 8, 9, 19, 20, 83, 101, 106–34, 142, 193–98, 202, 203, 206, 209, 210, 212, 213, 220; acute episodes, 125; adoption studies, 193; anoxia in pregnancy and, 202; anxiety in, 123; associated with organic brain pathology, 107, 108; associated with temporal lobe epilepsy, 108, 109, 126; associated with tumors, 109; behavioral ratings, 122; and birth weight in twins, 108; British vs. American diagnosis of, 116; changes with clinical improvement, 125; conservative diagnosis of, 116; disturbance of limbic system function, 107–112, 115, 119; disturbances of attention, 8, 107, 109, 110, 112, 113, 206; effect of distraction on memory in, 203; florid symptoms, 106; genetic influences, 107, 108, 134, 193–98, 202, 220; heterogeneity of, 116; mother-child relationship in, 196; obstetric and perinatal birth complications in, 8, 107, 108, 111, 202;

premorbid personality, 198, 212; psychological deficit in, 198, 203; reaction time in, 203; research with animals applied to, 107, 112, 114, 123; schizoid personality, 197; schizophrenogenic environments, 196; schizotaxia, 196, 197; schizotypy, 196, 197; severity, 125; social withdrawal, 5; twin studies, 193
Schizophrenic subtypes: acute vs. chronic, 116; based on research data, 106, 107, 122; clear vs. confused, 115; defect or residual state, 120; good vs. poor premorbid, see process/reactive; high vs. low redundant groups, 107, 110, 111, 133; institutionalized vs. noninstitutionalized, 116–19, 121, 122, 124, 127, 128; Kraepelinian, 106; nuclear, 107; paranoid (includes paranoid symptoms), 5, 96, 107, 110, 111, 125, 133; process/reactive, 106, 110, 125; relation to medication, 126; remitted vs. regressed, 115; responders vs. nonresponders, 117–34, 209–11; schizophreniform, 107; stability of responder/nonresponder subtype over time, 125; utility of responder/nonresponder subtype, 122, 126
Self-instructions, 167
Sensory input: disturbance, 199; gating, 109–11, 125, 140; modulation, 92–94, 201, 202, 205; processing of, 109–15, 125, 132; processing/ideational gating, 125; scanning, 140
Septal area, 109
Shock, electric, see Stimulation, electric shock
Sine spectra, in analysis of EEG, 146
Sinewaves, 145–48
Size estimation, 110
Skin temperature, 120
Sleep, 2, 4, 5, 7, 23, 31, 42–72, 202, 203, 206, 207, 209–11; actual sleep time, 51, 54, 56, 60, 61, 64, 65, 68–71; age and, 46, 52, 53, 55, 72; biological

need for, 46, 47; depth of, 45; drugs and, 210; early morning wakening, 47, 48, 51, 54, 56; methods of scoring records, 50, 59; onset, 47, 48, 51, 55, 56; PIPs (phasic integrated potentials), 59, 61, 62, 65, 66, 69, 71; quality of, 7, 47, 71, 72; REM pressure (or "need" for REM), 46, 47, 62, 63, 72, 206; severity of depression and, 52, 54, 55, 72; spontaneous awakenings, 46, 51, 56; stages of, 2, 6–24, 44–46, 48–72, 206; stages, selective rebound, 17, 18, 47, 62, 63; total sleep time, 51
Social disapproval, 169
Somatic activity, 181, 182, 188
Specific etiology, 194
Stability, *see* Reliability
Startle response, 21, 124
State-trait distinction, 15, 18
Stimulation: auditory, 27, 28, 31, 33, 36, 84, 87, 88, 93, 94, 106, 114, 117–19, 120, 121, 124, 125, 131, 132, 204; aversive, 205; background, 106; cue value of, 113; effect of interstimulus interval, 122, 124, 131; effect of rise time, 124, 125; effect of stimulus intensity, 94, 95, 97, 99–102, 113, 115, 120, 124, 125; electric shock, 21, 84, 85, 87–93, 171, 172, 204; as factor reducing differences between anxious patients and controls, 7, 30; laboratory as stimulus, 18, 63; *see also* Laboratory, adaptation to; noxious, 115; painful, 5, 6; registration of, 114; somatosensory, 32; thermal 22; visual, 29, 30, 32, 84, 93, 106, 140, 189
Stimulus conditions: preference for simplicity, 215, 216; selection of, 213–16, 218, 220
Stimulus input, *see* Sensory input
Stomach motility, 171
Stress, 2, 7, 169, 186, 188; *see also* Diathesis-stress
Striate cortex, 109
Stroke volume, 21
Sweat gland activity, *see* Electrodermal activity

Sympathetic nervous system, 21, 168, 169, 187, 188, 195
Symptom specificity, 5, 6

Tapping task, 36
Technology, as limiting factor in psychophysiology, 219
Telemetry, 215
Temperament, 139, 163, 189, 201
Temporal cortex, 109
Temporal lobes, 131–33
Thalamus, 159
Therapy, *see* Treatment
Trait, *see* Personality, traits
Treatment: autogenic training, 169; as confounding variable in comparing patients with controls, 210–12; progressive relaxation therapy, 169; role of transcendental meditation, 169; systematic desensitization, 168, 169; use of biofeedback in, 169; use of learned visceral control in, 169, 170, 186, 188, 189; *see also* Prophylaxis; Medication; Depression, electroconvulsive therapy
Tuberculosis, 194
Tumors, 109, 130, 131
Twins, 9, 108, 142, 144, 149–65, 193, 200; blood typing, 149; fingerprint ridge analysis, 149, 160; idealized distributions of differences between MZ and DZ, 158
Two-flash threshold, 6, 123

Ulcers, 195
Underarousal, 205

Vagal rebound, 93
Vagus, 182, 188
Variability: intersubject, 51, 52, 71, 81; intrasubject, 49, 64, 71
Vascular responses, *see* Vasomotor activity
Vasomotor activity, 6, 21–23, 85, 86, 95, 99, 100, 102, 113, 131, 168, 171, 172, 182; voluntary control of, 171
Ventricular fibrillation, 169, 170, 186

Visceral organs, 169–73, 181; control of, 167–69, 171–73, 181, 182
Volition, 167
Vulnerability, 66, 186, 194–96, 201, 202

Weight loss, 35
Will, 167
Wittenborn Psychiatric Rating Scale, 122